WHAT ABOUT

The LD Adolescent

WHAT ABOUT ME?

The LD Adolescent

Doreen Kronick

with contributions by

Elizabeth Adams
Lauriel Anderson
Mary Jane O'Gara
Sylvia Bleiweiss

1975
Academic Therapy Publications
San Rafael, California

© Copyright 1975

Academic Therapy Publications
P.O. Box 899
1539 Fourth Street
San Rafael, California 94901

Publishers of educational materials

International Standard
Book Number: 0-87879-095-0

Library of Congress
Catalog Card Number: 74-29558

First Printing, 1975
Second Printing, 1977

This book was set in IBM Century
8 point and 10 point medium
and medium italic type.
Chapter titles were set in
Varityper 20 point Univers
extra bold extended:
section headings were set in
IBM Univers 11 point bold.
The paper used was 60 pound
White Antique for the text;
10 point CIS for the cover.

Printed in the
United States of America

Contents

Preface

UNLIKE THE YOUNG CHILD, the adolescent is mobile. He lives, works, and plays in many environments. His experiences in each setting spill over into other realms. The events and feelings about what happens at home affect his school performance; and his successes and failures at school influence his feelings about himself—hence, they affect his ability to handle himself in the community. Consequently, a book concerned with the learning-disabled adolescent must be directed to all facets of his experience: family, education, recreation and vocation. In short, it must assume a comprehensive, integrated approach to the whole child.

The urgency of the learning-disabled adolescent's plight, and the poverty of knowledge about what "makes him tick" and how to meet his needs and the dearth of services, require accelerated techniques for alleviating his distress. In part, the solution will lie with parents learning about how teachers of the learning disabled feel: their frustrations, difficulties, and limitations of resources, the nature and depth of their duties and commitment. Similarily, teachers will understand and empathize more fully with the learning-disabled adolescent when they perceive the dynamics of the youth within his family structure: the family's joys, sorrows, and hopes. Once the process of understanding has been initiated, and concerns shared, a meeting of minds in mutual trust is easier to achieve. It is only by working together that we can hope to create the milieu within which learning-disabled adolescents in North America can learn, produce, create, achieve, interact, and—finally—recognize for themselves that they are the persons of worth that we who live and work with them know they are.

Before the volunteer associations concerned with the learning disabled were formed, almost all learning-disabled children in our land neither were being diagnosed, nor were they receiving any services or understanding. Now, a decade later, hundreds of thousands are being helped because parents cared and they fought relentlessly to ensure their children's right to respect and appropriate services. We owe no less to our adolescents. An ironic picture is emerging in North America. There are some fine services for the elementary-age child, and some emerging services for the college-age child, yet pitifully little for the adolescent. There will be little more in the near future unless parents mobilize the same energies that they did in the 1960's and produce a combined educational and social action push. We must bombard the secondary schools with panels, speakers, and movies. We need to invade the teacher-training institutions, backed up by committed professionals. There is so much that we have to teach vocational assessment and employment agencies. We have to fight for learning-disabled adolescents singly and collectively until every last adolescent in North America receives the understanding and help that he needs.

Parents can't look to others for the answers, because others don't have them. As Lauriel Anderson states, "If you ask a question, be prepared to find the answer." When she asked about vocational training she found that she had to become an authority herself, but in the course of doing so helped her own daughter and countless others. We can't bemoan the fact that no one does anything because no one understands or feels as deeply about the plight of the learning-disabled adolescent as we do. It is a difficult challenge. Can we accept it?

Part One

Chapter 1:

The Need for a Psychology of Learning Disabilities

As I UNDERTOOK the research requisite for writing this book on the learning-disabled adolescent, I was struck by a glaring gap in our current body of knowledge, the gap being the absence of a psychology of learning disabilities. I feel that until the theoretical framework for a psychology of learning disabilities has been developed, the programs we conceptualize and the techniques we propose to teachers and parents must, of necessity, be lacking.

There is relatively little in psychological theory to date that deals with the experience of the learning disabled. Freud developed a psychology of neurosis. Lang and others evolved theoretical framework for psychosis. The new therapists, Maslow, Berne, Glasser, Perls *et al*, mapped a psychology of the healthy person. Beatrice Wright, Tamara Dembo, and others delineated an impressive psychology of handicap. All of these schools of thought have much to say to the experience of the learning disabled, yet they fail us in critical ways. These failures, as I see them, center around the concept that, if given environmental influences are present or absent, humans will respond with predictable, delineated behaviors. There is little in the literature that deals with individual response to developmental influences, and virtually nothing which describes the altered perception that the minimally developmentally deviant person has of his environment and its consequent effect upon his psychological development.[1]

All of the psychologies seem to agree that a child's caretakers must make him feel safe, loved, respected, and provide him with feelings of belonging if he is to develop into a healthy person. Recognizing that learning-disabled persons are members of families in which these needs are met in varying degrees, let us concentrate, for the moment, on those families who are nurturing. We are left with the need to examine what happens to a child whose family has led him to understand that it will protect him. From the comfortable knowledge of this protection, he ventures forth, only to learn that his unstable perceptions, poor coordination, errors in judgment, lapses in memory, and inability to deal with some forms of complexity, create for him a hostile and dangerous world. Consequently, familial messages of safety do not suffice for such a person.

Even if psychology has devoted little attention to the learning-disabled child's intrinsic vulnerability in coping with the world, he and his parents recognize it; and, typically, the family provides the required protection. However, this very protection may prevent the child from conquering, withstanding, or overcoming, so that he continues to feel doubtful that he can. This holds true not only for coping with external dangers, but for the ability to control and delay one's impulses, and therefore to be unafraid of them.

There is a need to examine the quality of parental protection. There are many reasons why parents of the learning-disabled youngster feel that they are incompetent in their child-rearing practices and that the world is an unsafe place in which to rear children. These feelings have evolved because the parents of the learning-disabled adolescents of today have received little support or direction from professionals and little acceptance or flexibility from educators. They and their children are devalued, expendable, misunderstood, and the recipients of hostility. We have to examine what happens to family members who initially may have been secure but now perceive a pervasive lack of support in a complex society which must provide critical kinds of support if its members are expected to be functional. The quality of support that such families provide to their offspring must, of necessity, be lacking. The parental message is that the world is not a safe place in which to venture.

Coincident with providing protection, parents expose their children; and on occasion, the decisions concerning where to expose and where to protect tend to be erratic and poorly conceptualized. They are related to parental fears, anxieties, and misconceptions. If one is irrationally afraid of educators, or backlash or exclusion from the education system, one won't protect one's child from situations at school—regardless of how unrealistic the demands on the child may be. Conversely, if one becomes panicky about the adolescent's approaching adulthood, one will expose the youngster to situations requiring sophisticated coping abilities, but bail the youth out rather than live with one's pain while the youngster develops coping abilities. Parental distortion and confusion around the parameters of a poorly understood disability often cause them to protect the child from demands with which he could cope with some understanding.

Unresolved parental feelings of aggression and rejection add to the cycle of over- and underprotection. The parent whose life has revolved around his or her learning-disabled child may need to continue to do a great deal for the child; and the youngster, recognizing his parent's need, is likely to oblige by being needful. Some attention has been paid to the feelings of parents of the handicapped, which have resulted in inconsistencies in the quality of protection; but we have not examined the cycle of parental behavior that the truly vulnerable child establishes.

Part of our developing concern with the learning-disabled adolescent should include an examination of the types of ineptitude that such youth demonstrate which occasions dependence on family members. Persons who are dependent resent those upon whom they depend; and persons who are being depended upon—parents, brothers, and sisters—resent the long period of dependence and resent the dependor who has denied them the freedom inherent as a promise in all intact developing organisms. Since the learning disabled present themselves primarily as intact, their continued dependence is largely unacceptable.

The psychologies state that, in order for a child to develop a concept of self and develop into a secure being, he must experience a feeling of belonging to the primary family unit, the nuclear family. Without question, many learning-disabled children are born into families where they are wanted and cherished youngsters. As preschool children, many of their accomplishments may be enjoyed and rewarded; nonetheless, by the time they reach school age, if not before, their feelings of belonging and their family's feelings that they belong are likely to be undermined. Although they share the physical attributes with family members, they do not share the degree of achievement or conformity. The professional's child may be semiliterate, the athlete's child may be clumsy, and the socially prominent family may sire a socially inept offspring. Inherent in belonging is the necessity to achieve the degree of status acquired by others in one's family and subculture and the need to be awarded and to award one's family.[2] Since the learning-disabled child's achievements fail to meet most external standards, the family tends not to perceive them as worthy of reward.

Since the learning-disabled child or adolescent tends to be egocentric, his conversation centers around himself. He fails to notice the attributes and interests of others—thus excluding them from his interaction. Consequently, from others' point of view, he is not a very rewarding family member, friend, or acquaintance. I asked forty sets of parents of learning-disabled children to tell me something good about their child. Thirty-five sets of parents could think of nothing good. If parents do not feel good about their offspring, the child will not feel good about being part of that family. Family members do not share the child's learning disability; he is alone in his experience. The learning disability is not accepted as a facet of him, but is the target of extensive effort geared to its elimination. This means that the attribute that he does not share with relatives is considered to be of considerable magnitude by his parents, since so much time and psychic energy is directed toward it, and since it is considered undesirable. His unacceptable differences, therefore, are accentuated.

Let us look at the human need for status and respect. A percentage of learning-disabled persons are born into families where there is readiness to reward the child in very positive ways for achievements. Ideally, a child should be rewarded in terms of his unique developmental time clock and not compared to age-related expectations. This ideal is easily verbalized by professionals but is an impossible expectation in our culture. Even if parents can inure themselves to comparisons to friends' and relatives' children, there is the ever-present knowledge that their children must attain specific milestones in order to meet the social demands of the preschool set, and must acquire the readiness skill to cope with the school experience. As school-age children, their social and academic skills *must* be acquired at the same speed as their peers. Failing report cards, school interviews in which parents are confronted by their children's failure and nonconformity, and rejection of the child by other children, create an environment in which parents cannot allow their children to progress at their own rate and be rewarded commensurately. As long as society's expectations are rigid, parents must pressure all but the most profoundly incompetent to meet external demands. This means that the child who does not possess the readiness skills to compete will be a failure. His modest achievements won't be rewarded: status and respect will be meager.

Psychology states that emotional problems are created whenever there is not a fit between skill acquisition and external expectation. Psychological theory, however, is based upon unrealistic parental expectations; and there has been no examination of parents caught in an impossible cultural bind. How indeed can the child achieve respect and esteem if we are forced to pressure him to adopt the time clock of his more intact peers? The move to normalization in education was effected to maximize the child's intact qualities and remove him from the self-contained classroom in which his differences were paramount. One has to question how successful normalization has been, since we removed protection in the areas in which learning-disabled children are deficient—academics—placing them in situations in which they are unable to succeed.

Then we must look at learning-disabled persons who have been provided with an environment of love, safety, and respect; but because they have difficulty perceiving the expressions of feeling conveyed by others, they may not have comprehended or internalized these positive environmental factors.[3] Having not comprehended all the positive reinforcement they received, they would not have responded. Being less aware of their own expressions of feeling, the responses they did give may have been inappropriate and misinterpreted by their caretakers. So those who love and nurture the child are less rewarded for their efforts than they are with their non-learning-disabled children; and without adequate reinforcement, the most loving family will lose a degree of interest. The same phenomenon happens with negative reinforcement, in which the child does not seem to be efficient in perceiving or responding to negative cues, so that he is a difficult child to socialize, and persists in producing inappropriate behavior.

The learning-disabled person seems to lack the ability to cue his animate or inanimate world to react to him in ways that would provide him with the kinds of stimulation requisite for learning. We thus need to develop a psychology of learning disabilities that examines the ways whereby the learning-disabled child conditions his environment to be less nurturing than it is for other children. If we fail to do this, we will continue to observe learning-disabled persons creating their own deprivation—be it in socialization with family and friends, or in communication and movement experiences.

Psychology has done little to examine concepts such as strength, will, courage, and motivation; yet these likely are the most critical factors for creating change in the learning disabled. I have been on the staff of an agency which provides services to the learning disabled, and the children I have observed who have responded to remedial and therapeutic efforts have been those who are motivated. The children who had no commitment to change, who remained passive while the program was imposed upon them, made only the most minimal gains. (One should be careful to distinguish the child who is temporarily discouraged from the one who is truly unmotivated.) We must attempt to discern what innate qualities a person possesses which allow him to keep trying when he succeeds so seldom, and keep him fighting for his optimum survival in a hostile world. We have to explore what qualities in a parent are modelled by the young to create motivation. What kinds of environmental messages, if any, create courage?

Eric Berne postulates a fascinating theory that contends that children receive their life script from their parents by age six.[4] One either receives a "winner" script or a "loser" script. Since many learning-disabled children appear intact in their preschool years, we assume that a proportion of these youngsters receive "winner" scripts. The assumption implied in the script theory is that, unless one is profoundly incapacitated, one will carry out one's prescribed script. There is no reference to children who are unable to actualize "winner" scripts as a result of subtly intrinsic disabilities. We are aware of the self-defeating behavior of persons who receive "loser" scripts. Now we must examine what happens to "losers" who receive "winner" scripts.

Let us examine a few of the issues inherent in the development of adequate self-concept. We know that the development of self-concept depends, in part, upon one's ability to make a realistic appraisal of oneself and then maximize one's attributes within one's society and possibly the world. Therefore, self-concept cannot stop at the person, but must include the person's role in and relationship to the world. The ability to center upon the world rather than be self-conscious, egocentric, and gratification-oriented becomes more difficult the more need-deficits a person has. The learning-disabled person has many need-deficits, so that he has a collossal problem developing a realistic, positive, and healthy concept of self. In our attempts to remediate his disability, we focus a disproportionate amount of time and attention on his deficits, accentuating their existence as facets of him, and deemphasizing the more positive aspects of his being. The current explosion of knowledge in the field of learning disabilities and the proliferation of volunteer organizations concerned with the learning disabled has had one negative result: further parental absorbtion with the learning disabled and parents' resultant propensity to see the learning disability in all facets of their child's behavior. The lack of services, particularly for the adolescent, forces the child and the family to focus disproportionately on the disability to the exclusion of developing and enjoying other personality attributes.

We have not taken a hard look at temporal planning as it relates to the development of a self-concept, even though one of the more typical deficits shared by those who have learning disabilities seems to be the problem of temporal organization and conceptualization. Many learning-disabled persons experience difficulty planning their spare time, just letting time "happen to them"; or they plan the immediate activity, but give no thought to what they will do with their time throughout the day. They have trouble figuring out how much time to spend on each homework assignment and when to initiate work on a long-term project. Unless they receive external reinforcement for their efforts, they seem to "wind down."

Self-actualization is meaningless without reference to a currently active future. All our actions and decisions are based upon knowledge of what happened in the past and its effects upon future plans. If the learning-disabled child or adolescent possesses insufficient organizational ability to relate current action and judgment to past experience and its effects upon future plans, he is a slave to the present. He has no concept of his life as being an evolving, fulfilling process through time. Maslow states that reduction to the concrete is a loss of future and that only the flexibly creative person can manage future.[5] The thought process of the learning disabled tends towards the concrete, and they are notoriously inflexible. Consequently, we should examine these attributes as they relate to conceptualization of time and self, and determine whether we can inculcate attributes in the young person who is learning disabled which would assist him in perceiving his living experience on a continuum.

Our education system often is structured in ways which allow the learning disabled a more limited choice of future than more intact young people who may be no more intelligent. Inability to master some academic requisites may serve to exclude adolescents from open-ended school tracks. As a result of the limiting nature of their disabilities, few learning-disabled youth have the unlimited choice of future that is the legacy of the young in North America. The literature on learning disabilities and the parents of the learning disabled convey the expectation that the handicapped youth can be retrained and become another Winston Churchill. The adolescent's reality implies that his future will be the same failure that his present is, so that he doesn't know which message to believe in order to conceptualize a realistic future. Such children and adolescents seem to generate disproportionately large anxieties around current difficulties and too little anxiety around the future. Can we develop a modicum of future anxiety that would generate effort related to future aspirations?

I wonder whether we have explored the learning theories in sufficient depth as they relate to this population. Perls, Maslow, and their associates make a compelling case for the "aha" of discovery as opposed to the drill of repetition or the external awards of behavior modification. We should determine whether the "aha" of discovery is sufficient for integration of knowledge for the child with some poor memory systems. Since we have conditioned all learning-disabled children to the concept that learning is painful and negatively rewarded, we should look into the factors which cause some children to respond to the negative conditioning by retreating, while others continue in pursuit of the "aha."

We must become involved in much more depth exploration of the social problems of the learning disabled than we have done to date. Society demands a degree of conformity and, in turn, rewards the individual with group acceptance. Psychology has studied the child who refuses to conform and the child whose environment has crippled the desire of ability to conform, yet has bypassed the child who wants to conform but lacks the skill. We must determine why indeed the learning-disabled child fails to enter into this transaction with society and thus so often remains friendless.

There is extensive work to be done on the relationship between learning disabilities and delinquency. A number of studies have been conducted in the United States in which groups of juvenile offenders were tested. In each instance, significantly high percentages were found to have learning disorders. To my knowledge, however, learning-disabled groups have not been studied to determine the percentage who are delinquent. All the implications to date notwithstanding, we still do not know whether the presence of a learning disability predisposes an individual to delinquency or whether there are other shared factors which are not present in some who are learning disabled. Possibly the most logical place to start would be with the current body of knowledge of factors which predispose persons to delinquency, such as the use of language to project or express feeling, and impulse control. Additionally, we should examine the quality of parenting, the degree of community support the families received, the extensiveness and effectiveness of remedial services afforded the child, the degree to which the child has been allowed to be a contributor to family and community, and the community's commitment to evolving a social and job role. Until we explore these and a host of other factors, we have a moral commitment to stop drawing ludicrous relationships between learning disabilities and delinquency. After all, we don't know, at this time, whether such relationships are primary, secondary, or incidental.

Finally, as a conclusion to this plea for a psychology of learning disabilities, I beg that it include a study of how we can maintain and nurture individuality while still striving to make the child add, subtract, read, write, spell, participate in sports, and acquire adequate social skills. I fear that our efforts towards conformity may have crippled much individuality and that we must find a way of preserving that precious commodity.

Chapter 2:

They Come to Adolescence

THEY COME TO ADOLESCENCE overnight and with little warning. They come from sheltered classrooms, itinerant teachers, resource room programs, gross-motor groups, special club programs, and arranged outings with other children. They arrive with a backlog of years of effort, their effort and that of others behind them, yet often it is not enough. They come to adolescence with hope, with fear, and with anxiety.

They have known understanding, dedication, and love. They have experienced cruelty, rejection, and ignorance. Their childhood was not of the storybook variety, carefree and idylic. Theirs was earmarked by academic failure, social failure and indeed, it often seemed, failure to do anything properly. Regardless, all energies were directed towards eventual normalcy. And now those hoped-for years are here.

They come to adolescence immature, unready, and still with many needs. They have travelled a long way; and, if there were enough helping hands, perhaps they are not hopelessly discouraged. They have many positive attributes and skills if we create an environment in which they can be used. They enter a world wherein teenagers are expected to have mastered the city as their playground, a world in which the acquisition of many boy- and girl-friends is the earmark of success. They leave the understanding teachers behind and enter a school of many rooms, many teachers, and shifting demands. The concrete learning of the elementary school is replaced by the confusion of geometry, algebra, and computer science.

In the world of childhood many people knew something about learning disabilities and treated the young person with understanding. In the world of adolescence almost no one is aware that there is such a disability, nor are most people receptive to acquiring such knowledge. Fifteen years ago we behaved as if the young learning-disabled child was a nonexistent entity. Now we acknowledge his existence, but pretend that there is no such thing as learning disabilities in adolescence.

There are a few services for him scattered across North America, and we have some residential schools for those lucky enough to be able to avail themselves of them. These facilities notwithstanding, all but a few fortunate ones are thrust into adolescence and are expected to cope without having acquired many of the coping skills.

Some professionals don't like to learn of their reality. When I lecture about the learning-disabled adolescent, they say, "Why are you so negative? Why don't you tell about the good things that are happening and mention the good teachers?" There are good programs, of course, innovative, exciting ones; and there are sensitive, kind and warm teachers and understanding administrators. The problem is that there is no plan: no plan for good programs in every secondary school in North America, and no plan for teacher training or in-service training that would impart knowledge and (hopefully) empathy to every teacher in the nation.

In the past we parents of the learning disabled had to candy-coat our experiences. We were able to share the things that had happened to us only minimally, because whenever we exposed our full reality, we encountered disbelief and withdrawal. However, we have travelled a long way. Many parents now can relate their stories without bitterness, and many professionals can face and believe the family's experience without feeling that it is a personal attack on their competence.

In parts of this book I discuss how the adolescent and his family feel and talk about what happens to them. Some of these descriptions are raw, bleeding, and full of pain, because that's the way they really are. It is important for professionals to understand what we have been through, because only then can they understand us and our adolescents. It is helpful, as well, for parents to learn of others' experiences, so that they will realize that what has happened to them and their son or daughter has been shared by others. Somehow, when one knows that one is not alone, it is a source of strength. I hope, too, that these books will serve as the beginning of a dialogue between parents and professionals, a sharing of feelings and perceptions, so that we both can perform our respective roles more effectively.

Much of the reason that the learning-disabled adolescent is in trouble is that we have known him so briefly. The volunteer associations concerned with the learning disabled formed primarily in the early 1960's. They pressed for services for the elementary school-aged child, services which became relatively available in North America in the latter part of that decade. The first generation of identified children who recieved public assistance on a scale of any consequence now are in adolescence. So, it is only as we begin to live and work with them that we evolve assumptions and methods. Our involvement with them, being so new, means that there are few hard facts and fewer answers. To be of any value, therefore, a book such as this one will, of necessity, present issues and a few suggestions.

We have not, as yet, established the vehicles for serving the learning-disabled adolescent in our communities. Special education training in North

America has been offered primarily to elementary school teachers. The ancillary facilities of school boards, such as consultants and speech therapists, typically are utilized more by elementary schools than they are by the staff of secondary schools. The learning-disabled adolescent who enters the secondary school stream still may be deficient in some or many of the basic skills; and to date we have developed few facilities for the provision of basic remedial assistance for the secondary school student who, only now, may be ready to learn reading, writing, and spelling. Our most serious failure is likely the misunderstanding of the learning-disabled person on all levels of the secondary school education hierachy. Educators are unaware of behaviors of which they should have knowledge. They rarely know that the learning-disabled person is stress-sensitive, that he overreacts to situations, that when he feels overwhelmed he finds it difficult to reverse that feeling, that he becomes anxious and frustrated in subject areas that were difficult for him in earlier years. They expect the learning-disabled person to comply to the same rules and expectations as his fellow students. There are few sources of intervention; and, oftener than not, those few are ineffectual in producing change and understanding. Even parents who are articulate advocates for their adolescents become defeated by the incomprehension and absence of courts of appeal.

Who is the learning-disabled adolescent? Who are his brothers and sisters? Who are his parents? What has been their experience, and how do they feel? The learning-disabled adolescent is white, black, Catholic, Protestant, Jewish, wealthy, middle class, poor, tall, short, obese, thin, handsome, homely, delightful, or unpleasant. He is part of a healthy, intact family or a sick or broken family. In other words, there is no prototype. There is virtually as great a variety of learning-disabled adolescents as there are adolescents. The only factor that they share in common is their learning disability which, if one is to adopt the United States Office of Education's definition, is that "they have a disorder in one or more of the basic psychological processes involved in understanding or using language, spoken or written, which disorder may infest itself in imperfect ability to listen, think, speak, read, write, spell, or do mathematical calculations. Such disorders include conditions such as perceptual handicaps, brain injury, minimal brain dysfunction, dyslexia, and developmental aphasia. It does not include children who have learning problems which are primarily the result of visual, hearing or motor handicaps, of mental retardation, of emotional disturbance, or of environmental disadvantage."

Even within the confines of the above definition one finds adolescents who are slow intellectually and ones who are brilliant. There are young people who experience great difficulty expressing themselves and very verbal ones, athletic youth and the clumsy, adept readers and the illiterate, adolescents who can and can't spell, write, express themselves on paper, or handle mathematics. There are adolescents who have one disability, and others who have several; and each disability can vary from minimal to severe. Some have acquired impressive social skills, whereas others are socially inappropriate and friendless. If these variations weren't sufficiently overwhelming to frighten anyone from studying or writing about the learning-disabled adolescent, I must point out the intrinsic variables such as creativity and motivation and the extrinsic ones such as home life and opportunities for enrichment, diagnosis and remediation, and attitudes of educators and the community.

By the time the learning-disabled youth reaches adolescence, he presents a mix of learning problems and the emotional problems which likely resulted from his disability, so that it often is impossible to separate one from the other, even if someone were to wish to do so. Considering the variables, why have I attempted to write and compile a book on the learning-disabled adolescent? I feel that he often is misunderstood, penalized, shunted aside, and provided with minimal opportunities, be they educational, vocational, or social. Someone must add to the sporadic efforts that have been made to date to describe the learning-disabled adolescent, attempt to examine why he is the way he is, and discuss ways of maximizing his position. Those persons who have avoided this task, using the variance in presenting behavior as an excuse, may have been "copping out" of an area with which we must begin to cope.

In writing this book, if my coauthors and I had any type of learning-disabled person in mind, we were thinking about the young person who has moderate to consequential learning disabilities. After all, the adolescent whose only problem is that he can't spell terribly well and struggles with foreign languages really doesn't need a book written about him. This book will discuss many learning-disabled adolescents, and you—as a professional or parent who is interested in one child or a specific group of children—will relate to the material that is relevant to the children in question.

How Does It Feel to Be a Parent?

Parents of learning-disabled adolescents feel frustrated. We want so much to have our child succeed, yet that which seems effortless for other teenagers is insurmountable for him. We wish that we could do things for him. We are frustrated because we want so desperately to help him, yet are thwarted. As a young child he allowed our assistance; now he repulses it. We are frustrated because we know that a little compassion, knowledge, and committment on the part of educators, school psychologists, and recreation personnel would make the difference between inclusion and exclusion; yet few seem to care sufficiently to create an environment within which our child could be included. We are frustrated because we want to convey to our son or daughter that we are with him; yet our very frustration, anxiety, and impatience with his general ineptitude often give him the opposite message.

Parents of the learning disabled feel impotent. Our child rarely is understood or accepted by educators. Instead they think of him as stubborn, stupid, having a poor attitude, lazy, disturbed, odd, delinquent, or a clumsy oaf. Since his behavior is perceived as purposeful, it often is penalized. The corollary of not recognizing or believing in the existence of the disability is not providing for it. This being the case, our children are coming to grief in the schools; and they and their families are suffering deeply with no recourse. To whom can they turn when their child becomes upset about school or begins to falter? There is no one to examine the current difficulty, determine the reason for the non-coping, and initiate alleviating procedures.

Because no one intervenes, the situation deteriorates. One parent commented that it is like being told that penicillin would cure her child and then being denied access to it. We parents recognize that our children will likely achieve less than a child with a comparable intelligence who doesn't have a learning disability. Nonetheless, we know that our offspring can handle much of the academic program if he is provided with knowledgeable support and allowed to contribute in the ways that he is capable. We resent the fact that academic programs in some parts of North America are not sufficiently open-ended. As a result, intelligent learning-disabled adolescents too often are shunted into occupations or vocational programs. It isn't that there is anything wrong with the vocational track; we feel impotent because the choice of educational stream is a right belonging to others, but not the right of our children. It is difficult for parents to feel positive towards a society that is minimally committed to their child.

Parents of the learning disabled feel caught in a double bind. We know that there is an obsession in America with university degrees, and that the person who applies for a job without such a credential is at a decided disadvantage. Regardless, our offspring often are excluded from the secondary school stream which leads to college entrance.

We are older, and the years of effort have taken their toll. We have less hope, stamina, and fighting spirit. Much of our resilience is gone. As a result, when the umpteenth assignment arrives home with twenty-five marks deducted for spelling errors, red slashes through words, and angry exclamation marks, or the report card arrives home with, "Can do better if he tries," we explode. By this point, we have attempted to educate an endless procession of relatives, friends, neighbors, and teachers. Few seemed to comprehend learning disabilities, and many felt that we were making excuses for a stubborn, spoiled brat who really wasn't too bright.

Now that our child has entered secondary school he encounters a number of teachers yearly. We feel uncomfortable intervening for a six-foot-tall youth; and the teachers discourage our intervention by querying why the child can't speak for himself. By the time our children reach adolescence we parents are intimidated by educators, feeling that educators purposely have employed techniques to intimidate us, though some of those feelings likely are a projection of our own discomfort. Even parents who are unintimidated experience difficulty arranging to meet each of their offspring's teachers each school year. When such meetings are able to be arranged, they often are not too helpful. Few parents understand their child's disability sufficiently to interpret it to his teachers; and almost all of us are unfamiliar with current secondary school cirricula. Consequently, we are at a loss as far as suggesting the types of cirriculum modifications which would help our child, or which are reasonable to request. In many school systems the only person to whom we can turn when the teachers don't seem to understand our child's disability or ensure a minimal degree of individualization, is the school psychologist. If the psychologist does not prove to be understanding, we have run out of options. Some school boards have learning disabilities consultants; but typically they are unable to intervene unless invited by the school staff. Even if they do intervene, they only can suggest procedures; they have no "clout."

Parents of the learning-disabled teenager are angry. We are angry at the child who thwarts our dreams and hopes and makes a mockery of our childrearing practises. He has required so much of our effort for so many years and given us relatively little in return. We are angry that other parents seem to be less intelligent, industrious, or virtuous than we perceive ourselves to be, yet are blessed with adolescents who achieve meritously in academics, sports, and training for careers, while our son or daughter remains essentially a non-success. We are angry at educators who often don't seem to care or exert minimal effort on our child's behalf. Every time our teenager is embarrassed or demeaned in front of his classmates, we are deeply hurt.

We feel powerless when confronted by the syndrome, "You're damned if you do and damned if you don't." This syndrome is practiced by a few teachers who establish a set of demands which the learning-disabled student will be unable to meet behaviorally or academically. When he fails, the teacher's response is, "What can you expect from such a rotten guy?"

Parents of the learning-disabled feel eternally grateful to every teacher, employer, neighbor, club leader, and camp counsellor who has been kind to our child. We have been particularly thankful for every sensitive teacher who has gone to impressive lengths to make our offspring feel wanted and productive. There are thousands of teachers of this kind in North America; and every one of our children has had the good fortune to encounter at least a few. Each contact with such a teacher has appreciably changed their lives. Just as defeats and slights are so debilitating for the learning disabled, warmth, appreciation, and acceptance are tremendously ego-building. An adolescent can survive an entire school year of seemingly impossible demands and incomprehensible work if he has one or two accepting teachers with whom he comes in contact each day.

We are saddened by the haphazardness whereby secondary students are placed in classes with understanding teachers. It is a game of chance rather than a concerted commitment on the part of the educators to succeed with the learning disabled. In our large, depersonalized secondary schools, crippled by budget cuts and a tax paying public that is becoming increasingly disillusioned by education, educators cannot help but view the inefficient learner in their schools as a decided drag.

Parents of the learning-disabled adolescent fear exclusion. The states in which there is mandatory legislation to provide appropriate education to the handicapped have inadvertently created an incredible secondary benefit. The child's and parent's concepts of themselves have demonstrated remarkable change. Rather than being enrolled in school on sufferance, suddenly these children found they had the same rights to an appropriate education as the non-handicapped. At this point, however, few states in the United States or provinces in Canada ensure that the secondary school student has a right to equal but different education. Therefore, our adolescents are in school on sufferance; and we live with the constant, realistic fear that they will be excluded. In many parts of the land compulsory education terminates at age sixteen, and we parents can't help but feel that schools' commitment will lessen as soon as our child reaches the age when they no longer have to educate him. With this knowledge, we pressure our adolescent to conform to every behavioral and academic expectation. "Hand assignments in on time and ensure that they meet all the teacher's standards, regardless of whether or not you understand the subject matter. Don't become involved in student pranks or skipping school, regardless of the fact that teenagers have indulged in minor mischief throughout history, because even small misdemeanors might result in exclusion." This message is an affront to the adolescent's right to behave as a teenager and to indulge in minor testing of limits; but, more important, the injunction to conform regardless of the price is a cruel assault on one's dignity.

Ironically, many learning-disabled adolescents are conformists because they desperately want to please their peers and adults. Also, because they typically are functioning on a preadolescent level emotionally, they are too immature or insecure to be involved in breaking-away behavior. Since they want so much to be like everyone else, they are nonconformists by a twist of fate rather than by choice. The parental message to conform may well replicate their goal. Regardless, many of our adolescents find themselves in small and large difficulties caused by their learning disabilities. Their literalness, rigidity, disorganization, and faulty judgment create problems for them. Thus, they are as fearful as their parents that their acceptability as students is periously tenuous. It isn't that they enjoy being students—but they have no idea what they would do with their lives if the possiblity of attending school was removed.

Joe's school principal phoned Mrs. S. extremely agitated. He had walked past Joe's locker just as a bottle of beer fell off the shelf and broke at the principal's feet. To make matters worse, the only apology Joe proferred was, "It isn't mine, Sir." When Mrs. S. chatted with Joe on his return home the story emerged. The young man whose locker was beside Joe's said that his lock was broken and asked whether he could store a bottle of beer in Joe's locker. Being anxious for friendship, Joe complied. Since Joe's spatial judgment is poor, he placed the bottle too close to the front of the locker; and because his temporal judgment is faulty, he opened the locker just as the principal walked by.

Just as our teenager may be in school on sufferance, other facilities which are other people's right are his provisionally or not at all. Our youth may be denied access to jobs, recreation programs, and camps, even though their need for organized socialization far exceeds the needs of non-learning-disabled adolescents, since the latter create their own social experiences through informal opportunities.

Parents of learning-disabled adolescents feel alienated. We feel alienated from friends and family because they don't share our experience and so often refuse to understand it. We feel alienated from professionals because our children had to pioneer an infant field; this meant that many professionals refused to accept the existence of learning disabilities. Others saw it purely as a psychological problem. When we approached professionals for assistance, oftener than not we received yet another diagnosis with much of the information being withheld from us under the guise of confidentiality. When we found that no one was prepared to look at our child globally and prescribe an evolving course of treatment, we were forced to become knowledgeable ourselves, incurring the label "professional parent." Our search for treatment spanned an era wherein a host of therapies were embraced as miracle cures. Our time, energy, and finances were directed towards these promises of normalcy. As we observe our learning-disabled adolescent with his current ineptitudes, we feel somewhat discouraged and betrayed. The announcements about exciting new programs for younger children recomfirms our feeling that our children were born a few years too soon.

Our adolescent offspring were young children when the volunteer associations concerned with the learning disabled formed in the early to mid 1960's in North America. Before that time almost no one had seen a learning-disabled adolescent. A myth, therefore, arose that, with two or three years of remediation, our children would emerge "smelling like roses." This meant that parents who had been denied remedial help were understandably bitter. They felt that society had withheld the opportunity for normalcy. How discouraging it is to be told that one's child is one year too old for a program! Parents whose children received remediation believed that with one or two years of assistance their child would be "cured." What happened to the implied promise in the literature that our child would be retrained and emerge as illustrious as Thomas Edison or, at the very least, Winston Churchill?

As long as our child was young we felt that we had considerable time to remediate the disability before adulthood. The leeway time seemingly has disappeared overnight. In the early years the discrepancy between our child's behavior and expected behavior for that age was not untoward, so we were not too concerned. In adolescence the discrepancy between presenting behavior and expected behavior seems considerable; and recouping time seems to have run out. We are supersensitive to each instance in which he handles himself differently than we think he should. Being aware of the telescoping of time, we are impatient with his inappropriateness and his errors in judgment. While appreciating his delightful attributes, perhaps his good nature, willingness to help, and honesty, at the same time a nagging voice inside whispers to us that our child has grown into a rather odd young adult. At times we feel like muttering, "For goodness sake, kid, stop coming across like a jerk!" We have the frenetic feeling that we must create a "normal" person in a reduced period of time with sparse facilities for academic remediation, almost no facilities for social remediation, and a teenager who is resistant to being helped—an impossible bind.

When he was young he went to school like everyone else; and we arranged other experiences such as clubs, swim groups, and camps so that he seemed to be doing most of the activities of his peer group. When he had no friends we invited children to barbecues and outings. From these outward appearances, we could tell ourselves that he was much like everyone else, or certainly would be in the near future. In adolescence the school experience has terminated or will terminate shortly, and with it may terminate much of the semblance of normalcy. He has demonstrated incredible growth over the years, yet the discrepancy between where he is and where he should be appears greater than ever. The disabled child was appealing, so that people reached out to him; but people find a disability in adolescence less poignant.

Parents of the learning-disabled adolescent are weary. We were the generation who became involved in arduous home remediation. In addition we have spent the last thirteen, fifteen, or eighteen years being constantly on the alert, lest our child need us or lest he handle himself inappropriately. Even our sleep has had a half awake quality. Our child also is weary of being deprived of leisure time for extra help. We all would like to terminate remediation and devote our energies to the normal stresses of adolescence and the additional stresses that a learning disability places on the adolescent. The decision to forego remediation, however, means that we must come to terms with the foreverness of deficits, which is a weighty decision to make.

Our teenager makes little constructive use of his spare time; and those activities that he does do, he seems to repeat over and over. He doesn't know the recreation facilities the city has to offer or how one would take advantage of them. He is friendly, pleasant, and outgoing, and is able to initiate a friendship, but seemingly unable to maintain it. When we, his parents, suggest a hobby, a club, or a visit to the museum, our suggestions are rejected. His language is boring, and he talks about the same topic so often and so ponderously that we could scream. Whenever people visit our family, he tries so hard to socialize that he overdoes it by talking too much, repeating himself and monopolizing the conversation. He says things he shouldn't which embarrass us and make him feel ashamed when chastised. He looks too much to his parents, especially his mother, for companionship. Occasionally his boring conversation, his rigidity, and his limited interests and knowledge get on her nerves so that she loses patience, and then feels guilty at her impatience. We feel painful compassion. We ask ourselves why everything that is so simple for his peers is so impossibly complex for him. We wonder why the phone rings countless times a day for our other teenage children and the world is their playground, yet this child of ours lacks the wherewithal to become unglued from the television set. He has no dates, no job, and— seemingly—no resourcefulness.

Our anxiety around his situation causes us to magnify the coping aspects of his behavior and make a big deal of the small things that he does well. We develop "if only" thinking. "If only" he could find an understanding girl-friend, all would be well. We look for simple shortcuts to happiness. The K's encouraged their seventeen-year-old learning-disabled son to become engaged because the girl and her parents were kind to him. We pressure our adolescent to do things that will make him look like everyone else, yet are hampered by our lack of knowledge of the customs and clothing of today's adolescents; so we teach him adolescent behavior that is twenty-five years outdated. We push him into situations in which he is going to have to develop coping skills, but bail him out because we can't bear his pain. We tell him he must make friends, yet hold out lures which enhance his relating to us. We have a lurking fear about whether he'll achieve independent adulthood, so we give him mixed messages about whether he'll be able to or not and whether he should keep fighting to attain it or live at home forever.

We give him mixed messages as to whether he is a child or adult. We offer him a beer yet ask him whether he is wearing his rubbers on a wet day. When he expresses a desire to learn to drive a car, we panic.

We are confused about which aspects of his functioning are intact or handicapped, and so confuse him. Many of us are confused about what a learning disability really is and our child's specific learning disability. We are particularly hazy about the ways our child's particular handicap manifests itself in adolescence. Out of this confusion, we protect him from areas in which he should cope, and expose him to tasks and demands from which he should have protection. Being unclear about his own disability, he may avoid areas wherein he could experience success, and tackle assignments in which he is certain to fail. His setting of short- and long-term goals may be unrealistic in light of his abilities and disabilities.

By the time the child reaches adolescence, his parents are middle-aged. They are concerned about their own aging process, the slight indications of declining health and the dilemma around what they will do for the remainder of their lives. Their learning-disabled child likely absorbed the time in the past decade and a half that they might have devoted to their own education, career planning, or the development of a hobby. Certainly he imposed considerable stress on the husband-wife relationship and on their relationships to the other children of the family. Rearing him depleted time that his parents could spend on themselves, with each other, and with their other children. His parents may regret the way they allotted their time and certainly they may resent the continued demands on their time. The parents and their learning-disabled offspring may have developed patterns of interaction which are unrewarding and nonproductive, yet be unaware of and lack the wherewithal to alter them.

Many fathers find it difficult to establish a relationship with their young learning-disabled child who embarrasses them and disappoints their short- and long-term goals. The child's egocentricity and social ineptitude have made the establishment of a reciprocal relationship difficult. If the father has been unable to develop a positive relationship with his child before adolescence, the teen years may create additional separation. Both father and offspring may very much desire a close relationship, but by this time are locked into interactions with one another which only serve to alienate further. However, people can change and grow at any stage in their lives, so that a commitment to change on the part of father and child, and the direction and support to effect change, can result in relationships that are healthy and rewarding. It is only in adolescence that many learning-disabled persons develop the cognitive capacity to work on altering relationships.

All our problems and concerns notwithstanding, we love our learning-disabled adolescent; indeed, we would not be so vigilant and concerned if we did not care so deeply. We enjoy his positive attributes, his loyalty, love, honesty, kindness, courage, sensitivity, and pride in his accomplishments. It is because we realize that he has so much to offer that we are eager to ensure that he finds his place in society.

How Does It Feel to Be a Sibling?

The presence of a learning-disabled child in the family creates an atypical environment from the child's early years onward, which has an effect upon all family members. The level of parental stress, hostility, and frustration increases appreciably when one has a learning-disabled child. They are in possession of information that has negative emotional connotations and are uncertain of how or whether to share it—do you tell the child that he is learning disabled; and if so, will he think badly of himself? What will others think of him if they know? When there is a learning-disabled child in the family, there is an increased level of negative feeling between family members: feelings of anger, rejection and disappointment, and a fear of expressing such feelings because they are considered unacceptable. There is a disproportionate amount of parental energy expended in anxiety around the learning-disabled child's prognosis and opportunities. He is given considerable parental time and attention because he requires extra support and because parents need to devote such time in order to live with their feelings.

Consequently, the brothers or sisters of this child inherit a less-than-optimal environment which cannot help but have some effect upon them. Typically they resent the parental overinvolvement and may be jealous and ashamed of their sibling. Although he likely is less favored, they perceive him as priviledged, spoiled, and self-indulgent. Children have different ideas of cause and effect than adults. They may feel that a jealous thought caused the learning disability. After all, irrational guilt is not the prerogative of parents!

All brothers and sisters fail their siblings in actualizing their dream of the ideal sibling, and that is as it should be. All of us fail in large and small ways as parents, spouses, and siblings; and this disappointment of expectations teaches the expector that we are human. The learning-disabled adolescent, however, fails his brothers and sisters more thoroughly. They may have dreamed of a popular brother or sister who would bring high-status adolescence to the house; instead, he or she is a loner. They may be embarrassed by his ineptitude and social inappropriateness. The fact that he is in a special class or behind in school may occasion upsetting questions or comments by other children. The siblings may have been denied some social opportunities by being saddled by their brother or sister, and some have been held back scholastically so that they wouldn't surpass their older sibling. A group of siblings commented that their parents allowed themselves to lose their tempers and become frustrated with the learning-disabled child, whereas they, the siblings, were always expected to be understanding.

Preadolescent brothers and sisters of such a youngster often seem to have difficulty accepting the fact that the learning disability is bonafide, and instead perceive their sibling as purposely acting inept in order to obtain parental attention. As a result, he is resented. As they reach mid to late adolescence, however, if there has been sensitive parental orientation to individual needs, they often develop empathy towards their learning-disabled brother or sister and voluntarily shoulder some of the supportive role previously assumed by the parents. Many become people who are sensitive to the needs of others, and a number take on a volunteer or professional role with the handicapped.

How Does the LD Adolescent Feel?

The learning-disabled adolescent is frustrated. Throughout his middle childhood he sacrificed playtime for remediation under the assumption that such remediation would ensure effective future functioning. Now the future has arrived and, if anything, he is floundering more than ever. This does not imply that he hasn't improved. It *does* mean that his improvement hasn't kept apace of demands; and, as the discrepancy between demand and function increase, his untiring efforts seem particularly fruitless.

He is frustrated because he recognizes the fact of his good intelligence and areas of competence, yet is held back and penalized for his disabilities. He is frustrated because he is acutely aware of the awards of adolescence, readily accesible to others; yet they elude his grasp.

The learning-disabled adolescent feels impotent. We are living in an age when incisive studies and books have been written on the inadequacy of our education system, yet all of us feel powerless to alter the lumbering giant of education who stalks relentlessly onward. If respected, competent, organized adults who have the subtlety and wherewithal to change systems are rendered impotent by the magnitude of the process, how much more impotent is the learning-disabled youth to modify his educational experience! After all, no adolescent is as high-status a person in our culture as an adult, so that we pay proportionately less attention to his suggestions; and a learning-disabled adolescent is of even lesser status. He has, therefore, few opportunities to change that which is unacceptable or untenable, and few occasions to control his environment—be it at home or at school.

The learning-disabled adolescent feels anger. He is angry at a society that demands conformity yet will not assist him to conform. He is angry at the vast majority of people he encounters who won't accept the existence of his disability, and so view his behavior as purposeful. When he bumps into someone, they think he is careless; when he stands between two people conversing, they think he is being rude; and when his language is hesitant or disorganized, they grow impatient and ignore him. When he misspells words, they assume that he can spell properly; when his written assignments are poorly written or garbled he is penalized. When he fumbles the ball, he is the object of group ire. Even his parents and siblings, who know about his disability, lose patience with his ineptitude, balkiness, and repetitive behavior. He is angry at being excluded from opportunities both social and educational.

Regardless of how much misunderstanding he has received in the past, if he displays his culmulative anger, no one considers his previous experiences which contributed to the anger; rather, they react to the current hostility. Teachers and others tend to view the anger as a cause rather than a reaction. "No wonder he is having difficulty; look at his attitude!"

The learning-disabled adolescent is frightened. He is fearful of an approaching adulthood and his lack of readiness to cope. He is afraid that he won't be able to acquire the education requisite to holding a job, the independence skills necessary for living on his own, and the social skills to date and make a wise choice of spouse. As adulthood rushes relentlessly closer, he worries a great deal about these issues.

He magnifies his successes. Such an adolescent doesn't do a great many things very well, so he devotes a disproportionate amount of time and conversation to the hobby, skill, or interest in which he has developed a degree of skill or competence. This makes him feel that he is a worthwhile person. If he dwells too extensively on his narrow interest, however, rather than serving as a basis for social interaction, it becomes repetitive, boring, and turns people off.

The learning-disabled adolescent may be depressed. He likely is seeing some of his problems for the first time, and this can be truly frightening! Suddenly he realizes how behind he is in the acquisition of learning skills and the implications for "catching up." Much of his depression stems from his years of failure experiences and his inability to handle many facets of his life experience. If he is depressed and discouraged, he may no longer keep trying to succeed, since he has learned that no matter how hard he tries, he rarely can meet the demands of a situation—be they academic, social, or athletic. If he is depressed, he is depressing, and people won't find him enjoyable socially. The demands of our society seem overwhelming and he gives up on the seemingly impossible task of coping. Peter says, "I'm tired of messing things up." He doesn't keep his depression to himself, but takes it out on his family. The amazing fact is not that some learning-disabled youth are depressed but that, when they are placed in a situation in which there is warmth, structure and tasks related to their level of ability, they may shake off their depression and demonstrate that, despite years of failure, they still are motivated, and can be "turned on."

He looks for magical answers. Throughout much of his life things have seemed to happen magically—such as social promotions, even though he couldn't master the work. His parents practiced remedial techniques with him, and both he and they believed in the magical outcome. His understanding of cause and effect may still be somewhat underdeveloped, so that he expects solutions to "just happen." Consequently, he may not invest himself in schoolwork or other projects because, somehow or other, he expects that a magical solution will appear once again.

The learning-disabled youth feels alienated. Perhaps, in one sense, I should not state that he feels alienated because one cannot be alienated from something of which one hasn't been a part. However, if I look at alienation experienced subjectively as being feelings of meaninglessness, boredom, loss, and unrelatedness, it describes this adolescent. His life has little meaning because he often has not the diversity of academic skills to remain in the open-door educational stream with the concomitant choice of one's vocation and life style. Further, he still is confused by his own capabilities; and we compound this confusion by failing to apprise him of what he can and can't do, and modifying his environment so that he would be able to succeed in his areas of competence. We still ply him with mixed messages of lofty expectations and hostile reactions to his ineptitude. His life is rendered more meaningless by his isolation, dependence, and insecurity around manipulating the outside world. He frequently doesn't know how to behave in ways that would be meaningful to others, or how to find the facilities in the community to which he could direct his energies and make a meaningful contribution. He often is excluded from positions of responsibility awarded to status adolescents such as a seat on the student's council or the duties of a prefect. Since one of the stages of adolescent development encompasses altruism, hence involvement of youth in Civil Rights, Vista, the Peace Corps, etc., one can assume that the meaninglessness of the youth's life separates him from activities which would contribute to adult functioning; and that very separation further contributes to his isolation. Some learning-disabled youth will espouse social or political philosophies; but it is less often that one would mobilize himself to action.

The learning-disabled adolescent often is bored. His short interest span, tenuous feeling of the future, and inefficient use of time preclude the development of in-depth interests which he might pursue for his own satisfaction. Charles Drake refers to the field dependence of the learning-disabled adolescents which is their need for external reinforcement of their efforts.[1] Efforts pursued merely to satisfy themselves don't seem sufficiently worthwhile. Their slow, inefficient reading processes, as well as the unpleasant associations with reading, preclude reading as a pleasurable pursuit.

Alienation encompasses a feeling of loss, and the learning-disabled adolescent has lost the carefree childhood which is the expectation of children in our society. He has lost the mythical American chance to strive for the ultimate in achievement. Every child in our culture expects, as his right, to be endowed with a whole body and mind; and the learning-disabled teenager feels that he has been denied that birthright. All of us have circumscribed ideas about what we feel life is owing us in terms of inheritance and opportunities. Although fate rarely is as just as our belief system would lead us to assume, nonetheless, we adhere to the faith in our rights as human beings in the one life we live. To have a clumsy body, an inefficient brain, reduced playtime, few friends, and limited status and vocational opportunities is, indeed, to feel a profound sense of loss.

A facet of alienation is unrelatedness. The learning-disabled adolescent differs from other family members in ability, personality, affect, and, certainly, many of the attributes which make a person acceptable in that particular family and subculture. Because the demands of school and playground have highlighted his ineptitude, and as a result of the paucity of remedial services, the family has had to focus on the child's disabilities. As a consequence, many have lost their perception of their adolescent's positive attributes, of which he has a number. If parents don't feel good about their child as part of the family, certainly he won't feel like an integral member. He feels alienated from educators because they neither comprehend nor make allowances for his learning disability; and he has likely been a marginal member of the student body. He is alienated from the educational process because he has been unable to crack the system.

He is hopeful that a brighter future lies ahead, and we owe it to him to ensure that it is so.

A devastating list of familial feelings has been documented here. While it is true that these feelings seem to be universally shared to a lesser or greater extent by the learning-disabled adolescent and his family, they are by no means always debilitating. An incredible phenomenon is the positive life force that propells the learning disabled, their siblings, and parents forward. In the presence of considerable counter forces, they continue to struggle to succeed, to search for new answers, and to be sources of strength to others beset with problems. If strength does emerge from adversity, they are excellent examples of that premise.

What Does the LD Adolescent Look Like?

The learning-disabled adolescent may look very different than he really is. He may have a six-foot, two-hundred-pound body with a deep voice, yet be a little boy inside. Notwithstanding, people expect him to behave the way he looks. Conversely, he may be a mature teenager inside an awkward body; and people assume ineptitude based upon his clumsiness.

If there is a discrepancy between his verbal and performance scores on an intelligence test, the discrepancy, in terms of its implications for behavior, may be the most noticeable in adolescence. Although test results will likely indicate areas of strength and weakness, however, they may exaggerate or minimize the actual ability to function, and must be used merely as indicators, rather than as a definitive delineation of abilities and disabilities.

The adolescent's anxiety around handling himself in one area of functioning may spill over into malfunctioning in more intact areas. Students may do poorly in an academic subject as a result of anxiety about subjects that are genuinely more difficult for them to master. The highly verbal youth may display his anxiety by becoming verbose or pedantic.

The adolescent brings many of the deficits he had as a child to adolescence; but experience, remediation and altered demands may wreak some changes in the presenting disabilities.

He may have a language handicap. This must be assessed within the context of his family and subculture. An adolescent from a minimally verbal family or subculture may have normal language functioning, though he appears deficient in terms of our larger cultural expectations. Similarly, an adolescent from a verbally adept family may have a verbal intelligence quotient of 130; yet, if he demonstrates errors in grammar, problems of word recall, and difficulty expressing himself in an organized fashion, he may well be language handicapped.

The language-handicapped adolescent typically is not as obvious as his younger counterpart, due to the benefits of maturation and the additional years of exposure to language. The child whose description of events were hopelessly garbled may be the adolescent who can produce a sequential description but who tends to digress into tangents. The young child who reversed the sequence of word parts, saying things such as "pisghetti" and "hopsital," garbles less but still tends to do so, on occasion, whether it is in spoken or written language. He still may distort words such as saying "hostages" for "hostels," or confuse words that have a similar meaning, such as "cake" and "pie," "icing" and "dressing." His vocabulary may be scant for his age and background, just as it was in his younger years; and his face still betrays the genuine confusion that he feels whenever he hears or reads a slightly uncommon word. The poverty of stored words may hinder his comprehension of ongoing spoken or written language.

It has always been assumed that there were two types of language memory deficits: the deficit in which words were completely erased from memory, and the condition in which the words were in the memory bank but the problem was in retrieving them for use in spoken language. Having observed children with the latter problem reach adolescence, I now feel that in many of the so-called retrieval problems, there also exists some complete word loss, as well. Consequently, for these youngsters, their knowledge of vocabulary is more limited than it should be. Such an adolescent may have difficulty remembering words; but the deficit no longer seems to be on the basic level that it was in childhood when he asked, "What's a tablespoon?" or "Can I have that thing to eat the soup with?" Now he forgets the names of the people in his class, particularly if any of the names are atypical. Regardless of his memory problems, he likely is skilled at masking his limited vocabulary, having determined the adjectives and phrases preferred by the adolescent set and sprinkling his conversation with words such as "like."

The adolescent still may have difficulty processing rapid speech or large chunks of ongoing language, so that he may lose much of the content of subjects in which teachers use the lecture method. Earlier problems in auditory discrimination seem to have improved, although the occasional adolescent still demonstrates his confusion with the way words sound by his faulty articulation. Even though the youth now may be adept in his discrimination of the English language, if one of his earlier problems was in auditory discrimination, he likely will have a tin ear in foreign language study.

A few adolescents still are illiterate, semiliterate, or slow, inefficient readers who find reading an arduous, unpleasant task. If the teenager was an impossible speller as a younger child, he likely is a better speller currently; but by no means does he spell well. When we are uncertain how to spell a word, we write it down, look at it, and tell ourselves whether it looks correct or not. The learning-disabled adolescent with a poor visual sequential memory won't receive corroborative feedback when he looks at a word; it looks like a new word each time. He can study his assignment the night before a spelling dictation test, have the words all correct on the test, yet spell them wrong in a sentence or paragraph a week hence. His spelling errors seem to indicate that he failed to learn some basics in his early school years; and he still may confuse words such as "there" with "their," "whether" with "weather," and "where" with "were." His written assignments may demonstrate poor thought organization. If his handwriting was illegible as a young child, it has likely improved considerably; but it is far from beautiful. He may be a slow, laborious writer. The occasional youth cannot remember the shape of written letters, and may always need a set of raised letters that he can feel. One lad I know can read printing adeptly but can't remember the shape of written symbols.

Some learning-disabled children who had problems in mathematics comprehension responded to remediation and can handle higher mathematics in adolescence, whereas others find that the concepts continue to elude them. Some spatially disorganized youth can cope adequately with algebra, but can't handle geometry; they can comprehend chemistry, but are baffled by physics. Some of these adolescents have been confused by mathematics for so many years that they approach each new mathematics assignment with such frustration and feelings of defeat that one cannot ascertain the degree of ineptitude versus the degree of anxiety. Some learning-disabled youth can handle mathematics concepts, but fail to comprehend the language surrounding the mathematics questions. There is the occasional adolescent who still is so spatially disordered that he can't cope with a page of math problems unless they are ruled off into boxes.

Some learning-disabled adolescents are disorganized in space. They have trouble finding their way around the city in which they have lived their entire lives. If they enter the school through an entrance other than the one through which they typically enter, they are unable to retranslate the space in order to find their way around. Such a youth will likely find the first few days of school confusing, until he develops a learned pattern of where the gym, lunchroom, and his homeroom are. Whenever he steps out of a doorway he has difficulty organizing the building in his mind to know the direction in which to turn. The spatially disordered youth will have difficulty finding his books, his homework, his pen, his eyeglasses, and his locker. He'll leave a trail of belongings behind him and fail to claim some of them. He will keep his belongings in a haphazard fashion, so that his locker and bedroom are chaotic beyond belief or, conversly, will keep his belongings obsessively ordered in an attempt to counteract his deficient ability to order space and the objects in it. He'll have trouble reading blueprints, maps, and sewing patterns. Geometry and geography will present problems, as will the perspective lesson in art, drawing from memory, and possibly reading music. He will likely forget the steps in space involved in threading a sewing machine and will lack the spatial judgment or coordination to sew anything complex or to produce a sophisticated article in industrial arts. He will find it difficult to perform one motor act with his feet and another with his hands, so that learning to drive a car will require considerable practice.

This is the adolescent who will experience difficulty in physical education. He will be uncertain of the size and shape of his body, what it can accomplish at what speed, will be uncertain of the size of a ball, and have trouble predicting the distance it has to travel and the amount of time it will take to reach him. He lacks the eye-hand coordination to throw the ball into the basket or hit the tennis ball or birdie with the racket. By the time he reaches adolescence, he is inexperienced in the use of his body and is physically unfit. He may even be tardy entering his physical education class because he still has difficulty unlocking his combination lock, changing into gym clothing, and tying his sneakers.

The nonvisual learner is relatively oblivious to people's bodies and their attire. He may not notice facial expressions, body gestures, or clothing. As a result, he will be ignorant of current clothing styles, or items of clothing which match, so that his own attire will not reflect the current teenage fashions; and his clothing may appear ill fitting or improperly donned.

If he was hyperactive as a child, he is less likely so as an adolescent; but he still is lively. He has difficulty sitting in his seat for any length of time or devoting his attention to a lecture or homework assignment. He flits from interest to interest, and his attention and thoughts are easily diverted. His language is hyperactive, also flitting from topic to topic. He lacks the capacity to be a spectator to his peers' efforts, so that when he completes his own project he talks, fidgets, runs around, or gets into mischief. His speed and energy are attributes which, if he learns to organize and channel them, could be assets. The learning disabilities volunteer movement is successful because it consists of persistent, energetic workers, some of whom are likely to be hyperactive people who taught themselves how to maximize their energy and to translate perseveration into doggedness.

If the learning-disabled adolescent was hypoactive as a child, he still is the person under whom nearly everyone would like to light a stick of dynamite. He moves slowly, talks slowly, seems to think slowly, and may spend days on end in front of the television. He may set one small task for himself to accomplish in a free day, yet take days even to accomplish this. He finds it difficult to arrive at school or work on time, and has managed to resist everyone's efforts to speed him up. Even though he is not hyperactive, he may share the short interest span, distractibility, and fidgity mannerisms of the hyperactive. Both may swing their feet, touch objects, and rarely stay entirely still. Both demonstrate an inability to organize their tasks within a given span of time.

The learning-disabled adolescent is immature and narcissistic. E. Siegel comments, "He often converses mechanically rather than with feelings, talking at you rather than with you."[2] He is amused at situations, but does not necessarily find the same things amusing that others do. One frequently is impressed by the absence of affect or inappropriate affect, yet cannot help but assume that he feels many emotions deeply. He is eager to please both peers and adults, but seeks the company of the latter. His interests are limited. He is deficient in some forms of abstract thinking, such as Piagian problem solving, is gullible and, at times, literal. Ted did well in college philosophy, psychology, and sociology; yet when his new car instructions stated that his auto had to have a one-thousand-mile check-up, he was upset because the car would have thirty extra miles when he took it to the garage. His rigidity makes it difficult for him to alter the progress of his life—which means that he has problems altering his functioning no matter how poorly it serves him. He becomes anxious around changes and is easily discouraged and overwhelmed. He has failed so often academically and socially that he may program for failure.

He desperately wants to be part of a group and, if accepted into any peer group, may try to be "cooler" than the "coolest," even to the extent of indulging in activities against his better judgement. If, more typically, he is on the periphery of the culture, he may adopt a defensive bravado, rejecting society before it rejects him. "I don't want to be part of your stupid goings-on anyway!" He may develop one-man pursuits, almost autistic-like interests, perseverate when alone, such as playing the same record over and over, and antisocial behavior. Such behavior, however, typically represents lonliness rather than psychotic thought processes. Whenever he is instructed in the requisite social behavior to be acceptable, and offered an opportunity to be part of a group, he embraces it with pathetic eagerness. Nonhandicapped youth generally have been accepted by society; and, once part of a process, they are then able to remain with it or reject it. Unlike their nonhandicapped counterparts, many learning-disabled youth have found doors closed to them; so, they want to opt in. It is ironic that we have a society wherein we agonize about the young who have rejected its values, yet exclude those who are prepared to embrace those same values.

The teenager has shown great improvement since childhood. Some is due to normal growth, some to maturation which seems to assist growth in deficit areas, and some to the remediation he has received. One almost has the feeling that learning-disabled persons can be likened to a jigsaw puzzle whose pieces are mixed up. If a sufficient number of pieces are assembled, and the child taught the pattern, successive pieces fall into place even after formal remediation has terminated. The adolescent now can use reason to modify his behavior and to find ways around his deficits. He is beginning to structure for himself, to internalize the control that which was imposed from without. He is more efficient in determining his levels of tolerance and to seek his own acceptable relief from stress.

As a child people found his plight appealing; indeed, many people want to work with handicapped children. The plight of the handicapped adolescent in our culture, however, is not considered as touching, so that sources of help, be they educational or recreational, are more difficult to find. Siegel comments, "Since the individual is not mentally retarded, and since he is no longer a child, there is simply no excuse for his faulty behavior!"

Chapter 3:
The Concept of Self

IN THE COURSE of looking at the learning-disabled adolescent, one cannot help but wonder what has happened to make him different from others. One of the ways whereby I developed some assumptions about his differences was to look at normal development and hypothesize about which processes might have been affected. The learning-disabled adolescent typically is immature. His behavior often is socially appropriate—but it is appropriate for a younger child. He demonstrates aspects of expected development coincident with aspects of development that seem to be fixated at an earlier stage of growth, so that the picture he presents is one of discontinuity. This is as disturbing and confusing to him as it is to others. To complicate the picture, each learning-disabled child differs in the areas in which he has developed and those in which he has fixated; so, of necessity, we will look at a number of developmental areas from early infancy onward to discuss the points at which the learning-disabled adolescent might have experienced developmental breakdown.

It appears probable that some learning-disabled infants create a less-than-optimal environment for themselves from early infancy onward. Studies have demonstrated that apathetic or underactive babies will initiate and receive less contact from their mothers, and overactive babies will exasperate them.[1] The learning-disabled infant, with his difficulty in organizing his activity level, may be unrewarding from an early age, and create for himself an environment in which the responses and stimulation he receives are more limited or less positive than that received by infants who produce more acceptable levels of activity. Furthermore, we can assume that such an infant's poor ability to organize the mother's behavior, to perceive it with accuracy, and limited memory span, may result in inefficient ability to recognize positive reinforcement, remember it, and grow as a result of having received it. This means that he will be inefficient in acquiring the successive social skills that one expects the young child to acquire, such skills being reinforced by the recipients, so that the social, developmental processes may be rendered retarded and uneven from infancy onward.

The neurologically intact infant learns to cope with, organize, and control external stimulation through the processes of refining his perceptual and motor skills. The perceptually and motorically inefficient infant continues to live in a world in which he cannot organize or control stimulation efficiently, so that his environment remains chaotic. Cognitive and social learning cannot emerge effectively from chaos.

When the child is roughly between the ages of six months and two and a half years, he passes through a period in which he imagines that he is omnipotent. He cries, and his needs are met. Parents are indulgent, accede to his requests, and make few demands upon him. The learning-disabled child's poor coping skills extend the period of dependence upon parents, and the parents compensate for their mixed feelings about the child by making fewer demands upon him. The stage that follows omnipotence is one in which the child achieves status by identifying with the parents. In order to accomplish this, the child must produce specific behaviors and independence skills. Since learning-disabled children often are less adept at this, the omnipotent stage may be prolonged.

Some learning-disabled adolescents still appear to retain vestiges of omnipotent thinking. Their parents continue to be indulgent. They have experienced social promotions in school which surely are viewed as magical since they are unrelated to the child's ability or academic knowledge. They establish unrealistic goals for themselves; after all, do they not possess the magic to accomplish them? Ausubel states, "Since feelings of adequacy (self-esteem) are largely a function of achieving status commensurate with a level of ego aspiration, the retention of grandiose aspirations of volitional independence, and omnipotence in the face of a reality which constantly belied these pretensions, would obviously make him chronically vulnerable to serious deflation of self-esteem."[2]

Between the infant's ages of two and four, parents become less attentive and comforting than they were, demanding more conformity from him to their desires and cultural norms. During this period the child is toilet trained and is expected to acquire culturally approved habits of eating, cleanliness, and some independence skills. Parents expect more frustration tolerance and responsible behavior. The child's increased cognitive sophistication enables him to perceive more accurately his relative insignificance and impotence in the family power structure. The only way he can attain acceptable status is by acquiring a dependent and subordinate role to his parents.

Some learning-disabled children are culturable only with considerable difficulty. They are not easily toilet trained. Their poor coordination means that they are sloppy eaters, and prevents them from executing independence skills such as dressing themselves. Their frustration tolerance and ability to control aggression are limited, so that they are poorly equipped to handle the stage whereby one achieves recognition and self-esteem by conforming to parental demands. It also is possible that some learning-disabled children fail to acquire the cognitive sophistication requisite to perceiving their role in the family structure.

Up to this stage, whatever unstable behavior the baby demonstrated may have caused negative feelings toward the child; but those feelings largely were confined to the family; all infant behavior is expected to be somewhat unstable, so that society doesn't react to the unpredictable infant. When the child reaches the preschool years, however, and fails to acquire the culturally expected skills and behaviors, the parents continue to find him unrewarding—hence reward him less—but also have to cope with their embarrassment from a judgmental society. This creates parental feelings of inadequacy, anger, and guilt, and further alienates them from the child who provides them with scant opportunities to be proud of him. This is the child who, because of his difficulties in processing, organizing, remembering, and executing, seems to respond less to positive and negative reinforcement, so that parents feel thwarted in their child-rearing practices just as teachers, when confronted with these children, feel thwarted and defied in their abilities to teach.

As the child moves from the omnipotent status of infancy into the dependent status of the preschooler, to preadolescence and adolescence, there is a period of disequilibrium between stages. This persists until he acquires the independence skills and conformity requisite of each stage. The learning-disabled child, being less able than others to acquire the skills requisite for his new status or to conceptualize the new role adequately, prolongs the disequilibrium, in some instances, for many years. Consequently, there is an extended state of chaos. The learning-disabled person, being disorganized, requires structure to provide the needed stability to order his world. This extended chaos is likely one of the more serious environmental conditions to which we should direct our efforts.

It begins with the preschool child's problems becoming toilet trained and relinquishing tantrums, and progresses to the school-age child who won't go to sleep on time, get ready for school in the morning, or clean his room, is stubborn, resistant, loud, and overactive. It continues on to the adolescent who still is inflexible, repetitive, disorganized, friendless, resistant, imperceptive, and underachieving. Thus there is a continued and exaggerated conflict between parental expectations and the child's production, which reduces his ability to develop throughout the period between the preschool and adolescent years.

Neither parents or child can tolerate extended chaos, particularly the child, so that efforts are expended to create a more comfortable environment. Since equilibrium cannot be achieved via the channels through which it is acquired by most children, which is conformity to parental expectations, other means are sought. Thus we find parents who have achieved peace through permissiveness on the premise that, if the child is allowed to do whatever he wishes, there will be no battle. Alternatively, some parents have sensed their children's need for order, so have created a very highly structured environment. In order to maintain peace, the order is maintained and change avoided since change occasions upset, even in the adolescent. Unfortunately, learning is acquired through change, so that peace is purchased at the price of growth. In both instances, the child has dictated the environmental terms; and in both instances, they are detrimental to growth.

Parents of the learning disabled are confused about why their children sometimes fail to obey. There are virtually no "experts" available to observe the child's disobedience in the home to determine whether it can be attributed to poor memory, poor judgment or motor skills, inflexibility, or manipulation. The parent's perception is that the child has not conformed, and parental insistence upon execution of the task occasions a power struggle. To avoid such a struggle, some parents opt for permissiveness. This permissiveness retards the development of frustration tolerance, independent behavior, and motivation that is not related solely to the pursuit of one's ego-centric pleasure, because parents fail to demand independent accomplishment and are ready to assist or take over for the child. All efforts and concerns center around the child, so it is not too surprising that his interest remains self-concerned. Such parents fail to structure realistically the limiting and restrictive aspects of the child's world, making it difficult for the child to establish realistic goals for himself and to perceive his own role and boundaries of acceptable behavior with accuracy.

Just as the learning-disabled infant was inefficient in ordering his environment, the older learning-disabled child experiences commensurate difficulty creating perceptual constancy. One facet of this is a result of his problems in screening, attending to and discriminating stimuli, determining the relevance of stimuli, and ordering them in a context that takes into account previous experience, as well as of the current situation. The other side of the coin is the inconsistant environment which has arisen around the child. His parents tell him that he is intelligent; yet he appears unintelligent in school; and his peers call him "dummy" and "retard." His parents allow some behaviors; yet, when visitors are at the house, he is punished for the same behaviors. His parents relate his exploits in admiring tones, yet punish him for these same exploits. At times he is told that he does something well, yet that same level of production will be considered inadequate by others.

Furthermore, his status state is unstable as a result the games people play around the disabled. Most children possess sufficient ability to abstract, to comprehend, and handle discrepancies between the things people say and what they mean, between what different people say, and what the same person says but contradicts in another context. Because the learning-disabled child lacks the abstract ability and the ability to process complexities, mixed messages remain unresolved and contribute to the instability of his status state.

All children prefer sameness, so, will cling to a developmental stage for a period of time before progressing to the next stage. If there is less perceptual constancy, the child will likely cling to his current stage of functioning overly long, rather than risk a new set of perceptions and relationships; this is particularly true of those with learning disabilities. Each new ego state requires personality reorganization; and children with learning disabilities, being disorganized, are loath to relinquish the status quo. They are torn between the drive toward maturation and their need to cling to the known.

Learning-disabled children, because they often think poorly of themselves, tend to remain longer in the stage where they receive positive feedback from their parents and positive reinforcement for being a member of their family. They are particularly ambivalent about parting with the protection and security of dependency because they find long-range striving difficult. They are not self-reinforcers because they haven't been sufficiently rewarded to deem themselves worthy of reward, and their poorly developed sense of time precludes conceptualization of a temporal future. This retards the development of a life plan which is dependent on extended goal-setting.

Human behavior is ironic. If we fail to obtain ultimate satisfaction from a relationship or status state, instead of leaving it to seek a more rewarding relationship, we are loath to part from it and keep "bashing its door down," trying to seek from it that which we want it to give to us. That is why one sees children returning again and again to rejecting parents and emotionally needy children indulging in attention-seeking behavior. Conversely, the person who is secure in a relationship or status state can leave it knowing it will continue to support him. He is aware that he can progress to a new state and will likely succeed as well as he did in the last state. Therefore, even though the learning-disabled child may not have been ultimately successful in the state whereby he was expected to obtain status from the family, he still may cling to that stage hoping for the acceptance and the understanding that may not have been completely forthcoming, to date.

Ausubel comments that, before the child can accept volitional dependency and seek a derived status, he first must perceive himself as genuinely accepted and valued for himself.[3] The learning-disabled child, even as an infant and toddler, tends to be less rewarding than his non-disabled peers. As an infant he may have experienced difficulty sucking, digesting food, and organizing himself on a schedule. As a toddler he may be clumsy, frustrated with manual tasks, and slow in talking or achieving other developmental milestones. His hyperactivity is exhausting and embarrassing. The desperate steps which parents take to reduce the child's activity to the coping level, such as locking him in his room or hammering a door on top of his crib to contain him, curry negative reactions of outsiders, which adds to parental embarrassment. This causes parents to adopt even more repressive measures in attempts to create conformity. The child's value and acceptance, therefore, might be slightly tarnished; and he is likely to perceive it as such.

Even if the child wants to conform—and most learning-disabled children very much wish to do just that—his disabilities prevent him from achievement in some areas. Given that fact, he cannot identify as closely with his family as his siblings because he cannot achieve in the areas in which the family have achieved, which are the areas they and he value. His reference group is not other learning-disabled children, because he associates minimally with others with similar handicaps. Even if he attends a class, recreation group, or camp with the learning disabled, all his informal contacts are with intact persons; and it is the latter group whose values he integrates. Consequently, identifying less with the family, he achieves less ego satisfaction in the derived status state.

Children who are highly accepted at home are more willing to exert effort to hold the approval of adults, are more independent, and able to postpone the need for immediate gratification. Thus, the disability itself may lay the groundwork for environmental conditions uncondusive to subsequent academic learning and impulse control.

The child who fails to identify adequately with his parents to obtain ego status through such identification is someone who has ego aspirations which are unrelated to the situation or his ability level.[4] This might explain some of the unrealistic goal-setting observed in some learning-disabled adolescents and the extreme difficulty that many of them experience in coming to terms with their level of functioning.

The child who does not identify well with his parents fails to internalize parental values which should be examined by those who are concerned with the relationship between learning disabilities and delinquency. Such a person's primary goal is ego enhancement, which is particularly interesting when one considers the egocentricity of the learning-disabled youngster.

In middle to late childhood the child begins his final step toward mature ego development, a breaking away from the status state which is achieved by association with one's parents; and he begins to develop independent status. Ausubel states,

> First among the factors impelling change towards personality maturation is the cumulative impact of progress in cognitive and social capacities, which in turn induces modification of parental and societal expectation. During the period of middle childhood there is an unspectacular but steady gain in the child's ability to comprehend abstract relationships, to reason and to generalize. His level of sophistication in perceiving the attitudes, needs and feelings of others, the relative status positions of various persons (including himself) in the group and the distinguishing criteria of social class status is gradually pushed forward. Thus, understanding more thoroughly the nature of the environment in which he lives, he feels less awed by its complexity and more confident to

navigate alone and unguided. He feels that he now possesses a sufficient fund of social and intellectual competence to qualify for a more mature and responsible role in the affairs of his culture.[5]

The learning-disabled preadolescent and his parents are aware that he lacks the aforementioned attributes, the social, cognitive, and perceptual competence to warrant the seeking and awarding of increasingly difficult tasks and independence skills. Thus, regardless of whether the learning-disabled child experienced difficulty progressing through earlier developmental stages, he almost certainly is lacking in the capacities requisite to the acquisition of independent status. He may, therefore, linger in the preadolescent stage of ego development. This is why many learning-disabled adolescents seek considerable parental assistance and approval in matters such as homework and job hunting. The type of conflicts that they have with their parents may center around issues such as how much television to watch or whether they wash their hands before meals rather than the more typical adolescent-parent conflicts. They are dependent upon their parents for socialization, direction, and assistance, and are fearful of being thrust into independent living before they are able to cope. Some learning-disabled adolescents, being friendless, must continue to look to their families for approval and status. This immaturity means that, in some ways, the adolescent years of some learning-disabled youth are freer of some of the difficult conflicts which arise in normal adolescent-parent relationships. This is a situation appreciated by parents faced with the many other problems the learning-disabled adolescent creates. This also means, however, that families may perpetuate conditions in which a pleasant parent-child relationship continues at the expense of ego growth.

The process of maturing from status acquired from the family to independent status is facilitated if the child is accepted unconditionally, and if obedience and conformity are not made the price of independence. Parents expend so much effort on building appropriate social and academic skills into the learning-disabled child, and overreacting to inappropriate behavior, that many learning-disabled adolescents surely feel that conformity is indeed the price of independence. Furthermore, the adolescent recognizes his vulnerability in coping with the world, so is reluctant to initiate breaking-away behavior.

When the learning-disabled child was young he may have been allowed to practice his judgment around childhood issues because the issues typically were of insignificant consequence. The judgment arrived at would matter little, regardless of what the child decided. As the youth matures, however, he is confronted by issues of more import. When the learning-disabled child was young, his parents could be relaxed about errors in judgment because the discrepancy between actual behavior and expected behavior was not untoward. In other words, if a six-year-old child has a tantrum, it is not expected behavior for his age; but, it is not atypical for a four-year-old, so parents are relatively unconcerned about it. Furthermore, they feel that they have many years in which to alter his behavior. When the learning-disabled adolescent commits an error in judgment, however, his parents overreact because adulthood looms so close, and because they fear the consequences of errors in judgment. Thus they disallow him the errors that everyone makes. I would imagine that parental distrust in the learning-disabled adolescent's judgment retards ego maturation.

Let me trace some of the steps which an adolescent must take en route to adjust identity.

1. He must become familiar and comfortable with his changing body and integrate it with his new identity, because the body is very much a part of self.

2. He needs opportunities and encouragement in his efforts to learn how to express his new and complex feelings if he is to develop a healthy mode of relating to this aspect of his inner environment.

3. He needs to exercise his growing intellectual abilities.

4. He needs to know, as he experiments with new ideas and values, that he is free to make mistakes without risking rejection by "significant persons." Given this sense of security, he will likely be able to avoid some of the tragedies associated with decisions influenced by insecurity and fear.

5. He needs to break away from his parents, identify with the peer group, and integrate their values. He needs to try new feelings, new roles, new ideas, philosophies, and values on his peers until he finds an identity that is "him."

6. He needs to establish new social relationships with his parents, teachers, and peers of both sexes. He must learn how to develop a relationship with them commensurate with his evolving new identity.

7. He needs a best friend of the same sex and, subsequently, friends of the opposite sex.

8. He needs to identify with living, historical, or fictional adults who he sets up as his models and incorporate their habits and values.

9. He needs to prepare himself for adult goals and responsibilities such as post-secondary education, a job, marriage, parenthood, civic responsibility, and military service.

He wants to perform adequately, to have his adequacy acknowledged by contemporaries. He wants to reap the resulting material, sexual, and spiritual rewards. The adolescent in our society feels that one's activities should be rewarding, fulfilling, gratifying, and worthwhile.

Let us examine the stages of development mentioned above as they relate to the learning-disabled adolescent.

The Role of the Body as it Relates to Adolescent Identity

As the infant begins to differentiate his body from the external world, he begins to develop a concept of self until his sense of body becomes synonymous with the sense of self. We are well aware that the sense of body and of self are not well defined in those who are learning disabled. When the body begins to change in puberty, the awareness of self is shaken in all adolescents; and in the learning-disabled, it is undermined even more critically. He is uncertain about how to manipulate his changed body and finds it difficult to restructure his identity within the changed physique. He is frightened at the changes an altered body implies to his already tenuous self, and concerned that an emerging adult body creates external expectations for adult functioning and assumption of responsibility. His developing body implies and demands an expectation of heterosexual behavior, and his social inadequacy is such that he even is more uncertain about these expectations than are most adolescents.

Many learning-disabled children have not become comfortable with their bodies and seem not to have learned what to do with head, arms, hands, and legs; and this confusion is accentuated by the emergence of an altered body. Certainly the awkward youth does not develop the ability to use his or her body provocatively, or to telegraph subtle messages. Chapter five of this book deals with some of these adolescents' difficulties in perceiving "cool" ways of clothing their bodies, either to purchase "in" clothing, to coordinate shirts, slacks, shoes, and pocketbooks, or even to wear them in the "hip" way with the accepted buttons undone, shirts tucked out or in, etc.

Some learning-disabled adolescents are uncoordinated and excluded from the competitive sports of school and neighborhood. Whenever they might be included, their embarrassment at their own ineptitude, lack of comprehension of the spatial demands of the game, and anticipated anxiety about their production, causes them to exclude themselves. Consequently, they tend to be flabby with poor muscle tone. Their unhappiness, impulsivity, poor judgment of how much to eat, and lack of exercise at times results in chubbiness or obesity. The blemished faces of some of our youth reflects their clumsiness and poor body awareness when washing as well as poor awareness of the requisites of personal hygiene. These imperfections compound their problems, because the adolescent in our culture places considerable store on an attractive, athletic, or fashion-model body; and many of our children do not qualify. Furthermore, we have customs involving the use of the body in heterosexual relationships, and develop proficiency in these customs by practicing throughout the adolescent years. The learning-disabled youth, as a result of his immaturity and uncertainty, is less likely than others to take the initiative in heterosexual encounters; or if he does, may make an inappropriate choice of partner, or behave inappropriately—in either instance, reducing his opportunities for experience and proficiency.

Because he may feel that his body does not compare favorably with his peers, the learning-disabled adolescent may suffer a loss of self-love and self-esteem.

Need to Break Away from Parents and Identify with Peer Group

The adolescent needs to sever his attachment to his parents and seek other models with whom he can identify and experience emotional involvement. This is difficult, if not impossible for many with learning disabilities to accomplish, since they are more dependent than others on their parents. Because they have proven so inept in mastery of the world, their parents have protected them; and because their parents have protected them, they have not mastered the world. By adolescence, the lack of mastery and judgment still necessitates added vigilance and imposition of adult decisions, so that both the youth and his parents may have learned to depend upon extensive protection as a way of life. Several years previously the mother may have burned all her bridges so that she could make this child her life's work, and clings to her "raison d'etre." The youth realistically fears enforced independence, just as his parents fear his eventual independence, so that both attempt to maintain a child-parent relationship to prolong security while struggling with the ambivalence of desiring independent functioning. The parents don't want to be burdened with him forever; they want him to be a normal adult; and he, too, fosters that goal.

The messages that the adolescent receives—that he still is a young child who must submit to parental authority—conflict with their expectations of him to behave like an emerging adult, are ambiguous. This compounds the stresses that all adolescents feel when caught between the lures and awards of childlike and adult behavior.

Jerome F. X. Carroll discusses the adolescent's need to have ample opportunities and encouragement in his efforts to learn how to express his new and complex feelings if he is to develop a healthy mode of relating to this aspect of his inner environment.[6] He comments that too often internal conflicts and external pressures lead to the suppression and, ultimately, the repression of authentic feelings, such repression being of serious import.

Many learning-disabled persons fail to express their feelings verbally. Instead they resort to acting-out behavior or withdrawal. They may lack the vocabulary to put their feelings into words. Certainly, many lack the friends upon whom they can sound out feelings. In the past they may have found that their feelings were too painful for their parents to handle, so that suppression seemed the safest route. Certainly the general communication problems which seem to result in many families when there is a learning-disabled member, contribute to the decreased opportunities for that member to express himself. Parents of the learning disabled tend to be so alert to their offspring's needs that they are mobilized into action whenever their child retreats to his room or overreacts to a situation, without the child having to verbalize his feelings.

The learning-disabled adolescent's poverty of response to life situations has been mentioned by P. Wender, C. M. Anderson, A. Thompson, and E. Siegel.[7] Wender and Thompson feel that the learning-disabled person's ability to feel pain and pleasure is impaired. Siegel feels that the learning-disabled adolescent lacks the communication knowledge or skill to use communication as a vehicle for expression of feeling. Davitz and associates found that persons who demonstrate some aspects of learning disabilities have difficulty processing their expressions of emotional meaning and that of others.[8]

I feel that the occasional learning-disabled person may not have the depth of feeling that non-handicapped people have, but that they represent the minority. It has been my experience that learning-disabled persons typically feel sorrow and joy as deeply as others; but there are reasons other than the pleasure-pain principle to explain their lack of affect.

In the learning-disabled adolescent's childhood years he exibited an exaggerated response to stimuli, laughing or crying too loudly, moving his entire body in a plastic infantile response to excitement, and lashing out in anger and frustration. His parents, being concerned with the inappropriateness of this excessive emotionality, suppressed it. Consequently, part of the adolescent's poverty of response may represent inhibition; his parents may have done too thorough a job. Peter commented, "I'm not sure how to respond to a situation, so I do nothing."

There is a relationship between cognitive sophistication and emotional reactions. Therefore, the person who cannot perceive all the implications and nuances of a situation, or relate it to past and future occurrences, is unlikely to react appropriately. The shallowness of response may well be related to the poor ability to perceive the subtle abstract qualities of a situation, to attend to its salient features, and perceive it in a temporal context.

Many aspects of expected adult affect are learned behavior. After all, adults don't respond to emotion-evoking situations in the same fashion as babies. The adolescents who, on an intelligence test demonstrate high performance scores with lower verbal scores, being visual learners, seem to be more successful in learning appropriate expression of affect than the lower-performance/higher-verbal score youth. The former have perceived facial expressions, body gestures, and clothing styles, whereas the latter group seem to have more difficulty processing affect and learning social skills. It is the latter group that seem socially immature and are dependent upon their parents for socialization and other forms of assistance.

However, deficient language usage does play a role in expression of affect, since people who are uncertain about the appropriate response and lack the tools for finite expression of feeling, may, in self-defense, ignore feeling-evoking stimuli. Their store of language includes the polarities of feeling such as "good" and "awful," but the words to express the subtle gradations are lacking. This is similar to their early language behavior, when they learned "morning, noon, and night," but found concepts such as "evening" difficult to comprehend, and consequently the word difficult to remember. These adolescents can perceive extremes in vocabulary and life experience; the progressive degrees from one extreme to another are more difficult for them to grasp.

I asked a learning-disabled young adult why he fails to display any response to emotional experiences even though, in his case, I know that he feels things deeply. He replied that males are not supposed to be emotional. Possibly an overly literal interpretation of role-expectation may account, in part, for the flatness of affect. Finally, we can't overlook the learning-disabled adolescent's narcissism. If one doesn't regard the world outside oneself as important, one won't respond unduly to what happens in it.

Just as the healthy adolescent must learn to express his feelings, he needs to exercise his growing intellectual abilities and skills. This is difficult for some learning-disabled adolescents to accomplish, because their disabilities may have excluded them from remaining in an academic stream that challenges them intellectually; or, by not being allowed to acquire learning and express themselves through their intact modalities, they have been denied opportunities to be challenged intellectually. Brian felt overwhelmed by the content and demands of his secondary school cirriculum. He was behind in his work and had given up trying; his stimulation level was zero. When enrolled in a school for learning-disabled teenagers, wherein the content was geared to his level of comprehension and the program exciting, Brian became "turned on" intellectually and embarked on an academic career that embraced philosophy, sociology, and psychology.

The healthy adolescent needs to experiment with new roles and behavior patterns. The learning-disabled adolescent finds it difficult to initiate new roles because his perception of the variety of roles one assumes, and the contexts in which they are assumed, is poorly developed. Because there has been a paucity of honest feedback and honesty of feeling about the roles he has assumed to date, he has not structured them as accurately as the non-learning-disabled do, so lacks them as a firm foundation on which to erect new roles. He lacks the friends upon which he might try his new roles, ideas, and philosophies. His previous behavior being so erratic, both he and his parents are fearful of him trying new behaviors. His reasoning abilities may not be sufficiently developed so that he rationally can evaluate the ideas and values of his family, and then confirm or disaffirm the beliefs, laws, and customs with which he grew up. He may not feel free to make mistakes without being ostracized by significant others because his parents overreact to his errors and are fearful of the consequences of mistakes in judgment. When he does make decisions, he may be so convinced that he lacks the skill to decide well, that he will lack the confidence to make a good decision. His experiences and our feedback have told him that he is a failure, so that he programs for failure. This self-defeating behavior notwithstanding, he is tired of failing. The "poor me," "stupid me," or "helpless me" roles have worn thin; and the secondary gain has been worked to death. He wants to succeed socially, academically, and in the world, and may be more motivated towards growth than he ever has been, if we can meet his motivation with programs that will foster growth.

The learning-disabled adolescent needs to prepare himself for life tasks. This is difficult for all of today's adolescents and may be particularly hard for the young person with learning disabilities. Regardless of whether he still is or isn't receiving remediation, his ability levels tend to increase, so he may be genuinely uncertain about what his eventual ability will be. He does not know how long he will be tolerated in the academic stream, whether he will be allowed in college and, if so, in what course. He doesn't know which subjects he'll be required to take in the college program of his choice, or whether he'll be able to handle them. If he isn't destined for college, he is uncertain of the attributes he has and the jobs he would be able to handle. It is difficult for him to find a model to emulate because he is aware that he does not have unlimited opportunities for attainment.

Chapter 4:
Fostering Healthy
Emotional Growth

THE LEARNING-DISABLED ADOLESCENT has as much need to break away from his parents as his non-learning-disabled counterparts. The task is particularly difficult for him, however, since he possesses fewer of the coping skills. At some point, where educational alternatives seem to have disappeared and the adolescent is dead-ended, parents may say, "You can stay at home with us forever, if you wish." If the adolescent opts for that choice, his immediate problems will be solved; but he and his family will have chosen a living death.

We must recognize that the learning-disabled adolescent will be more dependent upon his family for assistance, direction, support, and socialization than his non-learning-disabled peers, so that ways must be found to continue to meet these needs within the family while encouraging breaking-away behavior and experimentation with new behaviors. Some parents are so concerned that their adolescent children will be delinquent if allowed to develop their own independent modes of behavior, that they allow them no leeway for growth. If the parents have become too emotionally involved in the child's dependence, and are frightened or resentful of his growing up, the process will be even more difficult for him than it already is; and he will have to rebel more vigorously and be more hostile than he might have been—or give up and remain a dependent forever.

Many of us parents become used to the way of life whereby we have offered a great deal of ourselves to our learning-disabled child. Sometimes the presence of a learning-disabled child in the family has served to disrupt the relationship between father and mother, so that the mother has turned to the support and strength that she provides to her child as a source of satisfaction. On the one hand, therefore, parents want their adolescent child to achieve independence and to be relieved of the physical and psychological demands he makes on them; on the other hand, letting go means that parents and adolescent have to change a pattern that has become comfortable, familiar, and carries certain satisfactions.

Parents who are wary of losing their children may interfere with the social lives that their adolescents are evolving. They harbor realistic and unrealistic anxieties about their teenage offspring and want to guide them through adolescence in ways which will obviate the making of mistakes. Parents want to minimize their child's pain—the normal pain of adolescence, and the added pain caused by the experience of being learning disabled. In the last analysis, however, if the adolescent is to acquire the requisite learning for the maturation process to develop, he must do his own growing up, be allowed to choose his own friends, make his own mistakes, and experience his own pain. As parents we should not look on each mistake as a manifestation of the disability. Unless their judgment has proven to be demonstrably faulty, we have to trust our adolescents and assume that their mistakes won't have dire consequences.

The progress through normal adolescence is a series of ups and downs. When things go wrong, the adolescent is certain that they never will be corrected, and may even convince his parents of this. The learning-disabled adolescent, who has had so many things go wrong in his lifetime and who has a minimal tolerance to stress, may become particularly discouraged. Because he is inflexible, he likely finds it difficult to alter the mood of discouragement to one of hope. Normal adolescence is a time of mood swings; and this can be distressing to parents of a learning-disabled teenager whose childhood was marked by too loud laughter and too fierce reactions to disappointment, both moods of which switched off and on at the drop of a hat. It can be frightening to the adolescent himself because he is unaware that lability of mood is to be expected at his age.

Adolescence is a time of cooperative compliance to parental demands and sullen refusal or procastination. "I'll do it in a moment" becomes the slogan, but "a moment" never comes. The teenager seems so selfishly concerned with that which is important to him that he loses sight of amenities which are important to other family members. The learning-disabled adolescent, who never was adept at organizing his time, organizes it more ineffectively than ever. He leaves everything until the last moment. The adolescent who never knew where he had placed his belongings is sloppier than the wildest dreams would imagine. To step into his room is an invitation to breaking your neck. He is upset at being unable to locate an item of clothing which eventually is found at the bottom of the pile of miscellany underneath his bed.

Adolescents typically make endless demands for money to purchase clothing and recreation items with little knowledge of the family's finances. The learning-disabled child may be particularly naive about the family's monetary position; and the parents may indulge the young person to "make up" for the friends and happiness he lacks. This indulgence may occasion sacrifices on the part of family members—which is unfair and leads to resentment. It denies the adolescent the opportunity to become involved in family planning of finances, and may make him accustomed to a standard of living which he'll be unable to duplicate in adulthood.

Adolescence, typically, is a time of deep commitments, be they to causes or people, unwavering stands for the period of time that they hold appeal, intense alignments and traumatic breaking away with the opposite sex, daydreaming, and overconcern with one's body internally and externally. The teenager is fussily concerned with clothing which, once purchased, is never worn. He becomes critical of everything the home and family stand for, their economic standard, their habits and manner of dress. If parents try to please their teenagers by complying with their wishes, they discover that this fails to work because the adolescent has lost interest in that attribute and is criticizing something else.

If our learning-disabled youth show some of these behaviors, we should be pleased that they have achieved adolescent emotional development. As parents, our most effective role can be to understand the adolescent's position, share his experiences because they are exciting, withal that they are traumatic, while maintaining our beliefs. Worshipping a Guru or a vegetarian diet may seem foolish to us, yet to him they are important; and, if we wish to share "where he is at," we must recognize that importance. This week's infatuation may seem to be just that, and the break-up may have the same soap opera quality that characterized the last five breakups. To him, however, the love is deep and real and the breakup acutely painful. The parental role is to take the adolescent seriously. Parents need to keep their own feet on the ground and, every so often, bring the child back to reality. They must try to keep lines of communication open; and, if they don't belittle the child's current commitment, he will likely share his experiences with them. At the same time, we parents should recognize that he may wish to withhold some ideas and feelings just for himself, or to share with his peers.

It is important for parents to keep reminding themselves of the fluidity of the adolescent. Today's attitude or behavior can be completely reversed tomorrow. Sue had always been a quiet, shy girl with expressive language problems. She preferred a couple of close friends (also quiet girls, or ones who were a little different, and thus excluded from the group), to being part of the "in" group. At age fourteen the "in" group suddenly had great appeal for Sue. She began running around with young teens from all over the city, staying out late at night, and testing all parental rules. She experimented with drugs, got into trouble at school, showed no interest in eating with or interacting with what had been, to that point in time, a close family unit. She belittled her family's religion, ethnic group, economic standing, and manner of dress. Her father bemoaned, "She's lost forever." By age fifteen she was a cooperative, reasonable, delightful, and mature young lady; and her parents were reeling from the incredible change.

So parents need to be patient, tolerant, accepting, and maintain a sense of humor. If both parents and adolescent can learn not to be too caught up in the disability, but can laugh at some of the situations it causes, they have passed one of the most critical survival tests. The adolescent needs to know that there are constants such as family traditions, beliefs, and habits upon which he can lean, to which he can return, and from which he can branch out without coercion to adhere. He should know that his parents are available, if needed, and will step in with limits if he extends himself. If he has the readiness skills and needs a firm push to fly in ever-increasing circles from the nest, his parents should assume that role.

The LD Adolescent in the 1970s

Life at the turn of the century had a certainty to it. Parents knew that they had the job of teaching their female offspring to be homemakers and the males to earn a living whose requisite skills often could be learned from one's father. Consequently, the child was instructed in these goals from early childhood. Children were observers of the adult world; they were taught its skills and attitudes so that the transition from childhood to adulthood was sometimes relatively effortless. There were clear ideas of right and wrong and parental confidence in instilling right and punishing wrong. Male-female differentation was explicitly delineated in the areas of dress, conversation, mannerisms, roles, etc. The behavioral expectations for persons of each age were clearly understood and unchanging. The adolescent was speeded towards adulthood because he had a clearly defined role awaiting him: jobs which he executed from start to completion, and whose contribution was basic, obvious, and appreciated. The church, the school, and the nation inspired confidence in their ability to perform their roles. The family was an ordered structure which fed into a higher order of religion, culture, and nation, all stable and predictable.

The youth of today has little feeling that his life in any way affects his sustenance. Food and clothing arrive at the house in ready-to-consume fashion. He is not required to chop wood, draw water, milk the cow, or tend the sheep. Girls feel that it is futile to sew or knit because far more elegant products can be purchased than one can produce. Similarily, far more succulent food is available ready-made than most people can cook, so that eighty percent of our foodstuffs are purchased preprepared; and the home-baker of bread is an anachronism. Household chores are minimal, largely meaningless, and rarely enforced. After-school and weekend jobs have largely disappeared. Products are produced on an assembly line in which one makes but one part of a commodity that has built-in obsolescence and will be purchased by a faceless public. There no longer are set behavioral expectations for age or sex so that they tend not to be consciously taught. We are quick to spot behavior that we deem atypical, however, and brand the producer of the unexpected behavior. Thus, the learning-disabled person who tends not to learn material that is not consciously taught nearly as effectively as the non-learning-disabled, is at a disadvantage with the amorphous quality of our behavioral expectations. Similarily, male and female role expectations are quickly melting away. This makes it most difficult for parents to teach clearly defined, expected behaviors, and prepare their offspring for future roles. Nonetheless, if the male produces behaviors that people feel are feminine, or if the female appears masculine in her mannerisms, people will be turned off.

What about the structure of church and nation? Many parents question the church's role in contemporary society, the handling of domestic and foreign issues by the government, and the sufficiency of our current "god of affluence." Our education system fails to prepare young people for the jobs that they hope to acquire. Indeed, our schools have failed so drastically to meet the needs of today's youth that the outrage at their dysfunction rocks our foundations; withal, they remain basically unchanged. Professions and trades tend to surround themselves with increasingly restrictive educational requisites for admission. Thinking parents are faced with the dilemma that they cannot morally raise their children to conform to institutions which, in their opinion, range from anachronistic to monstrous. Yet, if they or their children fail to conform, there is little allowance for the deviant or even the constructive dissenter. Furthermore, dissent rarely results in change and, oftener, in suppression of the dissenter.

The young person of today no longer has the warm, close family on which he can lean with the comforting sameness of tradition, the home that has been in the family for fifty years, the Fourth-of-July picnic, the maple sugaring, and what-have-you. Thus, all adolescents feel somewhat frightened and unsupported. The learning-disabled adolescent is bound to feel more overwhelmed by that which faces him, and wonder whether he ever will acquire the admission requisites to a highly developed, changing society.

What then can the family do? One can't go wrong by suggesting that the family who provides a secure base will be helping to prepare the adolescent for his forays into less known territory. Of course, the most essential security lies in relationships; and, if those are well established, material changes can be handled with aplomb. If the parents can supplement a healthy emotional climate with some physical constants, so much the better. This might mean living in the same house in the same community, an anomaly in our mobile society. It means activities shared by the family and traditions, be they Sunday brunch, Thanksgiving dinner, or a Christmas tree decorating ceremony. It might mean hobbies shared or songs everyone sings around the piano. The twentieth century urban pace is frenetic. Perhaps families of the learning-disabled might slow it down and take the time to share and build memories together.

You Have to Know What You Stand For

Most of us know only too well the dilemma of the thinking North American in this era, and how our uncertainty of belief and custom is conveyed to our youth. We even allow our young to blame us for the political and environmental state of our world because we are so insecure about our role. All adolescents could do with more security than our reeling world provides, but it even is more essential for the insecure learning-disabled ones. It is so easy for parents of the learning disabled to feel overwhelmed by the bureaucratic nature of society since it has acted contrary to their child's interests in the past; and they as parents may have been powerless to alter it's stand. Therefore, some parents of the learning disabled feel insignificant. But, if they wish to convey to their adolescent children that the world is a place over which one has mastery in small and large ways, they must grab their convictions by the tail and live them. This means that husband and wife, singely and collectively, need to determine what institutions and customs are expressions of themselves and solidify their lives with a commitment to that which has meaning to them, be it religion, politics, or a cause. It may mean a break with old affiliations because, if they have lost their meaning, continued involvement conveys duplicity to the young.

Practice your convictions in your relationships with your family and outsiders, and expand them into an active community concern. Religion or ecology can't be relegated to one day a week. Share with your children why you believe the way you do, and involve them in the practice of your convictions. Your learning-disabled adolescent needs the feeling of belonging and the companionship and acceptance that he can receive if he is an active member of a church, political party, or other group. He needs to experience the meaning to his life of doing something for others. Throughout his life he has been a recipient, and we have deprived him of the beautiful feeling of giving of oneself. (As long as everything centers around him, he is bound to be narcissistic; and as long as he has not contributed to society, he is unlikely to feel commitment to its laws or customs.) Once your adolescent has learned how to become involved in an organization outside the home, he then can branch out into involvements of his own, and should be encouraged to do so.

Assure that he has a meaningful role in the family. He should be part of family councils and decisions, and his contributions should be respected.

Include him in discussions concerning your work. I ask my language-handicapped adolescents for synonyms when I write, and consult them on word meanings and spelling, even though it is like the lame leading the blind! We discuss the courses that I take in college and the administration of the agencies with which my husband and I are involved. Make mealtimes, evenings, and outings a time of discussion in which every conceivable topic might be explored—from pacifism to homosexuality. You can talk about civil rights, the ways whereby our culture furthers or fails human dignity, and the positives and negatives of subverting much of our individuality in order to maintain society. Explore women's liberation, the abortion issue, and the problems of the developing countries. Discuss the way some of the most important statements of our time are expressed through fiction or drama. Take him to plays; the preponderance of small theatre companies means that plays now are no more expensive than movies. Discuss the messages of live television drama. If art interests you, include him in gallery tours, and discuss which art he likes and why, or include him in your interest in music. Many learning-disabled adolescents read minimally, have few friends, and rarely go anywhere besides the school and home. Thus their interests are limited so that they are uninteresting people. They are only vaguely aware of how the world outside their limited terms of reference works, and are clueless about the exciting pursuits that are available even to the nonreader. Any exposure that parents can arrange, without coercion, is bound to increase his knowledge, his interests, and his ability to utilize resources.

On Setting Goals

Some learning-disabled adolescents seem to cling to incredibly unrealistic goals. The youth who can't master grade nine mathematics wants to become a mathematician, and the uncoordinated wants to be a professional athlete. We are living in an era in which there is an overwhelming compulsion to actualize oneself. Today's youth believe that they should have a job which allows them full expression of their creative, humane, or whatever self. In fact, few people find jobs that end in being a joyful expression of self, which is a grave disappointment to anyone. The learning-disabled adolescent, with his disabilities, limited education, and job opportunities, is even less likely to find a job that is "him." We owe it to all our children to explode the myth that every minute of one's time must be fulfilling. Show them the repetitive, administrative, and unpleasant aspects of every job—be it housework or a profession—and also point out the ways whereby every job can be fulfilling. Furthermore, encourage your learning-disabled adolescent to seek his fulfillment in activities outside his job.

Some learning-disabled adolescents are obsessed with the desire to attend college. For some, this is a realistic goal. Others are not well suited to college. In assessing suitability, one should not consider intelligence only, but should take into account attributes such as reading ability, flexibility, degree of organization, and ability to handle stress. Some learning-disabled adolescents will want to attend college because their parents and most of their family, friends, and relatives are university graduates. Such youth will take their aspirations from family accomplishments rather than the goals that the family has established for them. Other youth will be determined to go to college because their families harbor the idea that no one can achieve anything in North America without a college degree. Such a concept is fallacious, so that such families will have to discard their misconceptions, and work with their offspring to alter their conceptions. The volunteer associations will have to eliminate the practice of publishing success stories, if success is perceived as college graduation.

Realistic small successes tend to diffuse unrealistic goals. Neil kept talking about his intention to swim lake Ontario; but, after a few good standings in school swim meets, he ceased talking about his unlikely scheme. This principle applies to social, academic, and other areas. Rather than involving him in lengthy discussions about the inappropriateness of his aspirations, attempt to steer him to arenas in which he has a reasonable opportunity for short-term fulfillment. As long as he remains motivated and undefeated, perhaps we should allow him some of his dreams. After all, progress consists of the fulfillment of unlikely dreams.

Don't Sell your Soul to the System

Parenting a learning-disabled child holds a few bonuses for us, the parents. Society does not allow us to float along with the status quo, sending our children to school year after year, commenting pleasantly on the good teachers and worthwhile practices, and reserving our criticism for coffee klatch and cocktail party small talk. We don't just send our children to Scouts, the "Y," the Little League, hockey, and on to college and jobs. Everything in the community that is other people's right is ours provisionally or not at all. Every poor practice of education and other community agencies that might be mildly unpleasant for our neighbors is a disaster for us. Rearing our children becomes a question not only of determining their bed time, whether they should drive the car, or whether to settle for hashish instead of LSD. Instead, we find ourselves involved in basic issues and are forced to make basic decisions around the really important values we hold for our children. A mother told me that in the past she would have been violently opposed to any of her children marrying out of her faith or subculture. Having a learning-disabled son, however, she now realizes that for her, the important values now are a kind, solid spouse for any of her offspring, regardless of one's religion or national background. We also are forced to take a good hard look at what our schools and agencies offer that is worthwhile, and what is uesless or harmful. Then we must decide how much foolishness we will tolerate (and we have to "go along" with a great deal in order to stay in the system with the payoff certificate at the end). However, at no time should we confuse the things we believe in with the things we tolerate, either in our own minds or our children's.

Several years ago I asked a teacher of a learning-disabled class whether I should tell my daughter that I agreed with her dissatisfaction with an obviously rigid, punitive teacher. The special teacher advised me always to uphold the classroom teacher. *She was wrong!* The most important gift of survival we can afford our offspring is to level with them. Teach them that there are many things that they will have to tolerate to reach the ultimate goal, but don't sell your soul and theirs down the river by pretending you endorse that which you don't. Don't urge them to respect that which does not lend itself to being respected. Acting obediently and respectfully is different than respecting. Whatever you do, don't allow educators or anyone else to put you in such a sweat about conformity or to hint at exclusion to the extent that you urge your child to do that which he is not able. Fight for your adolescent's right to be part of the system, contributing in the ways whereby he is capable. Never for a moment give your child the message that, because he learns differently, he must question less and be more compliant so as not to threaten his tenuous position.

Learning-disabled adolescents sometimes do a poor job of weighing issues and tend to overreact, regardless of the magnitude of the demand, the stress, or indignity. When your child reacts to an event at school, discuss it. Teach him to weigh the issue in terms of importance. He needs to learn to differentiate between issues with which one has to go along—just as all of us have to go along with much that displeases us and issues that are an assault on his dignity and must be altered. Teach him how to change the latter and back up his efforts with your support. If your adolescent feels that he has a role within the system and some autonomy over the way he learns a subject, he is liklier to feel that he is a person of significance than if decisions are imposed upon him. If we can demonstrate to him that we aren't intimidated by the system and will work constructively with the school and other agencies to ensure that his dignity is kept intact, he and others will take their cues from us and conclude that he is a person worthy of respect. By the time he reaches adolescence, he should be included in conferences or staffings on him.

Teach him that random or destructive anger accomplishes nothing other than backlash, so that fury must be released in the boxing ring, gym, or by running around the block. Conversely, constructive social action is his right; and, whereas it may result in pressure to conform or suppression, it also may result in change. In any event, it will protect him from enduring injustice, discrimination, or poor teaching practices in silence, which may help him to remain intact. I urge you and him to read *The Little Red Schoolbook*.[1] It is written for adolescent students and suggests ways whereby they can effect more exciting, relevant course content; if their efforts to do this fail, it describes several courses of social action and, failing that, how to amuse oneself while bored in school.

What about Psychotherapy?

Having to resort to psychotherapy does not mean that parents have failed in the ways they have reared their children. Adolescence is a time of stress for all children, and particularly stressful for the learning disabled. He alone, or with the help of his family, may be unable to work through some of the difficult feelings and changes one encounters in adolescence; or he may be so discouraged that he no longer is willing to invest himself in the educational process or in friendships, and requires skilled assistance. If he seems unable to resolve his role as a man or woman, or is extreme in his behavior, be it manifestations of aggression, withdrawal, or whatever, a therapist might be consulted.

In order to provide an environment that is most condusive to change and growth, the therapist might want to involve the family in therapy. Parents should not feel that this is a threat to them or an attempt to pry into their secrets. Therapy need not be a digging for and expurging of disease. Rather, it is a process of learning new ways of thinking, feeling, interacting, and communicating that can untie old structures and release people for fresh experiences, expanded horizons, and deepened relationships. It requires strength to enter therapy and an attitude that one made and will make mistakes. But, to make mistakes is human, and not so terrible that one must protect those mistakes from scrutiny. Parents should choose a therapist who is knowledgeable about and accepts the concept that there is such a syndrome as learning disabilities.

Many clinics, particularly those serving the adolescent, still adhere to the theory that all behavior is learned. If such clinics intend to serve the learning disabled, I feel that they must expand their thinking. Even if the environment exerts considerable influence, client change tends to be minimal if therapeutic approaches are not combined with special education services and practical suggestions for home and community management. The feelings of child and family can be worked with ad infinitum with minimal progress being accrued unless the disturbing problems of school, street, and home are improved. Furthermore, families who have spent years living with the "child who doesn't fit" and who have endured the agonies of his noncoping, the rejections, the prejudice, etc., will not take kindly to being blamed for the problem. As long as there are almost no suitable educational services for learning-disabled adolescents so that the family is faced with the daily nightmare of a totally unsuitable school experience, and denial of the disability by educators, no amount of working with feelings will alleviate the crisis. The therapist, therefore, might serve the family's needs most effectively at that juncture, by teaching them the ways of fighting for services, or arranging some very practical help for the child, plus intervention with the school. The child must be provided with a school environment where he feels he can contribute, is appreciated, and valued. As long as we permit him to feel confused, overwhelmed, defeated, and having to resort to deception, subterfuge, and withdrawal, how can we expect to work with him? Robert Coles quoted a teacher in the south, "If I see *any* child lonely or terrorized, I feel that if he is going to learn, something must be done about his terror as well as his answers to tests."[2]

Some of the most effective therapy is that which is directly related to the situation. If the youth has difficulty at work, the specific problem is dealt with at that juncture. If he has problems around interaction, the interaction is discussed with him and alternative modes of behavior talked over. In order to serve learning-disabled adolescents effectively, the therapist may have to vacate the traditional settings and join the youth where they are. The lag between a problem and it's discussion in the therapeutic hour may be sufficient time to render the discussion merely an intellectual exercise rather than one with carry-through value. Adolescence, for many learning-disabled persons, is a series of crises. The most effective therapeutic results might be obtained if the youth was worked with at the point of crisis; yet so often therapists leave no time in their case loads to accommodate persons in acute distress.

Chapter 5:

Socialization

IN E. H. ERIKSON'S "Eight Ages of Man" in *Childhood and Society*, he comments that the youth experiences "a sense of finality regarding the fact that there is no workable future within the womb of the family."[1] Thus the adolescent recognizes his need to establish friendships with other adolescents. This need is further accentuated in the North American culture, where today's family functions as a group of independent individuals. The home today's family functions as a group of independent individuals. The home becomes a rendevous for family members rather than a pivot around which life goes on. Notwithstanding his need to be part of a group, the learning-disabled adolescent often finds himself excluded from social acceptance as a result of the attitudes other adolescents have towards the selection of friends and the attributes of lack thereof that the particular adolescent brings to social situations.

Erikson comments, "Young people can be remarkably clannish and cruel in the exclusion of all those who are different in skin color, or cultural background, in tastes and gifts, and often in such petty aspects of dress and gesture as have been temporarily selected as the signs of an *in-grouper* or *out-grouper*."[2] Furthermore, adolescents are more selective about their acceptance of newcomers due to the increased sophistication of their group make-up. They derive status from the status of the persons with whom they associate. To associate with one who is much sought after is to shine in reflected glory.

The learning-disabled adolescent, being a low-status person, fails to provide the status other adolescents seek. Since we are identified, in part, by those with whom we associate, the learning-disabled adolescent is not considered to be an ideal friend. Some learning-disabled youth do stand out as different in dress or mannerism, glibness or grace. Some are unaware of the "in" clothing adopted by today's teenagers. Others may be aware of the appropriate clothing to wear; but when they wear it, they appear as if they were dressed by a blindman. Many are unfamiliar with colors, patterns, and cuts of clothing that do or don't match. They may not realize which clothing is worn for which occasion, or become overly fond of some items of clothing which then are worn over and over. Some heed their parents' suggestions of what to wear . . . so that Janet came to the club party in a frilly blouse and skirt only to discover that the other young people were wearing jeans and T shirts.

It is possible to pick some learning-disabled adolescents out of a crowd merely by the gawky manner in which they handle their bodies or the exaggerated quality of their gestures. Some tilt their heads awkwardly and never seem to know what to do with hands and feet. They are uncertain how closely to stand when they are conversing with someone, when to touch someone, put arms around someone, hold hands, when to stand, sit, hold open a door, or assist someone. They may react to excitement with their entire body, or underuse their body in expression.

Some have difficulty interpreting other people's nonverbal messages, what is being implied by the position and tone of the body, by gestures and facial expressions. A. Mehrabian, as quoted by Dr. Joyce Brothers, found that when an individual talks, the words themselves account for 7 percent of what he communicates; 38 percent is conveyed by his manner of speech, and 55 percent by facial expression and body language.[3] Since we obtain many communication messages from such channels, a problem in perceiving such cues or inattention to such cues will hamper a person's perception of what *really* is being communicated. If the teacher verbalizes a positive statement, but her body is rigid, arms akimbo, nostrils flared, and eyebrows compressed, most students will ignore the words and believe the body message. The student who has missed the visual clues and interpreted the statement verbatim very well might find himself in trouble.

Some learning-disabled adolescents have difficulty interpreting cues in space, such as what a person's clothing tells us, and what cues we can elicit from the extensions of one's body, such as a pocket watch, eyeglasses, hearing aid, pipe, cigarette holder, jewelry, or cane. We make many assumptions about people based upon their clothing, whether it is expensive or inexpensive, threadbare, clean or dirty, stylish, formal, or shoes polished or scuffed. A woman in a mink coat with her hair elaborately coiffed and wearing all the accessories will lead us to make one set of assumptions; whereas a woman in a housedress, tacky cotton coat, and run-down shoes, will evoke another set of assumptions. A man in overalls, denim jacket, thick shoes, and carrying a lunch pail will lead us to assume a number of facts about him, those facts being different, indeed, from a man with bowler hat, vest, spats, and walking cane.

We make assumptions around people based upon the setting in which we meet them, the people with whom they are surrounded, and what we know about their friends and relatives. (This is one of the reasons why learning-disabled adolescents are reluctant to befriend other learning-disabled persons: because people then will assume that they have the same attributes.)

Learning-disabled adolescents often are deficient in making these assumptions. Much of this is related to their problems in perceiving situations as a Gestalt (or whole), and making complex relationships. We think of a person as part of a family, subculture, socioeconomic group, member of a political party, who dresses in a specific manner, has specific habits, hobbies, beliefs, lives in a specific fashion, etc. Many learning-disabled adolescents have not learned concepts of relatedness properly, so are not able to perceive a person's relative status in family, subculture, and culture. In the past, their unselective attention and segmented attention meant that they did not attend to relevant cues or perceive them as a Gestalt, so that their acquired knowledge of the messages we obtain from nonverbal cues is uneven. It is almost as if the learning-disabled adolescent were deaf and blind for several years, and were then suddenly thrust into a culture wherein he is expected to have mastered incredibly complex communication patterns, most of which have been internalized by others and are practiced unconsciously. This means that persons who wish to consciously teach these patterns to others find it an almost impossible task.

A significant number of learning-disabled adolescents have problems interpreting the nonverbal aspects of speech. They are imperceptive to the communicative aspects of pauses, inflections, fast speech, or slow speech. They are uncertain of the propitious moment in which to interrupt ongoing speech. They have not perceived how long to talk about a subject or how much interactional energy is expected of each situation. In other words, a discussion of the weather between strangers at a restaurant counter calls for a minimal energy outlay, so that the person who extends a casual comment on the weather into a lengthy discussion, will likely be viewed as odd.

Similarly, those who have learning disabilities often are not perceptive in monitoring other's reactions to their conversation to determine whether their interaction is enjoyable, irritating, or boring to others. They fail to keep a running measurement of the other person's reactions and expectations. They tend to discuss topics of interest to them, rather than asking themselves what the other person expects of the interaction, and then presenting that which is expected, both in content and extensiveness. They don't know how to use aspects of their speech such as volume, pauses, or humor, to create desired effects. Siegel comments,

> If it is true that the minimally brain-dysfunctioned population, as a group, has difficulty in interpreting nonverbal messages, many consequences ensue which militate against the emergence of social savoir faire. If only the word—but not the mood—registers, a concrete approach to language as well as some degree of emotional 'unsteadiness' develop (characteristics, by the way, which are commonly ascribed to this population). It is not a case, then, of being unconcerned with others, but of not understanding them. If one cannot discern the meanings of facial expressions and body lan-

guage, then emotional messages of suspicion, unhappiness, boredom, hostility, discomfort, and anxiety will be missed, and inappropriate responses—that is, behavior—follow.[4]

Their hazy concepts of relatedness likewise work against social adequacy. They are uncertain about who holds which position in the greater family, in the neighborhood, school and community. Consequently, they are confused about the people to whom they should show respect, those with whom they should be chummy, those with whom one should have a casual relationship, and those with whom one should be intimate. This really is a more sophisticated form of their earlier confusion around whether to address a teacher as Mrs. or Miss, and what those terms meant regarding marital status, or, again, a form of their confusion around what an aunt, uncle, grandparent, or cousin was in terms of relationship. As adolescents they are confused about who to address by their first name, last name, or title; their errors too often are thought to be gauche or rude.

The learning-disabled individual wants to relate to others, but is insufficiently aware of how to use clothing, props, grooming, settings, and conversation to project a picture of himself that he would like to portray. Most of us attempt to convey an image of how we would like ourselves to be, our ideal self. Others respond to that projected image, assuming that it is an expression of our real self. This allows us to bridge the gap between our real and ideal selves. The learning-disabled adolescent often hasn't mastered the communication skills, perception of subtleties, or expressive ability to project an ideal self. He merely *relates* in a similar fashion, regardless of the situation or the person to whom he is relating. He is uncertain as to what he is portraying about himself; and, as is to be expected, he is inefficient in processing people's reactions to his communication. Because he has not picked up all the meaning behind their nonverbal and verbal responses to him, and because he doesn't possess a communication bag of tricks, he is limited in modifying future communication so that it could be more appropriate. This also means that he is not efficient in using communication to establish a continuously evolving concept of self which can be modified by interactional feedback in a circular process of projection, reaction, and modification.

Erikson comments that the adolescent is ready for intimacy, the capacity to commit himself to concrete affiliations and partnerships, and the ability to develop the ethical strength to abide by such commitments, even though they may call for significant sacrifices and compromises. He suggests that the child's danger, at this stage, lies in a sense of inadequacy and inferiority. If he despairs of his skills or his status among his partners, he may be discouraged from identifying with them and with a section of the work world.[5]

As Erikson suggests, adolescence is the time when the intact human integrates all facets of himself into a concept of the whole person, that is, himself as an offspring, sibling, grandchild, nephew, friend, acquaintance, student, Christian, North American, his physical self, his hoped-for self, and where he is now.[6] He organizes this into a complete picture of who he is and further refines this self by trying a variety of behaviors on friends. The learning-disabled adolescent finds the task of organizing his various roles into a totality that is "him," most difficult. He has not become sufficiently integrated to offer an identity to others or to become involved in the compromises and commitments of extended intimate relationships with others. If learning-disabled adolescents were to have a well developed concept of who they were, they then could be less egocentric and more other-directed. The stress upon twentieth-century western man is very much other-directedness, so that the acquisition of this trait seems particularly important. The non-learning-disabled adolescent's relationships are characterized by depth and intensity; those of the learning disabled, by shallowness. The learning-disabled adolescent, being locked into a concrete present, lacks the temporal projection necessary to develop a long-term commitment to others which would involve a concept of how the relationship might develop through time.

To become a friend means to become interested in, and somewhat knowledgeable about the other person's interests, be sensitive to their needs and feelings, compromise on activities, laugh off differences, be supportive, allow the other person freedom to interact with others and spend time with themselves, be elated by their successes, share their sorrows sensitively, be able to communicate your pleasure, displeasure and anger without such communication being destructive to either party, and change and grow as your friend changes and grows. I wonder whether many learning-disabled adolescents possess the sensitivity, empathy, flexibility, maturity, and generate sufficient interest and excitement to maintain such friendships.

Erikson states, "Many a child's development is disrupted when family life has failed to prepare him for school life, or when school life fails to sustain the promises of earlier stages."[7] As Erikson points out, if a child feels that he lacks the skills that his fellow students possess, he may be discouraged from identifying with them. If we are to render the learning-disabled adolescent sufficiently confident to seek friendships, we must ensure that he succeeds in school.

Summarily then, social interaction in our culture is a process that demands a high degree of complexity involving a lifetime of processing, storing, assessing, comparing, projecting, etc. The learning disabled experience difficulty processing complex situations, particularly in their areas of dysfunction. Some of their difficulties are related to early learnings of concepts such as relatedness, expectations, and nonverbal cues, which the non-learning-disabled normally acquire, but which those with learning disabilities acquire in a spotty fashion. Since everyone who comes in contact with them assumes that early learning has been mastered many years ago, they view the current behavior as being deliberate. The teenager handicapped in this manner, being unaware of the reasons why people don't find his friendship worthy of sustaining, cannot learn from friendships lost. The mannerisms that his family nag him to change may not be the ones which turned people off; but, since people don't often share with the irritant the cause of irritation, he works on the more obvious manifestations of gaucheness.

He is a poor judge of what he has to offer and who would be interested in "buying" his attributes, his good nature, and loyalty. He seeks friends on the level of his family's friends and is reluctant to befriend the lonely, who would welcome his friendship. He may look to his parents to satisfy his social needs, yet take much of his frustration and loneliness out on them, while being fearful that such behavior will cause them to push him into adult independence.

He feels inadequate and uncomfortable in the school community and in his present and eventual role in society, so he is discouraged from relating to his peers and their activities. School is the milieu around which North American adolescent life revolves. If one can't "make it" in school, one loses the prime vehicle through which friendships are made. So, learning-disabled adolescents' problems in socialization can be traced to rejection by peers, difficulty in social skills, and exclusion from an accepted and comfortable role in the institution attended by our teenagers: school. He becomes depressed by the fact that he has reached out to people with friendship for years, yet has been rebuffed. Once he is depressed, he becomes less appealing as a friend. Because his investments have resulted primarily in pain, he is less ready to invest himself and, indeed, may program for failure.

How are we going to attack these problems? There has been little research on the development of social skills in the learning-disabled adolescent. In fact, there is no finite cataloging of the sequence of social skills the intact human acquires and the ways whereby they are acquired. There have been studies relating environmental factors to some aspects of social and emotional development, but we still are a long way from being able to develop a sequential social learning program as we have done for motor or academic skills. This means that everyone who now works on changing the learning-disabled adolescent's social effectiveness must, of necessity, be a pioneer and an experimentor. It is well and good that there have been suggested some hypotheses about the reasons for the learning-disabled adolescent's problems in socialization; but one is on shakier ground suggesting solutions. We have no choice but to try, however crude our initial efforts.

The first point of attack and the one which lends itself most readily to know improvement, lies with the learning-disabled adolescent's place in the school. As long as he finds secondary school confusing, overwhelming, impersonal, and pressuresome, he will stand out as a non-coping member of the system, surely no one to befriend if one is seeking "with it" friends. Neither will he feel comfortable enough with himself to seek friends. All his energy will be directed to the coping aspects of academics, and all his emotions directed to the sense that he is drowning. This returns us to the never-changing beginning point for the learning-disabled child, which is that we must create an educational milieu in which he can be comfortable and productive before we can embark on a program to effect social change. Some of the ways whereby this might be achieved are dealt with in the section in this book on the academic process.

Then we need to examine the adolescent's social functioning and ask ourselves the areas in which he is deficient and what that deficiency represents. In this I plead for an eclectic approach, since so often we lean towards the simplistic. The behavior that one observes in the learning disabled neither is all learned, nor is it all related to organicity, so that it requires a multifaceted approach. One will have to be a careful observer over a period of time to determine the gaps in social learning. Then we must determine the ways of closing these gaps, ways that will be acceptable to the adolescent in terms of the teacher and of sophistication of content. Some compliant adolescents might be receptive to working with their parents. Others would respond more positively to a college student, a club leader, or "Big Brother" as described in the next chapter.

It might be beneficial to read chapter 7, "The Communication Components of Time, Space and Relatedness" in my book *A Word or Two About Learning Disabilities.*[8] This chapter deals with the ways whereby temporal, spatial, and relatedness concepts are used in communication, and suggests ways whereby some of the deficiencies might be remediated. You will have to sophisticate the procedures to suit the adolescent's level. Even if you imagine that the youth has a firm grasp of an area, test it out; you may be surprised at the gaps that he demonstrates in elementary knowledge.

Ascertain whether he knows all the stages of man, such as infant, baby, preschool child, preadolescent, adolescent, young adult, middle-aged or senior citizen, and the ages one is when one falls into those categories. Determine whether he is aware of who are included in the global categories. Test his ability to predict by taking a walk along the street, and have him suggest the quality and price range of stores, restaurants, and merchandise. Have him predict the clientele stores serve by the window layout, sign lettering, and type of goods displayed. Go into restaurants and talk about the effect created and how furnishings, accessories, and sound were utilized to create different effects. Go into clothing stores and discuss the messages conveyed by the layout, attire, and manner of salespersons, etc. Go into homes and have him tell you all he can about the family's habits, type of life, ages, income, etc., by the messages conveyed through furniture, color, odors, books, toys, and other props. Try this out in different rooms of the house.

Have him tell you which items convey which messages, and then ask him what behavioral expectations there would be of him if he were to visit that home. Ask him how he would behave at that home if he were at a supper party, barbecue, or visiting someone his own age.

Take a subway or bus ride with him, and ask him how much he could tell you about the people on the bus: their ages, incomes, types of jobs, ethnic background, personality, and habits, and what cues led him to make those assumptions. Have him observe people on the bus and tell you what their mood is and which cues were a clue to their mood. Point out mannerisms that might indicate whether a person is anxious, in a hurry, happy, etc.

When he is in the process of developing a friendship, ask him what the new friend's interests are, and encourage him to discuss the other person's areas of interest with them. Have him play a game with family members and friends in which, within two minutes, two people determine how many interests they have in common and how many areas of differences there are between them. Try to have him tell you, before he embarks on an interaction, whether it is a minimal, moderate, or maximum energy interaction, whether he should contribute one short sentence to it, or whether it calls for an extensive investment on his part.

Many learning-disabled people have difficulty expressing how they feel so that, although they may talk volubly, they may not share much of themselves with others. Siegel says, "It is simply a style, an ability level, a reflection of his concept of the function of conversation. Instead of genuinely listening and then 'levelling' (i.e., conveying the essence of his thoughts, beliefs, and feelings), he frequently adopts a role, which seems to stand as a buffer between himself and the other party."[9] The learning-disabled adolescent seems to need practice recognizing his feelings and learning how to express them. Encourage him to share his feelings with family members and friends. If you have arranged a "Big Brother," have him also work on this area. In order to develop an awareness in the learning-disabled child of what it is that is bothering him, you may have to start at the beginning of the day and ask him how waking up went, breakfast, etc. As long as he is unable to verbalize his feelings, he is bound to feel alienated from others. When he has learned acceptable ways to express his triumphs, his anger, and his pain, he will receive and give more to friendships. He needs, however, to learn the difference between sharing himself emotionally and buying friendships.

Guide him in the type of commitments one must make in order to maintain an in-depth friendship. Encourage him to develop a variety of interests so that he is an interesting person. Then, if he is unable to handle in-depth interactions, perhaps he can develop several casual friendships around his areas of interest. Don't allow him to perseverate, that is, spend too much time talking about the things which interest him, because this causes people to avoid him rather than seek him. Don't be fussy about his friends, provided they meet minimal standards of decency and conformity.

Encourage him to establish himself in a new environment, obtain a job at a camp, in another town, or take a bicycle trip across the land. Often, learning-disabled adolescents have difficulty making friends in their own neighborhood or town because their old reputation persists. Their current behavior may be quite appropriate, yet their peers have them pegged as "dumb" or "crazy." Being stuck with that stereotype means that the youth recognizes that he is expected to be dull or bizarre; and one can't behave effectively with those expectations. He needs to be able to make a fresh start with people who haven't known him in the past, people who will accept him on his current merits. Ray has one friend in the city where he lived for twenty years of his life, yet made several lasting friendships in the colleges he has attended and with young people he met while travelling and working in Europe.

Just as we teach learning-disabled adolescents about their disabilities as they relate to school functioning, we must provide them with knowledge around the skills that they find difficult socially. When they are unable to handle an academic assignment, or comply with a teacher's request, or are unduly punished for areas in which they can't cope, hopefully they will explain their disability to their teacher so that he or she will be more understanding. Similarly, when the adolescent finds that he has missed an important social cue, or has said or done something which has not been well received, if he can explain his deficit so that his behavior will not be perceived as purposeful, people may be more understanding.

Once again, this harks back to the necessity for the parents to become intimately familiar with the child's disability so that they can interpret it to him and others. If the parents are unfamiliar with their offspring's disability, they should seek a professional who has had contact with the young person and can explain the "why" of the social disability to the adolescent and his parents. He then needs to be taught the language to use to interpret the disability to others. This knowledge and skill not only will allow him to intervene on his own behalf, but it will provide him with the tools to monitor his output and continue to remediate himself socially. Most importantly, it gives him control over his social environment.

A number of learning-disabled adolescents are inappropriate because they fail to recognize the impact of their behavior on others. They may not realize that they are being sarcastic, aggressive, impatient, loud, repetitive, or what-have-you. They should be asked whether they wish to have the behavior pointed out unobtrusively whenever it occurs. Many learning-disabled children from an early age onward are master manipulators. Unfortunately this manipulation may prevent the young person from developing honest relationships or meeting his responsibilities. It requires a special and trusting relationship to convince the adolescent to alter behavior which may have been his defense against the world, and to learn instead the positive rewards of facing situations. The extent to which the adolescent will acquire more appropriate social skills under adult tutelage is dependent upon the relationship they develop. Both parties must realize that the adult is attacking the behavior—not the person. The adolescent whose social skills change in such a relationship is one who is willing to have the adult as a reinforcer.

Some parents ask whether they should move to a new neighborhood to escape the old reputation which stigmatizes their learning-disabled adolescent. That is a tough question with no pat answer. Every family personally must weigh the pros and cons of moving, judge their ability to handle a move financially, gauge the adjustment demands it will make upon all family members, obtain the assurance of a comfortable school placement for the learning-disabled member in the new school, and ascertain whether his social skills are sufficiently polished for him to have a fighting chance of making friends in the new neighborhood. Possibly a less drastic solution might be to enroll the adolescent in a group around which he has a special interest, or in a carefully chosen club group at the community center. This would give him an opportunity to interact with people who didn't know him from the past, while providing a structure around which some friendships might be based.

Some language-handicapped adolescents are uncomfortable using the telephone. North American adolescents seem to have the phone as a permanent appendage to their ears, and the youth who avoids telephone chit-chat is at a decided disadvantage. Steve double-dated for his first date; and the next day, when his friend phoned to rehash the date Steve queried, "Is that all you phoned about?" You may have to point out to your child the way adolescents use telephones and encourage him to phone his friends and become involved in discussing the minute events of their lives. The selfsame behavior that drives us crazy in our non-learning-disabled adolescents, ironically, is the behavior we may need to teach and encourage in the learning disabled.

What about Dating?

The prerequisite behavior for dating is that one know how to be a good friend, so that all of the preceding material in this chapter is important for the aspiring dater. He must learn how to be interested and interesting, caring and solicitous without being possessive, and must be aware of the small kindnesses practiced by people interested in one another. He or she will likely have to have some of these behaviors pointed out to him and be given hints such as, "Compliment your date on her appearance," or "Hold the door open for your date and help her on with her coat." Many of our adolescents are unaware of the evolution of a friendship which precedes dating, such as eating lunch at the same table in school with a girl, walking her home, buying her a coke, going bike riding together and, then, an appropriate activity for a first date such as a movie or ice skating. Tell him the price of the snack one might treat the girl to after the movie, and alert him to protocol in the restaurant such as holding the chair for his date. From his preteen years, have him help the female members of the family off and on with their coats, hold doors open for them, and the other gallantries, so that by the time he reaches dating age, it will be ingrained behavior. My husband instructed our boys to do this at an early age, and I appreciate the gracious touch this lends to our lives. It does not deter the women in our family from actualizing themselves. If your offspring can become a member of a group, he then can date as part of the group, which is far less stressful than individual or double-dating. The current generation of adolescents tend to become involved in boy-girl friendships and informal time spent together in a group, rather than the kinds of dating in which their parent's generation indulged. Ascertain that your adolescent know the facilities the city has to offer for recreation: museums, planetaria, outdoor restaurants, boutiques, parks, zoos, sports facilities, etc.

What about Sex?

Some parents of learning-disabled adolescents are concerned that their children will be unable to enjoy a normal sex life. I understand from my friends who teach learning-disabled adolescents that this is an unnecessary concern. Learning-disabled adolescents are capable of, and many do, become involved in sexual behavior. Consequently, they should receive as much information on sex as one would supply to any adolescent and in the same manner. If one or both of the parents feel sufficiently comfortable to discuss sex with their children, this is likely the most effective method of communicating both factual information and attitudes such as the respect that one must have for one's partner, the sexual act being used as a means of conveying love, and the reasons against promiscuity. Do a particularly careful job of teaching the adolescent about birth control and venereal disease. If you wish to provide him with reading material, you might give him *Facts About Sex For Exceptional Youth* by Sol Gordon, available from The New Jersey Association for Children with Learning Disabilities; this is simply and effectively written.[10]

What about Engagement and Marriage?

Learning-disabled people can marry and have a family like everyone else. However, they typically are less mature than their peers and have fewer opportunities to socialize with the opposite sex than do others. Thus they should have ample opportunity to mature, to spend time with other young adults of both sexes, and become settled in a job before marrying and being tied down. If at all possible, try to ensure that the dating years are not circumvented, that the youth does not go from little dating right into marriage.

How Do They Manage as Spouses and Parents?

The feedback that I have had from teachers and parents is that, similar to the rest of the population, learning-disabled adults fare from disastrously to very well as spouses and parents. My concerns about some learning-disabled individuals as spouses and parents would be whether they had learned communication skills, initiative, perseverance, organization, are perceptive, flexible, and had been able to develop some of the subtleties in dealing with people. Every spouse, in relationship to his or her mate, assumes a variety of roles. At different times he is parent, spouse, child, protector, protected, indulgent, firm, helpful, and helpless. Hopefully, the learning-disabled person will have learned to perceive the role expectation of his spouse. He should be able to express tenderness and joy, be able to give and receive love comfortably, tolerate delays in gratification, and be self-reliant.

Marriage for a man or woman is the undertaking of a never-ending responsibility for oneself and others; and he must be ready to undertake and feel comfortable with such responsibility. He can't have a tantrum when he fails to get his own way; and she can't scream in frustration when the food burns; they can't be at the mercy of every pressure they feel. They must have a commitment to the marriage and parenthood that survives boredom and stress. They must be able to carry through on decisions, tasks undertaken, and difficult assignments, and not over- or underrespond to situations. They must be able to tolerate disappointment, frustration, and be philosophical about situations which they feel are unfair.

Throughout childhood and the early to mid-teens, the learning-disabled child and adolescent may be the scapegoat of school or neighborhood. As he reaches late adolescence and young adulthood, however, he will likely experience less scapegoating, because adults are more tolerant of individual differences than are children. Unlike children, they are less concerned that their status is closely related to the persons with whom they associate. (This is one of the reasons that learning-disabled children and adolescents avoid socializing with their peers, preferring to interact with adults.) Although adults tend to be patient with learning-disabled adolescents, so that interaction occurs, one must not necessarily conclude that the adolescent possesses adult social skills. When he is an adult, his skills will likely be as deficient in relationship to other adults as they were in relationship to his peers on a child or adolescent level. However, the learning-disabled adult's social inadequacy is partially related to his immaturity so that, with opportunities for, and an environment condusive to growth, his social skills can be expected to improve as indeed, everyone's do, throughout our lives. Furthermore, in all the stages of man's life, adulthood is the stage wherein one has the greatest flexibility as far as choosing friends. Dress, mannerisms, and the ability to play hockey no longer are requisite behaviors for friendship. The learning-disabled adult can avoid his areas of inadequacy and concentrate on his areas of interest and intactness in vocation and avocation. This person must, however, learn to move into the community and seek friends. Since many learning-disabled youth have the techniques to initiate friendships, they must develop the most important skill of all: that of maintaining friendships.

Chapter 6:

A Friend in Need

CHILDREN ARE SOCIAL BEINGS who need social experiences. To that end we should make our homes as enticing to the young as we possibly can, perhaps by having a billiard or ping-pong table, tasty food in the refrigerator, a monthly make-your-own-pizza party, and show our children's acquaintances how pleasant we find their presence without overdoing it. Then, if that is insufficient to provide your child with social experiences, you will need to look to organized recreation. Since learning-disabled persons' social maturity is not necessarily related to their age, this chapter will deal with some issues concerning readiness and recreation which the reader then can match to the child in question, regardless of his age.

I am disconcerted at the way too many parents of the learning disabled in the United States and Canada have attempted to meet their children's social needs—which is by initiating gross-motor groups. They fail to take into account whether the child is ready for one-to-one interaction, one-to-two interaction, sheltered, or integrated recreation. It also is unlikely to do a good job either of effecting social learning or of meeting the children's gross-motor needs since, typically, it is an undifferentiated program staffed by volunteers. It even is unlikely that the child will feel that he made friends in the group with whom he shared companionship. Such programs typically fail to take into account whether the child needs gross-motor training and, if he does, whether he already is receiving sufficient remediation in that area in school and elsewhere. I feel that we would be of far greater service to children if initially we concentrate on one goal only, remedial or social. After a social program is well under weigh and running smoothly, a remedial element can be introduced as an integral component of recreation. Until you reach that point, however, I think that it is best to attempt to meet one need only, but meet that need well. *Remediation can be fun, but socialization should not be work.*

Learning-disabled children, because they have fewer social contacts than others do, and tend to learn less from the contacts they have, need more concentrated social experiences than other children. They cannot obtain much varied interactional experience on a walking board. The child needs to learn how to make small talk with his peers, be aware of activities that he can suggest that they might do together, and have interests that he can share with others. He needs a degree of knowledge and expertise in the activities which interest his agemates. Then he needs to test his increasing knowledge, skill, and interactional abilities with his peers. He needs to receive feedback (which the leader assists him in processing without distortion), be helped to modify his behavior, and try new models of behavior and interaction on other children to ascertain how they are received. This can happen only in a well-rounded program, most probably a club program.

Parents always hope that, in some mysterious way, a recreation program will decrease their child's learning disabilities. That is why they confuse remedial and social goals, initiating fine- and gross-motor groups so that their children will interact with one another. Parents should not expect direct improvement of the disabilities from a recreation program. The program is not connected with the remedial assistance the child receives, so it cannot be part of a coordinated approach. If your child attends school five days a week, he has discharged his work commitment and has a right to pure recreation which is just that: re-creation. He needs to make up for the many unenjoyable experiences he has had through the week by having fun with peers and adult leaders. Possibly, if he feels good about the successes he has within the club, his good feelings might carry over into his school work as greater motivation, which is central to overcoming disabilities. We don't know, however, to what extent good feelings are situationally determined, so we should not anticipate even indirect academic benefits from a recreation program. We should be more than happy to settle for socialization as our only goal. A recreation program can expand a child's horizons and knowledge, but not cure a learning disability.

The adolescent is unlikely to improve his coordination appreciably with formal gross-motor training, and he might find formal gross-motor activities childlike and demeaning. His needs are served far more effectively if he can be a member of a group that participates in sports with no emphasis on competition, or indulges in activities such as running, swimming, bicycle riding, jumping, and skiing, because he probably can become reasonably proficient in these activities.

Recreation plays a large role in making the child or teenager feel that he is a valued member of the peer group. Neil was finding senior high school discouraging and overwhelming. Except for the kindness of his geography and mathematics teachers, each school period was a greater nightmare than the period before. However, the one factor that made school tolerable was the swim team. Neil is quite uncoordinated, having been diagnosed as spastic cerebral palsied when he was young. Regardless, his swim instructor at camp spent many hours working on swim skills with him. By the time he reached secondary school he was sufficiently proficient to swim on the team and be hired by the school and the city to teach swimming. Although Neil didn't win many swim meets, his school coach entered him in each one, including the provincial finals. Neil's teammates called him "tiger" and pounded him on the back in camaraderie. This young man identified so strongly with the team that, ill or well, he arose at six a.m. daily to attend swim practice. At one meet his trunks slipped off and Neil continued to swim naked rather than let the team down.

Calvin attended a nonspecialized camp from ages nine to seventeen. He was so much a part of the camp that, when he arrived each summer, he remarked, "I feel like I have come home"; and after camp each year, he felt let down. In addition to functioning as a member of a cabin group, he appointed himself the official camp host, greeting visitors affably. When Calvin grew too old to be a camper, he took the job as camp dishwasher; and Neil became one of the camp's swim instructors.

Calvin also attends a sheltered club program in the city. He eagerly looks forward to each meeting, lining up his classmates to enroll in the club and travelling to and from club meetings with his new-found friends. The integrated camp was a good choice for Cal because the director is a social worker with a learning-disabled son. He hires mature staff, supervises them well, is flexible, and encourages individual skill development rather than competition. But, because Cal is very immature socially, and the city lacks an integrated club program with the safeguards afforded by the camp, the sheltered club was the preferred choice. Consequently, one must consider the child's or adolescent's readiness as well as the options available before deciding whether to opt for one-to-one, one-to-two, sheltered, or integrated recreation.

Some of the issues you might consider in selecting program options are:

1. Can the child relate appropriately to a large group of peers, a small group, or relate only if he has adult monitoring?

2. Is he fairly realistic about his strengths and limitations? Is he comfortable with his disabilities? Is he well coordinated?

3. Is he knowledgeable about community facilities?

4. Is he much less mature than other children his age?

5. How stable is he (outbursts, tantrums, aggression, frustration)?

6. Can he remain with a task for a reasonable period of time?

7. How independent is he?

8. Is he affable and well motivated?

9. How sophisticated is the integrated program you are considering?

10. How much expertise have the leaders in working with the learning disabled, or willingness to learn and commitment to working with

the learning-disabled child and modifying their program commensurately?

11. What are the demands the program will make of the child? Even sheltered programs have some demands that are too threatening for some children.

12. What is the leader-child ratio? Would the provision of another leader for the total group increase the possibility of the child being able to handle the program?

13. How much supervision do the leaders receive? What is the commitment of the supervisor to try alternative methods of programing until he achieves success? Examples of flexible approaches are:

- use of volunteers to improve leader-child ratio
- extra leader in group or crisis help on call
- shorter period of attendance
- matching task the child is assigned to his abilities or providing him with a partially completed project which he completes, thereby making him feel part of the activity by ensuring that he can succeed at the task he has been assigned
- recognizing when the child requires assistance, clarification, or calming down

Each alternative of sheltered programing, be it one-to-one or a sheltered group, should have an active social learning component so that most of the participants can progress to nonsheltered recreation. Parents and recreation personnel should guard against the tendency to place learning-disabled children in sheltered programs because they are an easier route than integration, promise greater security, and provide an increased likelihood of a successful experience. In fact, recreation personnel sometimes keep a child in a sheltered program longer than necessary, because it is easier to serve the child in that fashion than make the necessary arrangements to ensure success in an integrated group. Or the leaders become attached to the child and the progress that they feel they are making with him, and are loathe to graduate him to a more exposed experience.

Parent's Expectations of Recreation

It is true that a sheltered program, by virtue of the ages, training, commitment, ratio and supervision of the staff, and the degree of program planning, is almost guaranteed to succeed. Conversely, placing a child in an integrated program carries greater risk. Nonetheless, if we choose the integrated program carefully, using some of the criteria mentioned earlier, the risk can be minimized. If parents are truthful with the program supervisor, sharing information on the child's social skills, attention span, athletic proficiency, and behavior, the supervisor is more likely to be able to arrange the safeguards requisite for success. He or she should be told if the child has problems reading, spelling, with mathematics, or fine-motor control, so that he can be protected from embarrassment. We parents always hope that our children will handle themselves normally in a recreation situation, and feel that if we catalogue a description of their behavior, it might serve to frighten or prejudice the personnel. Consequently, we may fail to supply the very information that would make successful functioning more likely to occur. We tend to fear that, if we are honest about our child, he will not be accepted into the program. If the staff is unequipped or unprepared to handle him, it is not a suitable program for him, in any event. It is far better to determine this in advance than withhold information, enroll him, and encounter failure. Even if you don't understand the psychological information on your child, or it has not been shared with you, you still know own youngster—how he behaves and relates to others—and this is what the recreation staff needs to know. This information should be supplied to the supervisor, and he then will use his discretion as to how and when to share it with your child's leaders. Forewarn him about any critical events in the family (such as a divorce) so the leader can avoid upsetting the youngster.

Have the leader and supervisor meet the child at a time preceding his enrollment into the program. This not only permits them to become acquainted and comfortable with the youngster before the program begins; but it structures it, as well, for your son or daughter. He now will be familiar with the building in which the program takes place and the people who will work with him. They can describe the first session to him in detail, as well as outlining some additional activities which will occur.

Is Sheltered Recreation a Wise Choice for the Adolescent?

If the learning-disabled person does not possess the social skills to become an integral part of his peer group, and such skills can't be acquired, or the situation altered to ensure success, we must opt for socialization with other disabled persons. Since adolescence, however, is the time whereby the human sheds his old identity and develops a new one, primarily through interaction with his peers, the very soundest adolescent may provide flimsy support to the identity struggles of his contemporaries. The learning-disabled adolescent, already hampered by his confused childhood identity and equally confusing adolescent self-image, is likely to be of limited usefulness in assisting his contemporaries in moulding their new selves. The imperceptive and nonresponsive learning disabled are not the best people to provide behavioral feedback to their peers, and people who are uncertain of what behavior to produce themselves are poor judges of others' output. The leaders, having grown away from adolescent expectations, also can't provide the necessary feedback. A sheltered program can, consequently, alter gross forms of social inappropriateness; but it is difficult to modify the subtle social ineptitudes without competent peer interactors. Since adolescents harbor strong feelings about being associated with other learning-disabled persons, it may be preferable to utilize a program model such as "Green Light" as described in this chapter, in which the teenager can be in a position of prestige and responsibility. Otherwise, some of the more socially competent siblings or classmates should be included in the group—but only to the extent that they can be absorbed without being a threat, or impatient with ineptitude or the simple level of the activities.

Because many adolescents prefer to remain friendless than socialize with other learning-disabled youth, it is important that we begin teaching social requisites to the young child and complete the stages of sheltered recreation, if required, before adolescence. Then, hopefully, by the time the child has reached his teens, he will be able to cope with nonhandicapped friendships. He still may need to be encouraged and directed to groups which revolve around a specific area of interest—and his own interests certainly should be taken into account. This will provide the structure he may require, enable him to become knowledgeable in some area, and provide him with something specific around which to converse and plan with others. Parents should not be judgmental about the type of group their child elects to join unless it's philosophy is so repulsive that the parent morally cannot tolerate the choice: A mother complained to me that her son had joined the psychedelic phenomena group!

Our children tend not to adjust to new situations with ease. It is important, therefore, that they allow a new program a chance to succeed. Establish your ground rules before the child enters the program. I would suggest that he be expected to attend a minimum of five sessions before deciding whether or not he wants to continue. Some of our children have been rendered so sensitive by past social slights and failures that they may become upset with minimum provocation or imagined rejections. Before you allow your child to drop out of the program, check with the leader to determine how well he has been accepted and how he has been managing. Before deciding that the program hasn't worked, determine the specific areas in which the child was not coping, and try alternative approaches.

Big Brother, Big Sister Model

If you feel that one to one interaction is a good place to start, the model used by the McGill University, Montreal, Children's Hospital Learning Center, might be worth considering. They have a "Big Brother, Big Sister" program utilizing college students. The Big Brother or Sister becomes involved with one or two children, depending on the child's readiness, expanding the activities to involve more children as the "Little Brother" becomes more socially proficient. The Big Brother takes the child into the community, teaching him how to travel alone and familiarizing him with the facilities the city has to offer for recreation, shopping, etc. He teaches the child independence skills such as shopping for Christmas presents. Under his tutelage the Little Brother practices the popular childhood pursuits, be they bike riding or baseball. Finally, if there is any spare time, he may tutor the youngster. Throughout these activities the Big Brother is actively monitoring the child's behavior so that he can achieve readiness for expanded interaction.

When the child appears ready his horizons are extended. The older student may become Big Brother to two boys, or he may join another Big Brother, encouraging the two youngsters to telephone one another and handle the planning of activities, times, and places. As the final step, he will determine what type of group the child would like to join, be it church choir, Young Democrats, or a club, and possibly arrange to function as an extra leader in order to provide the Little Brother with protection and direction. By protection, I mean that perhaps the child is becoming over-stimulated after half an hour the first few times with the group, so that he and his Big Brother could leave while he still has control of the situation. Or perhaps he requires extra assistance with a task which the Big Brother unob-trusively could proffer. If you are considering emulating this model, I feel that it is important to extract a commitment from the Big Brother to remain with the program for a predetermined period of time. Learning-disabled children have been "let down" by so many people that it is impor-tant that this experience not become another desertion.

Noah, a learning-disabled eighteen-year-old became Big Brother to Tom, a learning-disabled twelve-year-old. Tom loved making models; and he and Noah would figure out how much money he had, how long he would have to save in order to buy a model; and then they would travel around the city, seeing what kinds of models the stores had. Their mutual work on models encouraged Tom to read, follow instructions sequentially, and develop his fine-motor skills with Noah intervening to prevent frustration. Noah prac-ticed skating, swimming, and billiards with Tom, helped him with school work, and consulted several people on the best remedial techniques he might use with his charge. He and Tom went on many outings together and spent pleasant afternoons watching ballgames and perfecting Tom's checker-, chess-, and card-playing skills. Then Noah's younger brother was included in the games, and he and Tom became involved in extensive transactions of trading hockey cards. Because Noah had so few friends of his own, he was able to devote a great deal of his time to his Little Brother.

One of Noah's problems had been that he didn't monitor his own social behavior well. Soon after he began working with Tom, however, he made comments such as, "Tom never will have friends if he burps in people's faces." I encouraged Noah to monitor Tom's behavior, teaching his young charge amenities such as the inappropriateness of asking for pop and cookies each time he entered our house. Noah also learned to limit Tom, to help him appreciate that he had other claims on his time, and clarify the number of sessions a week that they could spend together. When Tom asked Noah to engage in an activity which encroached on Noah's areas of deficit, Noah explained that he couldn't do those things well because they were his own areas of disability. This was a wonderful example to Tom of matter-of-fact acceptance of disability. Whereas previously Noah's conversation had been primarily self-concerned, Tom expanded Noah's world to encompass a sensitive, conscientious concern for another person, and made Noah feel genuinely needed.

Operation Green Light

Several parents of learning-disabled children ages twelve to eighteen were eager to arrange a sheltered club program for their socially isolated offspring. A group of college students volunteered their services as club leaders, and their club house to be used as the meeting place. One of the students was appointed administrator and coordinator, and I was consultant. The students and parents met to share ideas on what type of program might best meet their children's needs, discuss what their children were like, and establish some ground rules (e.g. how expenses would be handled; who would be responsible for the children's safety; the leader's expectation that the children would be taught how to travel to the program and henceforth travel on their own; the criteria for enrolling and maintaining a child in the program, namely sufficient social and behavioral skills to benefit from and handle oneself in the program, with termination of a child's membership occuring at the discretion of the coordinator). Subsequently, we met with the parents in mid-winter to discuss their perceptions and ours on how the program was progressing.

After the meeting with the parents, the college students then met with the prospective club members to elicit their ideas of the type of program they wished to have. Everyone realized that the age range of twelve to eighteen was not a viable programing unit, and the young people decided that the sixteen- to eighteen-year-old youth should join the college students as club leaders. Each learning-disabled club leader or college student took one or two of the younger children as their special charges, to telephone during the week and with whom to work on social and behavioral skills. Once a week, all the leaders, learning-disabled and otherwise, met with me to discuss how the program was progressing, future program ideas, and their successes and concerns about the children who were their charges. After the meeting there was coffee and an informal get-together.

When the program had been under weigh a couple of weeks we found that the learning-disabled youth were arranging to travel to the club sessions and meetings with one another, or meeting early and having a meal together. Many of these youth were the selfsame people who had elected to spend the rest of their lives in front of a television set rather than socialize with others with learning disabilities. Nonetheless, because they had the responsibility of being club leaders with a prestigious group of college students, they could rationalize their socialization with other learning-disabled adolescents, around a specific goal, thus diminishing their loneliness.

We taught the leaders how to break activities down into small chunks for their charges, how to structure programs, and how to monitor behavior. Just as in Noah's case, they transferred this awareness of other's social behavior to an increased sensitivity to their own behavior and it's appropriateness. We discussed which children were ready for integrated programs and why, and this sensitized them to the requisites of interaction with others who do not have learning disabilities. For the first time in many of their lives, they were doing something for someone else, rather than having others' attention always centering on them. In the process of seeking program possibilities for their group, the adolescents learned what the city had to offer recreationally.

This program, "Green Light," came about because a group of people asked themselves what the needs in a community were, explored resources, and devised creative methods of matching resources to need. When we view learning-disabled persons as donors rather than recipients, we expand our resource pool.

Integra Foundation Sheltered Program

A pilot sheltered recreation program for socially inappropriate learning-disabled adolescents was initiated by the Integra Foundation, a provincially funded, private agency. The first year, the screening process eliminated severly acting-out and behaviorally retarded adolescents. All other applicants were accepted; and we consequently found that our population was not socially inappropriate, merely immature. We discovered that several of the teenagers in the program already had an active social life, so that our group was an additional program for youth who really weren't in need of such a program.

Initially, the group was organized on an activity-centered basis in which the children rotated from activity to activity and ended the evening in a discussion group. However, we discovered that within such a structure, they did not interact with one another but, instead, worked side by side much as preschool children do. A change of professional staff allowed us to restructure the group into clubs. Interestingly, the change of some of the staff and program structure proved to be profoundly upsetting to the adolescents. The clubs allowed the young people far greater diversity of activities. We discovered that, whereas there had been a reluctance to engage in discussion within the formal discussion period of the original program model, as the teenagers became engaged in club activities, they began to share their experiences and feelings.

Since this group of youth was quite socially appropriate, we felt that the adolescents in the group who were loners had ended up in that position because they were less mature than their peers. Additionally, they had been bussed out of their neighborhoods to sheltered classes for an extended period of time, so that they lost contact with the young people in their neighborhood. They felt sufficiently ashamed of being in the "dummy" class that they lacked the courage to reinstate friendships. To further compound the problem, some were considerably overprotected. At year's end we deployed our staff to integrate this group of adolescents into nonsheltered programs in their own areas of the city.

The following year we found a group of truly inappropriate adolescents and began again. We discovered that the young people avoided interacting with one another, preferring to use behaviors that they felt would be appealing to the leaders. These behaviors invariably were discussions of something of interest to the adolescent himself, the very egocentric behavior we were supposed to modify. The leaders, charged with the desire to be kind to and patient with handicapped adolescents, responded to these overtures and required considerable encouragement to limit their responses and steer the teenagers to peer interaction. The reluctance of the adolescents to socialize with one another persisted through activities such as bowling and skating. We found that, when activities were organized by the leaders, the young people tended to relate to and through the leaders rather than with one another.

Parties at the club members' homes finally broke the ice. The adolescent host or hostess planned the evening's entertainment and made the refreshments. Even activities that one would suspect would be "corny," such as darts, ended up being fun and excellent ice breakers. Some of the party hosts or hostesses invited a few neighborhood teenagers to join their club party, and this proved to be very successful. The local adolescents had fun and didn't seem to perceive this group as being anything different from a "normal" club group.

Integration with non-learning-disabled adolescents occurred, as well, when the club members brought their brothers, sisters, and schoolmates to the club meetings. Since the club took place at the "Y," the learning-disabled adolescents began to interact with other "Y" members in the cafeteria and pool. This was an excellent opportunity for the leaders to render active assistance in interaction skills, particularly when the club members were trying to relate to the opposite sex. Bob met a girl in the pool and arranged to get together with her in the cafeteria after the meeting. Once in the cafeteria, the girl and her friends sat in a booth whispering while Bob maintained his distance on a stool. His club leader dropped in and gave Bob the needed encouragement to join the girls. This turned out to be so successful that one of the girls invited Bob to her house.

We found that none of the club members had major interests, so it was almost impossible to have them perceive other club members' interests and talk about things which interest someone else. The leaders used some films designed to promote social adequacy, but found that the accessible films tended to be so far ahead of our charges' functioning that they were unable to bridge the gap. Drama was introduced, in which the club members were supposed to imagine themselves as people in a variety of situations. Although this technique has proven successful with younger learning-disabled children in our programs, the teenagers found it difficult to project themselves into another pair of shoes and a different place and time, and were threatened by the very exercise. They managed more successfully when acting in a play, and then discussing how the characters felt. They were uninterested in discussing hypothetical, ethical, moral, or behavioral situations; they were far more interested in discussing real situations affecting them. The leaders used basic techniques to foster interest in others, such as having the club members bring photographs of themselves from infancy onward which fostered discussions of areas of mutuality such as pets.

The club leaders chose a president for the month. This person had to phone each member in mid-week, remind each one of items to bring to the meeting, and other details. This was an impressive and frightening responsibility for some of our adolescents. A few of them were uncomfortable using the phone; but all were delighted to receive calls, since the telephone so rarely rang for them.

We found that the members were understanding and patient with behavioral deviations. They would sit quietly and wait out the speech of their peers with expressive language problems or that of the hypoactive slow talkers. They ignored inappropriate laughter and running around. The leaders dealt with inappropriate behavior largely by ignoring it, and rewarding appropriate output or discussing appropriateness as situations arose, such as when it is appropriate to discuss sex. Within the context of the group many of the members' behavior had become more appropriate; but we have yet to determine how much of that appropriateness has been generalized to other situations. Some behaviors lent themselves more readily to change than others. We were least successful in altering hypoactivity and aggression, and found that aggression was contagious.

In seeking members for our club groups, we found that youth from low socioeconomic areas of the city were prepared to enroll but that middle- and upper-middle-class youth typically shunned the sheltered program, regardless of how desperately they needed it.

In planning a sheltered program for adolescents, there are several considerations to take into account. The program should serve a narrow age range, young adolescents, mid-adolescents, or young adults. The intake worker should seek some compatibility of members in terms of physical size, maturity, and intellectual capability. This is not a snobbish bias to exclude needful youth, but a recognition that each group should have sufficient homogeneity to be able to function.

The group sponsors will have to decide whether the program will serve learning-disabled adolescents within the strict confines of the definition, or adolescents whose parents say they are learning disabled, in which latter case there will likely be a mixed group which will include the learning disabled, culturally deprived, slow learners, and emotionally disturbed. The only purposes for limiting enrollment to the specifically learning disabled would be if the group was designed to examine and modify specific learning behaviors in order to test a research hypothesis. If the enrollment is limited to the learning disabled, the sponsors might encounter difficulty obtaining psychological information. Such information, even if accessible, may be several years old; and school boards or clinics may be reluctant to share it with a mere recreation program, particularly if a registered psychologist is not on the program's staff. The best source of learning-disabled adolescents is likely students enrolled in a secondary school remedial program, where such programs exist, and who the remedial teacher says are learning disabled. Regardless of whether a pure population is served or not, there should be behavioral criteria for admission. The competency and number of leaders, the structure of the group, facilities, and back-up staff will determine the extensiveness of behavior problems that can be accommodated.

Social group workers or recreation personnel should be consulted concerning program design, supervision, demands on staff, insurance, safety procedures, liability, etc.

If we are to add to the sparse knowledge currently available on the development of social appropriateness in those with learning disabilities, the people who are attempting to bring about such changes should document their results and impressions. I feel that, in their documentation, they should separate the ways that they modify emotional problems, such as aggression, from behavior that is assumed to be more directly related to organicity such as inattention, attention to segments of a situation rather than the whole, and perseveration. We already are aware of methods whereby one to alter emotional problems, but do need to learn of ways whereby social learning can be enhanced, which behaviors respond to which techniques, and which fail to respond. Since the majority of learning-disabled persons expect to function adequately in the non-handicapped adult world, our current goal, realistic or not, is adequate social functioning. Therefore, our present attempts are not to create a veneer of appropriateness but internalized knowledge of what to do when. Our task, in the next few years, is to determine whether such a goal is realistic, and, if so, how it can be implimented.

Parental Responsibility

Having one's child spend some time each week in a recreation program offers relief to the parents, and allows the child to feel that he is a member of a club, Scouts, or activity group like other children. Nonetheless, parents must not expect that their responsibility ends when they deposit their offspring at the "Y" door. We parents cannot assume that it is our right to have the recreation agencies serve our children, so that the problem of how best to meet our child's needs and the possible need for supportive services is dumped entirely into their laps. Many recreation agencies know little about learning-disabled children in general and, of course, know nothing about our own child; so our job is to educate them about the disability and how recreation programs can best meet our children's needs for social interaction and skill development. With the help of the local volunteer association, we should line up possible consultants and suitable reading material for the agency. If extra hands are required, we should assist the agency in soliciting volunteers from secondary schools, colleges, and church groups. If additional paid staff is required, we parents should be prepared to underwrite the added expense, or find a service club that will. If the child initially can tolerate only a short stay in the group, or his behavior is uncertain, we should remain—unobtrusively and without interfering—in the hall or nearby room. When the child finishes each session, we should not crowd the doorway to query, "How did he do?" He'll have good days and bad days, so instead, a brief chat with the leader or supervisor once every month or two will provide a more global picture.

I have known of situations in which the best-meaning parents or recreation personnel initiated groups for the learning disabled, supposedly to meet a critical need, only to have no one show up. This can be very embarrassing, after one has convinced the agency of the necessity of such a program, and had them rearrange their pool schedule, hire leaders, etc. Usually the embarrassed initiator blames parent apathy and disinterest, yet has never bothered to determine whether a supposed need is an actual one, or whether the structure that one has chosen actually will meet the needs. Before approaching an agency to initiate a program, ascertain what programs currently are serving the learning disabled in your community, and find the parents and children who desire the intended program. Then involve them in planning the type of program they wish to have, and the times it should occur. If you intend approaching an agency to initiate services for the learning disabled, I suggest that you read chapter 14, "For Recreation Leaders and Administrators," in my book *A Word or Two About Learning Disabilities.*[1] If you approach an agency to initiate a sheltered program, ask them, as well, to integrate those learning-disabled children who can cope, into their "normal" program. We parents can involve ourselves in considerable recreation with our children and adolescents, but their greatest enjoyment and feelings of worth and belonging will be derived from socializing with their peers. A friend in need is a friend indeed!

Chapter 7 :

The LD Adolescent
in Home and Community

DISCIPLINING THE LEARNING-DISABLED adolescent is a difficult issue for parents. In the early years, the parent may exert authority by means of power. (Even if it is not verbalized, the assumption is, "Obey, because I'm bigger than you are.") By adolescence, however, power cannot be utilized, if only because of the child's size, nor should it be. The preferred form of discipline for the adolescent is reason, with the adult laying the groundwork of expectations based upon reasonable premises. This assumes, however, a supposition that the adolescent can judge his own actions and the actions of others, and then make a mature choice involving critical thought. He needs to develop logical theses around why he should or should not follow a line of action; and, if he elects deviant behavior, he should comprehend the consequences in advance. Although learning-disabled adolescents have reached this level of conceptualization, some have not. The parent's dilemma is, if authoritarian control must continue, does he or she maintain it by capitalizing on the adolescent's fears of being thrust into the world? "Do what I say, or you can't live here any more."

The young person is more likely to accept limits if he has been part of the decision process, but *really* a part. It does no good to pretend that he's involved when, in reality, parents have made their minds up ahead of time. Issues should be examined with an open mind; the young person may have a valid point of view. The learning-disabled adolescent who has problems with judgment needs more practice judging than others do and more exercises in determining consequences. He needs to make mistakes and learn from them by discussing what went wrong.

Rules should be clearly understood. We may think that all family members comprehend the rules; and they may think that they are slightly different than we perceive them, particularly if any of the family members have problems with language processing or memory. Those slight differences can be a source of great friction. Have a family evening in which everyone states then writes the rules down. *After* they are written down, issues of fairness and changes can be discussed; but first, have them in black and white. Then, if the learning-disabled member is not carrying out his chores, honoring his bedtime, or whatever, ask him what needs to be done so that he will comply, perhaps a checklist, or help in organizing his time, etc. Whatever structure he decides that he requires in order to put the rules into effect, is a structure that he must take the initiative in implementing. Otherwise, the parents will continue to nag, remind, and organize the adolescent; and he'll depend upon their props rather than take the responsibility for organizing himself, and meeting his own responsibilities. Although parents may have to assist the adolescent in establishing the initial structure, subsequently it should be his own ball game. Tom was having difficulty planning his time. He'd come home from school, watch television, tackle his homework sometime in the evening, do it halfway through the night, then be too weary after school to do anything but watch television. Thus the unsatisfactory cycle perpetuated itself. The important issue was for Tom to recognize his problem himself and agree to try a changed routine. Then Tom and his parents figured out a typical homework load; his parents worked with him determining the amount of time and commitment each type of assignment typically requires; then they drew up a plan. Tom would allow himself forty-five minutes after school to unwind, then he would tackle his homework. He allowed himself an hour for supper, then continued homework, if any, after supper. His time then was his own until bedtime. Steve's family posted a list of daily chores for every family member. As chores were completed, a check mark was placed in that day's column. Those who defaulted had to execute double chores the following day. Parents often fall into the pattern of continuous nagging about broken rules and neglected routines, rather than determining what the problem is and selecting a vehicle for implimentation that depersonalizes the process. A checklist with a default clause serves to avoid name-calling such as lazy, selfish, sloppy, etc.

Rules should be open-ended and available for reexamination whenever a family member wishes to suggest them for discussion. Families should be flexible and creative regarding ways of having family members comply to rules. Rules should be applicable to everyone, with alterations based upon age, maturity, and demands upon one's time. There should be reasons for rules; it isn't good enough to impose a rule by virtue of parental authority.

The flexible family who has open, warm relationships and good communication might encounter a few months here and there in the adolescent years when rules are flaunted, but generally, shouldn't find rules and chores a large problem. In my home there is a free-and-easy trading of chores with little concern that someone is being overworked. If one child is in a hurry, another will take over his chores—knowing that the favor will be reciprocated.

Parents have to veto some adolescent behaviors because their experience and maturity have taught them that some behaviors are unsafe or unhealthy. However, they shouldn't veto until they know with certainty that the child is indulging in destructive behavior, or that the friend really is a bad influence. Regardless of parental veto power, the adolescent should enjoy the respect of a person with thoughts and feelings in the decision-making process. All adolescents encounter some unfair and disrespectful treatment in our schools. Decisions are made and punishments imposed without the adolescent having his say. The learning-disabled adolescent is a more frequent recipient of such treatment than others, which provides a cogent argument for respectful treatment at home.

Parents of the learning disabled have to ask themselves regularly whether they are exacting enough from their growing children. Do they shoulder their portion of the chores? Do they market, run errands, clean, cook, wash dishes, keep their room clean, babysit, help prepare, serve, and clean up when the family entertains, tend bar, rake leaves, mow the lawn, shovel snow, wash windows, clean eavestroughs, make home repairs, and hold down an outside job? Every adolescent should realize that work goes into the provision of food and creature comforts. When parents spare their learning-disabled adolescent their share of chores, they may create anxiety in him that he is very different. Parents who lack the courage to demand responsibilities of the adolescent should not be surprised to see him grow into an adult who expects the world to be served to him on a silver platter.

Paul A. Clarke comments, "The adolescent from an overprotective environment has difficulty in making decisions about anything; he always wants to be told what to do and how to do it; he is relatively unable to evaluate his own work; he is highly suggestible and easily influenced by his playmates as well as adults."[1]

Communication

Having a learning-disabled child seems to be so destructive to family integration that many families seem to lose some of their ability to handle communication effectively and openly. The father bottles all his feelings about having a learning-disabled child inside himself; and those feelings serve as barriers between husband and wife, and particularly between father and child. The mother may do somewhat better at verbalizing the way she feels; but even she imagines that some of her feelings such as guilt, anger, disappointment in the child, resentment and sometimes even hate, are unacceptable, so she also keeps them to herself.

Then there are families who are so consumed with shame that they won't even allow the learning disability to be discussed. They won't even allow discussion about the fact that the learning disability can't be discussed! A mother phoned to tell me that she had enjoyed reading my book. "Which one of my books?" I inquired. "I can't tell you the title," she responded, "because my son is listening." I suggested that, whichever of my books she had read, she had missed the message and would do well to read it again.

Many families feel that only good feelings can be shared and that mistakes must be kept secret. Despite the fact that these attitudes are prevalent, they amaze me because they imply standards which are applicable only to gods. Real people have all kinds of feelings and these include disappointment in spouse, and in our children, feelings of being cheated, wronged, hate, and many others. These feelings aren't bad, merely human; and expressing them is good. One just has to learn how to express such feelings without being destructive, and authors such as Virginia Satir and Hiam Ginott teach us how to do this. We also need to remind ourselves that just because we hate someone, that doesn't preclude loving him or her at the same time.[2] Relationships aren't one-dimensional; and simultaneously they can include elements of pride, disappointment, envy, delight, irritation, warmth, aversion, and so on.

There is no feeling or mistake that need be kept secret, because secrets are barriers to communication. If family members are aware that we have human frailties, they will realize that they aren't expected to be perfect. If we share our so-called bad feelings with other family members, they'll feel free to express theirs to us. They must be allowed to comment on their impressions of our actions and expressions of feelings. It is only through this openness that the learning-disabled person can have his impressions and conceptions clarified, either corroborated or adjusted. This is vitally important to the learning-disabled adolescent who, through unselective or imperfect perception, may have failed to perceive the critical aspects of a situation so that distortion might have resulted. This allows him, as well, to discuss his disability openly and clarify his conceptions about it. Open discussion conveys the message that no feeling, mistake, or disability can be terribly bad; it is the perfect dragon killer.

If the father found the adjustment to having a learning-disabled child particularly difficult and closed himself off from his wife and child, it is never too late to change. I found it effective to share my feelings of disappointment and frustration with my husband and talk about the reactions I had observed in other fathers of the learning disabled. It took some effort to bring him to the point where he could talk about how he felt, but talk he did. Once the feelings are verbalized, they lose the ability to haunt us and, after a while, may dissipate entirely. Some parents of the learning disabled, particularly fathers, are skilled at side-stepping a discussion of *feelings* by manipulating the conversation to a discussion of *issues*, such as what type of class the child should be in. Don't go along with the game. Return to the discussion of feelings, possibly with a reminder, "Hey, you're intellectualizing again." He may not want to revert to intellectualization, but it is likely a long-standing habit.

The father who didn't develop a relationship with his young learning-disabled child will have to put forth real effort to become close to his adolescent offspring. He will need to learn communication skills that many people in our society have not acquired. If he can't develop these skills on his own, he may need the direction he might find in a family-life education group, or from a social worker or counseling group for parents of the learning disabled.

He'll need to learn to level with his adolescent. Mark was a case in point. He was having extensive academic difficulties and also many emotional problems at home. Mark blamed himself for his parents' divorce. He was home alone and friendless daily until his mother returned from work. At that time she sometimes found him attired in her clothing. I suggested a residential school for learning-disabled adolescents, and Mark was enrolled. The school did a beautiful job of dealing with Mark's learning and emotional problems. He refused, however, to give the school a chance, either to adjust or to make friends, because his dad told him that, if he didn't like it, he didn't have to return the second year. The parents discussed this with me, and I urged them to have their son remain in the school. Mark had said that he wouldn't return home if it made his parents unhappy, and the parents were going to lean on that statement. I urged Mr. S. to level with Mark and tell him that he erred when he made the promise, that it was a big mistake to have made, but that the school was his only opportunity to receive the assistance that he so urgently needed. The father found it impossible to level with his son in this manner. We are so used to playing games, to using communication to coerce, lean on, evoke pity or guilt, to blame, shame, put down, inveigle, and every conceivable indirect route to achieve our ends, that many of us have lost our facility to state our case in a manner that doesn't arouse negative response in the interactor.

So play it straight with your adolescent. It's OK to say, "I blew it again. I wanted to enjoy your visit home from college, yet it began with me becoming impatient with you." Can you as a father or mother of a teenage learning-disabled person express your tenderness to him? Does he know that you'd like to become closer to him and are looking for ways to accomplish this? After years of strained relationship, it will take him time and practice to learn to relate more satisfactorily. Chuck and his father care for each other deeply; but Chuck's father had never been able to relate much to him, so that Chuck's close relationship was with his mother. At age twenty, Chuck and his dad were driving him back to college after a visit home, and his father initiated many topics of mutual concern. Father returned home elated at one of the few good discussions he had had with Chuck. When Chuck's mother commented on this to her son, he replied, "Yes, but I didn't try hard enough to relate to Dad." So both recognized the need to develop a closer relationship and the effort that was required to do so.

Should He Drive?

He is sixteen, wants to take out his learner's license; and we parents are in a panic! His reflexes are slow, his hands and feet don't seem to be able to do things simultaneously, and his spatial judgment is in left field. Regardless, if he is willing to try, we have to allow him to do so. He may have to take a great many lessons and try his driving test several times; but, if he is prepared to persevere, we must support him in his efforts. Then, if he passes his test, we must allow him to drive. Certainly, the driver with slow reaction time and questionable judgment is greater risk than are more intact drivers, but he can't live his life in cotton wool. Driving will open entire new horizons to the learning-disabled adolescent. He'll become more independent, learn his way around the city, and state, have access to recreation facilities such as ski hills, be able to transport a date or a group of friends, and possess an invaluable skill for use in a job and other pursuits of adult life. If he can't handle the reading portion of the driving test, the parent will likely have to intervene with the authorities on his behalf.

What about Clothing?

A clothing allowance can encourage the youth to plan his season's clothing requirements, apportion his money, determine the best buys in town, become more appearance conscious, and use practical mathematics. Insist that he or she set money aside for essentials such as coats, boots, and good clothes, and not spend all the money on shirts and jeans.

What about a Job?

A part-time job can be an important experience for the learning-disabled adolescent. Since his social life is so meager, a job can be a source of companionship. Within the job he can feel productive and competent. The Children's Hospital Washington study found that the non-learning-disabled control group saw jobs as stepping stones to upward mobility, whereas the learning-disabled adolescents looked on jobs as a source of satisfaction unto themselves, and hence, were good employees.[3] A part-time job can teach the adolescent how to apply for a job; how to dress and what to say in the interview; to handle the "gaff"; how to meet the job demands—temporal and otherwise; how to organize his time and surroundings while working and to interpret his disability to his boss and coworkers so that they will institute the necessary props. The latter might be able to write a list of his duties rather than tell him verbally, to explain things slowly and simply, or point out the location of items in the stock room to the illiterate. Parents might have to fill out the job application form for the illiterate, the sloppy writer, or impossible speller. They also may have to role-play the job interview in advance of it actually taking place.

Many vocational assessment agencies currently do a poor job of meeting the needs of the learning disabled. They should determine the applicant's strengths and interests, and steer him to jobs that will capitalize on these. Additionally, they must determine the requirements en route to the job, union admission requirements to trades, or college courses requisite for professions. Parents may already know that their son has a way with animals. What they need to know is all the demands en route to becoming a veterinary surgeon, and whether their son is equipped to cope with college level sciences.

What College Should He Attend?

In other parts of this book I discussed the fact that college should not be perceived as the be-all for every young person. I also dealt with the attributes other than intelligence requisite for college functioning. These cautions notwithstanding, some youth can and should attend college, or are determined to attend college and will have to discover for themselves whether they are capable of handling college demands. The next issue is to select an appropriate college.

Currently, there are four colleges in the United States in which there is a special unit established for the learning disabled. The students study the regular college curricula, but are provided with considerable support, assistance in study skills, remediation; and, most probably, some orientation is provided to the college staff at large. In some of these programs the students tape their lectures and make notes from the tapes. For the student who could learn to make notes directly from a lecture, however, such a prop only serves to increase his study time considerably and delay his development of note-taking skills. Consequently, the students who enroll in sheltered programs such as these should be the ones who require a considerable degree of support. A list of these colleges can be obtained from the Association for Children with Learning Disabilities (ACLD). Parents and the youth should visit the colleges they are considering to determine whether the special program for the learning disabled seems appropriate for them, and whether the college courses and orientation meet their needs.

The ACLD also publishes a list of colleges which are prepared to accept the learning disabled. Once again, the family should visit the college. Some institutions are prepared to enroll the young person with a learning disability; but then he becomes a nameless face on the campus; and, unless he seeks assistance, he is lost in the masses. A few colleges have a staff member who has elected the role of intervening for the learning-disabled student, and who will make a point of speaking to each of the student's instructors. So, in selecting a college, the family should determine how much intervention and direction the youth will require, whether he can obtain it through the regular remedial and counseling channels of the college, whether he will seek assistance when required, and how much interpretation he will provide on his own to his teachers.

As a general rule of thumb, a small college is preferable. Then it is helpful to select a college that reflects your way of life. A southern religious college will have a different orientation than a northern liberal college, and your son or daughter will be most comfortable in a college that feels like "him."

Chapter 8:

What about School?

THE OCCASIONAL LEARNING-DISABLED adolescent finds himself in a secondary school program that is specifically geared to his needs. The majority of learning-disabled adolescents in North America, however, are in non-specialized secondary school programs; and, if they receive the understanding and support that they require, that is a most suitable placement.

The learning-disabled teenager needs a principal who is committed to his succeeding, because he or she will translate that commitment to the school staff. If he is committed to success, his student will most likely succeed. Conversations in the teacher's lounge will provide feedback to the principal on whether the teacher feels that the prevalent message in that school is to scapegoat or support the student. The principal and the staff really must believe that the student is not "stupid," but has the intelligence to do well. He must encourage his teachers to individualize and work with them on ways that they can do so that will not make unreasonable demands on their time. He should be creative in encouraging the teachers to utilize in-school and community resources in order to provide the personal approach and the drill that the learning-disabled student requires. Perhaps he should train volunteers specifically to work with the learning disabled as they have done successfully in many parts of the country. Volunteers can be fellow students, housewives, retired teachers, etc.

Once there is the commitment to success, each area of difficulty should be examined. One must ask whether there are alternative routes that can be travelled to ensure success. This might be simpler reading material, a student reader for the slow, inefficient reader, projects using photographs and tapes, tracing and verbalizing large geometric symbols that have been drawn in black magic marker, or producing a handkerchief in sewing while the other girls produce blouses. Before the decision is made for a student to drop a subject, the area of difficulty should be ascertained. One needs to determine whether he truly cannot handle the subject matter; whether he doesn't comprehend the language the teacher is using; whether he can't produce the written work; whether he feels confused, overwhelmed, behind, and frustrated; and whether he requires remedial help or merely tutoring in order to gain confidence and keep apace of his classmates. If he truly cannot handle a subject, perhaps he could take the same subject on a less advanced level. He should not be placed in a lower educational track because he cannot master one or two subjects. Learning-disabled adolescents should be allowed to take as many of the subjects as they can handle in their areas of competent functioning without being penalized for their deficits, and remain in as open-ended a stream as possible. Since many of them have developmental lags, they continue to improve; and some of the intelligent but very disabled have done better educationally than their elementary or secondary school teachers ever would have dreamed was possible.

Every learning-disabled student in a secondary shcool needs an advo-cate, be it a guidance counselor, psychologist, principal, interested teacher, or resource room teacher. The advocate must ensure that every one of the youth's teachers is aware of his disabilities at the beginning of each semester and aware, as well, of implications for the student in coping with each teacher's course of studies. The advocate must ascertain how the course is taught and the specific demands on the student. James did well in biology for years until he reached grade twelve. Investigation of his current failure showed that the current biology teacher used graphs extensively and also had the students work in pairs. No one chose James as a working partner, which earned him the label of "uncooperative"; and the production of graphs was disastrous in light of James' spatial organization problems. If none of the school personnel understand the learning-disabled student's disability, the school psychologist or the student's parent should meet with his teachers and explore ways whereby he can maximize his assetts.

The advocate must ensure that the teachers are aware of the learning-disabled adolescent's need for organization. His teachers should spend a few minutes with him each week teaching him how to organize his assignments in terms of content, headings, organization on the page, when to start, and how long each assignment should take. The learning-disabled student needs assis-tance in organizing his study habits and homework from the time it is assigned to completion. Of particular importance is temporal organization. Learning-disabled persons have trouble determining the amount of time each assignment merits and planning a daily homework routine. A teacher or their advocate should work with them on developing a structured after-school homework time, a system for remembering the daily assignments, and the books and materials to take home. He should paste his weekly schedule on the front of his binder and check it before each period. Teachers must be sensitive to the literalness of the learning-disabled pupil, who will take the teacher at her word so that she, in turn, must mean what she says.

One of the most critical awarenesses that the teacher must have is of the learning-disabled adolescent's vulnerability to stress. He becomes easily frustrated and discouraged; and, if he feels that he is lagging in a subject, he gives up and, after a short ime, feels so hopelessly behind that he is certain that there is no recouping. The teacher, therefore, should check with the student regularly to ensure that he understands the lessons and assignments, and can organize and cope with the combined work load of all his subjects.

When the learning-disabled teenager first enters secondary school, he will require a few days of extra support and structuring which could be handled by his advocate or, preferably, another student. The spatially disordered youth will have difficulty finding his way around the school, finding his locker, remembering how to open his lock, remembering to take his belongings from place to place, finding his seat in each new classroom, etc. He may exert so much energy worrying where the washroom, gym, and lunchroom are that he has none left for academics. Learning-disabled persons do not adjust easily to change, and it will take the young person a couple of weeks to handle himself comfortably with a new classroom and new set of demands every forty minutes.

The advocate should meet with the youth a few times yearly to determine how he feels he is doing, to solve areas of difficulty, and to offer support and direction. These meetings can highlight areas in which the advocate should intervene on behalf of the student with some of his teachers. He also should check with the student's teachers regularly to assess the extent to which the student is coping, and encourage the teachers to seek him out at the first hint of a problem, rather than have it accumulate. The learning-disabled student often feels too powerless and too poorly about himself to intervene on his own behalf; he is uncertain about how to describe his disabilities to teachers in a method that would evoke understanding; and he fears that telling a teacher about his disabilities will result in penalization, or that it will be interpreted as a ploy for preferential treatment.

The learning-disabled students who have problems in spelling should not be penalized for misspelled words, since no amount of lost marks will assist them in remembering the correct spelling. Students with poor fine-motor coordination shouldn't have their sloppy handwriting prejudice the way assignments are recieved. If possible, they should be encouraged to learn to type, though it will likely be a skill that is acquired through long and frustrating effort. Smith-Corona and IBM produce a keyboard called "Dvorak" that is much easier to learn than the standard keyboard. Students who are planning to be secretaries or reporters should learn on the standard keyboard, but "Dvorak" may be a fine choice for others. When a student has difficulty with written or spoken language, the teacher should ignore the garbled quality of his production, and determine whether he knows the subject matter. If he does, he sould be marked accordingly. Students with spelling problems may be unable to spell foreign languages, but may be able to handle them auditorally. Conversely, students with auditory processing problems may be able to learn foreign languages visually, but not speak them. Both types of students should be allowed to take the subject if they can learn it on some level. Latin often can be coped with for two or three years because it is systematic and seldom needs to be heard. Spanish is an easier language for the language handicapped to master than French, though both are impossible for some. Computer Science presents grave problems to some learning-disabled persons because the material has to be organized and translated into a symbolic system; and, after all, a learning disability is a problem in symbolic functioning and in organization. The student with spatial problems will find the perspective lessons in art difficult to master. His artwork will be immature; but, in an era that values primitive art, I hope that his productions will be deemed valuable. Since written music is a symbolic system, it will be difficult for some learning-disabled students to learn to read music; and most find music theory confusing. However, many have good singing voices and a deep appreciation of music.

Physical education, industrial arts, home economics, and all soft-core subjects should have philosophies of inclusion, not exclusion. Every student should be allowed to produce on his own level and feel a comfortable member of the class. There is nothing more upsetting than spending all day dreading physical education or sewing, and such a feeling can color a student's feelings toward all of his subjects and his school experience. The learning-disabled student may not be able to remember the steps in space to thread a sewing machine, be unable to thread the needle, or find reading a pattern impossibly confusing—but be able to produce beautiful embroidery.

Learning-disabled persons tend to overreact, be it to depression, excitement, upsets or changes in routine or plans. They need a place in the school to which they can retreat before they become embarrassingly frustrated, anxious, overstimulated, or angry. This could be a small room with a comfortable sofa, or, if nothing else is available, a corner of the nurse's office. They need ready access to someone with an understanding ear: the nurse, secretary, janitor, or what-have-you.

If learning-disabled students are intelligent and not severely academically retarded, they should be allowed to remain in the college entrance stream, if they wish. If they enter vocational school, there should be as much understanding of individual needs as there is in higher-level tracks. Both streams should offer remedial reading and remedial written language organization, high-interest, low-level reading courses such as a study of children's books, and remedial mathematics. The vocational schools that expose their students to a "smorgasbord" approach must recognize that their learning-disabled students will experience great difficulty handling some of the subjects—be they tailoring, drafting, or the mathematics of merchandising. Vocational courses should be open-ended to allow for upward mobility for the student who was erroneously placed in a terminal track, or for the late bloomer who reads his first book spontaneously in his teens and blossoms intellectually from that point onward. When a student is uncoordinated and disabled in learning, his area of greater strength should be assessed. If he is steered to a trade, it should be one such as landscape gardening or merchandising, because they don't require extensive coordination. If the student is steered to academics, he should receive all the support he requires to survive comfortably in secondary school.

Every school district in North America should have professional development days in which the learning-disabled student in our secondary schools should be the topic explored and attendance should be compulsory.

We cannot individualize a student's academic requirements and forget his social needs. If he is not "making it socially" he may be too unhappy to commit himself academically. Some learning-disabled students are so angry or rebellious by the time they reach secondary shcool that they require professional therapy; and the therapist should know a great deal about learning disabilities. Others merely require support and direction. The guidance counselor or advocate should ensure that the student has an opportunity to be in a prestige position—be it on the swim team, prom decorating committee, or student council. The larning-disabled student who has far fewer demands on his time than his non-learning-disabled peers will do a conscientious job on any committee, and may only require help in organizing his duties. The advocate should steer the adolescent to structured social groups in the school or community. Since the learning-disabled person has difficulty determining his assetts and finding someone who is prepared to "buy" his assets, the advocate could arrange projects in which the learning-disabled student is paired with lonely, shy, unattractive, or—for whatever reason—unpopular students who would welcome the learning-disabled teenager as a friend. He could attempt to teach the young person the type of social behavior that is valued and behavior that "turns people off." Additionally, he should instruct the youth in appropriate behavior with the opposite sex and the sequence of steps which precede and are a part of dating. He must remember that social behavior that is learned by the non-learning-disabled through observation and modelling is unevenly learned by the learning disabled, and requires conscious instruction.

Parents tend to be intimidated by secondary school structures. Even parents who have established a fine rapport with each successive elementary school teacher tend to be less confortable approaching a series of secondary school teachers. The content of our current secondary school cirricula often is foreign to pre-computor-age parents, and they feel less comfortable intervening for an emerging adult than when they paved the way for a dependent child. They find secondary school teachers difficult to contact, and, at times, unreceptive to their information. By the time they have intervened on their child's behalf for fourteen years with an often uncomprehending world, they may be weary and discouraged. Include them in your planning and problems. They are aware of their child's behavior, limitations, and difficulties. Parents can provide valuable insight and suggestions. They must feel that you are not going to "kick their offspring out," but want to work with them on ways whereby he can learn and enjoy his school experience. If they feel that both you and they are on the same side, they and their son or daughter can be valuable members of the team.

We cannot wait for all school systems to institute special programs for all learning-disabled adolescents. Most don't require such programs; but, in any event, they are in our schools now; and each year that we wait we lose a generation. We can't exclude many of them from the college entrance stream, because they are intelligent and have the same right to professional choice as any intelligent person. We must, therefore, begin to provide for them now. If we believe that they are valuable and worth teaching, we will find inexpensive and effective ways whereby they can be productive members of our schools.

Part One / Notes

Chapter 1:

1. H. G. Birch, A. Thomas, S. Chess, M. E. Hertzing, and S. Korn, *Behavioral Individuality in Early Childhood* (New York: New York University Press, 1971); L. J. Stone, H. T. Smith, and L. B. Murphy, *The Competent Infant* (New York: Basic Books, 1973).

2. A. Zaleznik, "Discontinuities in Status and Self Esteem," in *Human Dilemmas of Leadership* (New York: Harper & Row, 1966): 100-121.

3. J. R. Davitz *et al.*, *The Communication of Emotional Meaning* (New York: McGraw-Hill, 1964): 43-55, 61.

4. E. Berne, *What Do You Say After You Say Hello? The Psychology of Human Destiny* (New York: Grove Press, 1971): 38, 97-100, 193, 216, 225-227.

5. A. H. Maslow, *Toward a Psychology of Being* (New York: Van Nostrand Reinhold Co., 1968): 15.

Chapter 2:

1. Charles Drake and J. J. A. Cavanaugh, "Teaching the High School Dyslexic," in L. Anderson (ed.), *Helping the Adolescent with the Hidden Handicap* (San Rafael, California: Academic Therapy Publications, 1970): 61.

2. E. Siegel, *The Exceptional Child Grows Up* (New York: Dutton, 1974): 35.

Chapter 3:

1. H. G. Birch, A. Thomas, S. Chess, M. E. Hertzing, and S. Korn, *Behavioral Individuality in Early Childhood* (New York: New York University Press, 1971): 40, 44-45, 57-58, 60, 62, 64-66, 69.

2. D. P. Ausubel, *Theories and Problems of Child Development* (New York: Grune and Stratton, 1959 and 1970): 289.

3. *Ibid.*

4. M. Mead, "Age Patterning in Personality Development," *American Journal of Orthopsychiatry* 17 (1947): 231-240.

5. Ausubel, *op. cit.*: 302.

6. J. F. X. Carroll, "Understanding Adolescent Needs," *Adolescence* 3:12 (1968-69): 381-393.

7. P. Wender, *Minimal Brain Dysfunction in Children* (New York: Wiley Interscience, 1971): 169; C. M. Anderson and H. B. Playmate, "Management of the Adolescent with Learning Disabilities," *American Journal of Orthopsychiatry* 132 (1960): 492-500; A. Thompson (from a lecture delivered at the CANHC/ACLD Conference, Los Angeles, January 1973); E. Siegel, *The Exceptional Child Grows Up* (New York: Dutton, 1974).

8. J. R. Davitz *et al.*, *The Communication of Emotional Meaning* (New York: McGraw-Hill, 1964): 43-55, 61.

Chapter 4:

1. S. Hansen, J. Jensen, and W. Roberts, *The Little Red Schoolbook* (New York: Pocket Books, 1971).

2. R. Coles, *Children of Crisis: Part One* (Boston: Little, Brown, 1968): 159.

Chapter 5:

1. E. H. Erikson, *Childhood and Society* (New York: W. W. Norton, 1950 and 1963): 259.

2. *Ibid.*: 262.

3. A. Mehrabian (as cited by Joyce Brothers, PhD), "The President and the Press, *TV Guide* 20 (September 1972): 23-29; also in E. Siegel, *The Exceptional Child Grows Up* (New York: Dutton, 1974).

4. Siegel, *ibid.*: 32.

5. Erikson, *op. cit.*: 33.

6. *Ibid.*: 261.

7. *Ibid.*: 260.

8. D. Kronick, *A Word or Two about Learning Disabilities* (San Rafael, California: Academic Therapy Publications, 1973).

9. Siegel, *op. cit.*: 33.

10. Sol Gordon, *Facts About Sex For Exceptional Youth* (reprint; Toronto: Canadian Association for Children with Learning Disabilities, n.d.).

Chapter 6:

1. D. Kronick, *A Word or Two About Learning Disabilities* (San Rafael, California: Academic Therapy Publications, 1973): 197-206.

Chapter 7:

1. P. A. Clark, *Child-Adolescent Psychology* (Columbus, Ohio: Charles E. Merrill, 1968).

2. Virginia Satir, *Peoplemaking* (Palo Alto, California: Science and Behavior Books, Inc., 1972); Haim G. Ginott, *Between Parent and Child* (New York: Avon, 1965).

3. E. S. Greenberg, "Brain Damage in Adolescence: A Ten-Year Follow-Up Study of the Children in the Montgomery County Project, Children's Hospital, Washington, D.C.," *American Journal of Orthopsychiatry* 40 (1970): 333-337.

Part Two

Chapter 1:

But When We Die

Elizabeth Adams

THIS SECTION IS WRITTEN, not by an attorney, but by a parent who has been through the experience of finding out about wills, trusts, and estates. It is written in the hope that it will serve as a guide to you when you, too, come to the day when you think, "We really *ought* to write our wills."

Without some knowledge of the nature of a will and the procedures to be followed, the normally uncomfortable process of thinking about your own death (with the fear of what will happen to your learning-disabled child when you can no longer shelter and guide him), can become a nightmare of indecision and worry. This writing represents the search we made for the best provisions for our child, and will perhaps offer you shortcuts to the resolution of your own estate planning.

First of all, you need to realize that your family may pay heavily if you die intestate, without a will. A heavy tax-bite can be levied on your estate before any distribution can be done. In addition, it is not wise to assume that the surviving spouse inherits everything automatically. In my state, an equal distribution is made between spouse and children, in addition to the heavy taxes intestacy produces. This could be more than awkward for the surviving spouse, who must pay debts and taxes out of a much smaller share of the estate than she or he may have expected to inherit.

Contrary to most people's expectations, the best technique in estate planning is not to rush straight to your attorney to discuss the terms of your will, for several reasons.

One of the most pressing immediate reasons for getting your own thoughts planned ahead of time is that, with the care of a handicapped child, most of us already are faced with higher-than-normal family expenses. An attorney's time does not come cheaply. If you spend an entire afternoon—as a couple I know did—discussing all the ins and outs of your *intentions* for your will, you may end up with a sizeable bill for his advice before you even get down to drafting the actual documents. Again, you are hiring the attorney to carry out the intricacies of expressing your desires in the legal form of a will. So it makes good sense to plan ahead of time just what you will require him to draft for you. We spent weeks discussing and sifting possible guardians and executors and calculating the size of our estate before visiting our attorney. When we did get in to see him, it took not more than a half hour to explain our situation to him and provide him with the facts necessary for him to proceed to his research in order to word our intentions clearly.

Your first move, therefore, is to determine just what your will is. In the case of a tiny estate such as one in which I was recently involved, the entire documentation was a single paragraph, dated and signed, dividing a tiny estate equally between two brothers, and naming one of them executor. The testator had no real estate holdings, stocks, or valuables.

Most of us, however, face more severe complications in the form of real estate, shares, life insurance, savings accounts, and, more important than those strictly material aspects, our intentions regarding the future education and income of our learning-disabled children.

It follows that, before you venture into the maze of legal language surrounding your will, you must decide in plain terms exactly what you want to happen after your death, for your child's benefit. Courts take very seriously this aspect of your will; and this can be crucial to your child's future if you die before he reaches legal age—or if he is of legal age but incapable of making wise financial decisions for himself.

At the beginning of our research into wills, we were babes in the woods as far as such items as trusts, income tax demands on estates, and liquid assets were concerned. If you too are in this position, your next move, having expressed in plain language just what you want to happen to your income for your child's benefit, is to determine just what size of estate you will be leaving. The table which follows is adapted to one you can request from your local bank, when you make an appointment to see their trust officer. That move will come a little later, after you have consulted your records and filled out the table for your own use.

Calculate the Approximate Size of Your Estate

Determine the approximate value of your estate, using the guidelines on the following page. A ballpark figure is good enough at this stage. Usually the full value of your property is includable in your estate. And remember to include the face value of all your life insurance.

Once you have this approximate figure in mind, you will have a guide to the tax which will be applicable to your estate, from the form you can also request from your bank.

Most people are surprised at the size of their estate. Even where your family income plus your mortgage and beat-up old car seem to indicate a tiny estate, once you add in life insurance, personal property, and bank accounts, you too may find you're worth a good deal more than you thought.

Bank Accounts: Checking and Savings	$ _____
Real Estate	_____
Stocks and Bonds	_____
Mortgages, Notes, and Cash	_____
Life Insurance	_____
Jointly Owned Property	_____
Personal Property (Jewelry, Furniture, Car, etc.)	_____
Retirement Benefits	_____
All Other Property	_____
TOTAL	$ _____

Now that you've collected a basic financial background for your will, your next consideration is your executor and your guardian. Between them, they will administer your estate and carry out your intentions. One bank officer I talked with recommends that *three* guardians be named, to ensure continuity should the guardian die while your child still needs him, plus an executor. You have a number of options about naming the executors.

You could choose more than one, possibly naming your bank plus a private individual. Or your guardian and executor could be the same person. These are points to consider when talking with the trust officer at the bank, whom you will go and see after considering your possibilities as guardians and executors. He may suggest to you that, if guardian and executor are the same person, there would be a minimum of complication in the case of say, the guardian wanting to send your child to a specific school, and the executor's having to arrange to release the funds necessary to pay the fees. Or, if you appoint the bank the executor and a person as guardian, this could also smooth out such situations. However, you need also to remember that both the duties of guardian and executor are legally heavy, and that it might be beyond the ability of one person to act in both capacities for your children.

The person you appoint as guardian must be considered by you with great care. You need, at best, someone who will not only be able to give your child a warm, thoughtful upbringing if necessary, with care in selecting his schools, and knowledge of his problems and talents, but must also be able to handle discussions with attorneys, bank officials, medical personnel, and all the school officials we as parents of learning-disabled children have learned to handle. And remember that you're asking him to take this on in addition to his own family responsibilities. If all this sounds like an impossible combination of virtues, then you may be able to find a relative or friend who has all the warmth and willingness you require, and who would be capable of acquiring knowledge about children like yours, if he is not already well-versed in learning disabilities.

At this point, it is well to realize, as I mentioned earlier, that the law takes a very serious view of your intent as expressed in your will. This means that if you name an executor and a guardian, the courts will look on them as such as they probate your will. You are requesting that these individuals assume a serious legal obligation. Hence it is essential that you consult them first and be certain you have their considered consent before you proceed to write your will.

Since the guardian has a long-term responsibility (the executor's work is normally finished once the estate is settled), you may need to shop around for a relative or friend with the qualifications your child needs in a guardian and the willingness to take on this responsibility. We handled this in writing, after I had secured the verbal consent of our would-be guardian. He wrote me a letter, dated and addressed, agreeing to be our child's guardian after the death of both parents, and specified also that his wife was willing to continue this role if he, too, died before our child was legally of age and/or capable of living independently. As you are probably aware, the guardian would only be called on if both parents have died or one survivor is incapable of carrying out the work of parents. Usually the law assumes that where one spouse survives and is capable, he or she automatically retains parental rights over the children.

You may elect to have your executor continue to handle the estate on a long-term basis, if you feel your child will only be able to handle his financial role either much later than normal or possibly never. In this case, you need to spell out for yourself and the executor exactly what you plan for that child. You may decide to leave the management of the estate up to the executor until your child reaches a specific age, which you can specify. You may incorporate a provision that extra funds for your child be available during his adult years, at the discretion of your executor. He will be responsible for determining whether your child can handle money, and how much. It's possible that, as your circumstances change, you may revise your will, which is not too complicated a process. Better to have a will you may want to revise than to leave no will at all.

Once you have named the guardian and the executor, however, you have certain moral, if not legal, responsibilities to them. We felt it essential that they be kept informed at intervals of our child's record—what schools attended, what district school personnel have handled his records, where his medical and school records are, which doctors have examined him, what procedures to follow to secure special education, therapy, benefits, and so on.

I prepared a list with all this information, dated and detailed, plus the name and address of our attorney, and close friends who could pinch-hit as parents if it took more than a few hours for the guardian to arrive on the scene.

If your prospective guardian and executor do not know what they will have to do if their services are required, find out and let them know now. Will the guardian, for instance, have to appear before a magistrate to take charge of your child, and if so, which, and how?

With all this information collected, you are still not ready to write your will.

Your next move is to the bank, where you can make an appointment to consult, at no charge, their trust officer. He can give you not only excellent general advice on setting up trusts for your children (always better than leaving property and money directly to the learning-disabled child, since he will then have a trustee to guide him); he can also, using the table you prepared, give you an estimate of what federal, provincial, or state taxes you will be liable to. He knows the laws of your state or province, and can suggest how to organize your intentions as stated in your will to cope with legal requirements. He has supplies of pamphlets which give tax tables, and can explain just how setting up trusts for your children can help you legitimately avoid extra tax burdens. For instance, he may explain to you the workings of the Marital Deduction Fund, a scheme whereby a husband, in writing his will, divides his estate in such a way that his wife is faced with a manageable tax bill on his death.

You may want to discuss with your trust officer the relative merits of appointing a person or an institution as your executor. One of the benefits of appointing an institution is that you will have an executor who cannot die—if your bank is executor, there will always be an officer available to administer your estate. This can avoid the complications that could arise from naming as executor an individual who just might die shortly after you.

Ask the trust officer to describe exactly the benefits of leaving your estate in the form of one or more trusts, rather than leaving it outright to a person. "Leaving it outright" is a lay term that your attorney might refer to as "vesting in the person." This can be a poor choice if it leaves your child wide open to heavy tax liabilities, which in some states, it can. A trust circumvents this by preserving the capital intact and distributing the income to your beneficiary. You need a trustee to supervise that distribution, and your trust officer will discuss with you whether your guardian or executor should also be your trustee, or whether you, again, should appoint an institution, such as the bank, as trustee, for the sake of continuity.

Estate planning, using a trust rather than leaving funds directly to your child, has a special significance to parents of the handicapped. True, many of our children will be able to handle their own lives as adults. But some may need care in an institution. And in some states, where a child who inherits an estate is cared for in an institution at the state's expense, the state is empowered to seize from the estate all the expenses incurred by the child, retroactively. If your trust provides that the child cannot handle the capital, however, only the income from the estate, the state cannot seize what the child himself could not have access to.

What a trust really does is to carry out and accomplish basically what you want for your children long after you have died.

Your trust officer will be able to enlighten you on the taxes due to be paid from your estate before any distribution can be made. Since taxes are due on a specific date after death, and must be paid in money, you need to be aware that, unless you leave enough liquid (that is, accessible in currency) assets, your survivors might be forced into the unhappy position of having to sell property in order to settle the tax bill. The tax people cannot accept an interest in a business, for instance, in lieu of the cash.

Apart from the many forms of trusts, your trust officer may be able to suggest possibilities for the disposition of your will, for instance a tax-avoiding provision that, if husband and wife leave everything to one another but both die, the property be converted to a trust to be administered for the benefit of the children. There are many facets to the question of trusts. For instance, it is possible to word your intentions regarding a trust so that the principle is invested and will ultimately go to whichever relatives you choose, but that the income goes to the prime beneficiary as long as she or he lives.

On the subject of trusts and trustees, now that you are almost ready to make that appointment with your attorney, note that he may use the term 'guardian' in two ways. One means guardian of the estate, in other words, trustee, and the other means guardian of the person, which is what you and I mean by a guardian for our children.

At this point you are finally ready to consult your attorney. It is a sound idea to canvass friends and relatives for advice on who is really experienced in the intricacies of wills and estates, since attorneys specialize, and since you want a man who grasps instantly what you intend in your will. Contacting other parents of learning-disabled children may be a help. When you find him, you will be competent to explain exactly what you want your will to do for you and your children. Though still open to suggestions, you will basically be in charge of the intentions of your will and can safely leave him to use the exact legal language to convey your intent.

Although, of all the processes we go through in planning for our learning-disabled children, the executing of a will is probably the least appetizing, you will find, as we did, that a peace of mind settles over you once it's done. You realize you have now carried out one of the most basic and long-term responsibilities of a parent.

Chapter 2:

Vocational Blues

Lauriel Anderson

JOB POSSIBILITIES run the gamut of variety for the person with minimal brain dysfunction; but only a small proportion of those with this disability get jobs at all commensurate with their potential. Why? Because there are many barriers along the way.

The "system" focuses on their failures rather than on their strengths. By the time they are ready to think of jobs, they are defeated, bitter, turned off. Teachers, geared to the development of conventional academic skills, do not know how to develop non-academic skills; counselors, with heads filled with test scores and college admission requirements, chalk off the MBD student as non-achieving; parents, seeing their children rejected, become overprotective and contribute to their immaturity; agencies designed to "help the handicapped" rarely understand the needs of the person with this invisible handicap.

If one is blind, he obviously cannot take a written test, and so a reader is provided; a person in a wheel chair is provided with ramps and parking privileges; the mentally retarded are provided with sheltered workshops to protect them from the threats of a competitive world.

But what about the person who, since birth, or as a result of illness, accident, or genetic quirk, has some abilities impaired? What of the person who appears whole and healthy, but has subtle neurological deficits? What of the person with good eyesight who has dyslexia because that portion of the brain designed to decode written symbols is underdeveloped or damaged? What of the person who can hear a pin drop, but who gets only garbled messages from a noisy world whose meanings he cannot separate and interpret? What of the creative person who can invent new devices, but who scores low in spelling and is written off as "stupid" in the conventional world? What of the person, in other words, who appears to have no handicap, who is in no position to explain his problems, but who is severely vocationally incapacitated as a result of them?

Some Have Found Jobs

Oh, it is possible to succeed with such handicaps . . . and a few have made it despite the barriers. Among some remarkable exceptions are the following:

- An award-winning British actress who is dyslexic, and memorizes her lines after a reader gives them to her.

- A neurologist whose nurse reads him the charts.

- A famous rock musician who has converted his hyperkinesis to superb skill and durability on the drums.

- A high official in the U.S. Department of Weights and Measures who was a genius in math and only learned grammer, history, and reading when they were presented in number concepts.

- A Hollywood writer whose growing years were painful because distorted visual perception made his world a confusion of double images and unreal forms.

- A non-writing policeman who somehow convinced his traffic violators to write their own tickets.

- A school principal who made his way through college and graduate school because an understanding wife wrote his papers from his dictation and summarized his required reading.

- A tutor of the learning disabled (herself with MBD) who claims that her own atypical approach to problem solving made her especially understanding when her bright brain-injured students devised new ways to find correct answers, or original ways to get directional clues.

- A successful broker who dictates his letters so that no one knows he cannot spell.

How and why did these people succeed? We can only guess. Most seem to have had an inner drive which wouldn't let them quit trying; an inner conviction that they could make it despite a world that thought they couldn't. Perhaps this was because they had experienced enough success to carry them through the failures; or perhaps they were raised by people who emphasized what they could do rather than what they couldn't do. Perhaps they discovered by accident that they could compensate in acceptable ways (like the dyslexic art student in school who carved bone joints out of soap in lieu of taking a zoology exam). Perhaps they were fortunate to be in a school system which was not rigid but acknowledged a wide variety of learning styles. Perhaps Uncle Henry had the necessary connections. Maybe they were just lucky.

In fact, for the many who have "made it" there are no records. The disability itself has only been recognized in the last ten years, so its presence is mere guesswork. A New England engineer wrote me that many engineers, including himself, have MBD. Who knows how many? Teachers, counselors, and social workers not infrequently have mild neurological problems according to a physician versed in the disability who is himself married to a teacher. How do they function? With one superior perceptual skill open, they can teach; and their deficiencies in athletics do not matter in the classroom. Salesmanship is a perfect occupation for the very verbal, hyperactive, compulsive person who learns to use, in positive ways, his peculiar combination of abilities. And who knows how many housewives, not rigidly required to be organized, on time, efficient, are, in fact, living with an undiagnosed hidden disability?

The Odds Are Poor

But in spite of known successes, we now are realizing that job failure rather than success is the way the betting odds are stacked for learning-disabled adults. Many are not finding jobs at all. Why? Why are they the ones dropping out of school? Why are some, even with remediation, ill-prepared for work? Why are they drifting into society's subcultures? Why are researchers now discovering that they heavily occupy our juvenile institutions and adult prisons? Why are many of them wasting away at home with overprotective parents who fear to push them out of the nest? Subtle, hidden neurological handicaps are not imposed on a person at adolescence. In most instances they have existed since birth. It is a tragedy that they are not being recognized until failure is established. Something is very wrong. The personal tragedy and social cost is enormous. In fact, a knowledgeable psychiatrist has written a book entitled, *Society Pays: The High Cost of Minimal Brain Dysfunction in America.* [1]

Research is grievously lacking about this deviant segment of America's population. What are young adults really like with this handicap? How prepared are they to hold jobs? What are the prime limitations to their functioning? What services do they need to bridge the gap between unemployment and employment? These are questions without answers. As a starting point, a pilot project has been undertaken in California.

CANHC Vocational Project

To find out what MBD young people are like, the California Association for Neurologically Handicapped Children (CANHC) in cooperation with the Department of Rehabilitation is conducting a small pilot project for twenty out-of-school young adults. Specifications state that they should be of normal or above normal intelligence, in their late teens or twenties, and should have a minimal neurological deficit with no other primary deficits such as blindness or deafness, epilepsy, crippling, psychosis, or drug addiction.

Individuals have randomly applied, usually on referral from parents, teachers, or rehabilitation counselors; but communications have been with the participants themselves. Case histories have been collected, extensive physical, psychological, sensory-motor and visualization tests have been made, remediation has been designed, and future steps are to be developed. The project staff, consisting of the CANHC coordinator, psychologist, physician, occupational therapist, visualization specialist, and rehabilitation counselor, meets regularly to discuss the cases individually.

Although the project is not yet completed, it already appears that the disability is more vocationally severe than expected. The majority of these young people need extensive help in order to become employable. Specifically, they are receiving three kinds of rehabilitative help:

1. An experimental physical program adapted by an occupational therapist for adults to improve the sensory-motor processing of the brain. (Ironically, most earlier therapy received during their developing years was at an academic symbolic level which bypassed the more basic developmental lags which interfered with their learning.) Hopefully it is not too late to improve such functioning.

2. Reality counseling and ego-therapy designed to overcome unreal expectations, improve coping mechanisms, and overcome attitudes of depression, hostility, or apathy.

3. Creative living skills designed to help with the basics of budget-planning, job pursuit, money management, travel, and independent living.

In addition to remediation, vocational skill training is a necessity. Almost all project candidates arrived at adulthood totally bereft of job entry skills. Vocational education departments have as yet made *no* adaptations for our young people and reject them; and special education curriculum still hammers away at academics without even pre-vocational preparation. Excluded from college prep courses, they drop out or even graduate with nothing to take to a job.

Schools Must Help Prepare for Jobs

Vocational help can and should begin in school . . . and with the special educator who recognizes that a child has a learning problem. As soon as such a child is discovered, a red light should be attached to his back to let everyone know that it is essential for this particular child to succeed! *This is a high-risk child!* Without such a warning, he will be surrounded by negative messages as a result of his observable learning and behavior responses . . . and he will soon reflect back his realization that he is a failure. To counteract this, the special educator and all his teachers must find ways for the child to succeed. The positive aspect of his potential must be developed. His entire future life—and certainly his job potential—will depend upon how he views himself. (In California, some of the federally funded drug prevention programs are focusing on image-building in the earlier years, on the theory that a person who cares for himself and has a strong feeling of himself will resist drugs when offered. This is true of all self-rejecting exceptional children as well.) A good self-image is important for everyone; but it is enormously harder for the limited child to achieve it unless someone takes this on as a major goal. Family reinforcement is essential, but meaningful success must be experienced in school somehow. Only a good self-image can fuel the effort necessary to build vocational adequacy after the adolescent completes school.

Specific vocational help should also be the task of the special educator, yet most teachers of exceptional children are not vocationally oriented. Pre-vocational skills must be taught and overtaught to these children at the level of their understanding. Excellent curricula along this line have been developed by some teachers. Such teaching materials should become essential ingredients of all special education programs in the nations's high schools.

Academic remediation at the secondary level could become "Occupational Academics" as is done in Archway School in New York. Here appropriate job skills are taught to a high level of efficiency after the staff realistically assesses the possibilities for each student. With the goal of training each person for a cost-productive job that will not put him in the Mentally Retarded (MR) category of the labor force, motivation for learning increases enormously. The academics, adjusted to specific learning styles and specific occupations, become relevant and important. And, as the designer of this program explained, "Unless your child is to work for Uncle Henry, he should become a totally equipped, cost-productive employee from the community standpoint." The success of this new program, small-scale though it is, seems to bear this out.

Vocational education is a reality in many school systems, but is rarely available to the student with learning problems. Too often there is no communication between the special education teachers and the vocational instructors. Beautiful equipment, skilled instructors, job-knowledgeable specialists in vocations are available for the non-college bound, providing he has no handicaps. But with handicaps, he is rejected. "He'll hurt himself," says an instructor observing awkward John at the power saw; "He can't read the manuals," says another. And yet special money is available in America for adapting vocational education programs to the handicapped or the disadvantaged. Often it is unspent because no one knows how to use it. For starters, wouldn't it be great to hire extra aides to assist the special student who learns more individually, at a different pace, or in a different manner? Perhaps he could have the manuals taped, and could strap on the earphones when he needs them. Special educators should aggressively seek out the vocational services of the schools and see that they are made available in prescriptive ways to the MBD non-academic teenager. Skill teaching can and must be learned for vocational success, but in a different way.

Work experience, voluntary or paid, is invaluable and should be made available. Since many atypical learners must experience something fully in order to understand it, real job stations with real working conditions and with supervision built in, serve the need for concreteness. A work coordinator must see that each MBD student is ready for the job assigned, that he understands the demands of the job, that he performs adequately or receives further training. Sometimes, as in Novato, California, this person is jointly hired by the school district and the Department of Rehabilitation, and works with the student even after he is out of school on a paid job, to assure his success.

Let's Not Forget Social Skills

No one seems to know why social inadequacy is almost universal among MBD young people, except those who suffer from specific developmental dyslexia with no other concomitant handicap. Most seem unable to make or hold friends. They do not seem to act appropriately in social situations. They often seem emotionally younger than their chronological age. As a result, they suffer rejection. Some then give up and retreat; others become aggressive and act out; most are insensitive to the effect of their behavior on others or the way to read subtle meanings into body language. Where most people learn this automatically by trial and error, it may never be learned by the MBD adolescent without overt help and contrived practice. Furthermore, it has been discovered that a prime reason for job failure is not skill inadequacy but the inability to get along with coworkers and supervisors. For this reason, if for no other, development of social skills must become a part of vocational training.

To our knowledge, only a few attempts have been made to deal with this problem. Sol Gordon in New York and Charles Weening in New Jersey have developed socialization programs in cooperation with the Department of Rehabilitation. But more is needed than social experiences and the development of social graces and manners. Behavior modification is a possibility; group counseling would seem useful; practical social laboratory sessions in social situations would give practice. But, again, research in the whole area of interrelationships is a crying need. Both causes and remediation must be better understood. And since, characteristically, these young people even in childhood do not seem to respond to typical psychiatric or counseling approaches, I would suspect that some entirely new approaches need to be devised.

Let me say a word here, however, about the acceptability of aloneness. Some people are loners out of choice and learn to live comfortably with it. They prefer jobs with a minimum of social contact, and are satisfied to be spectators. If this is the adolescent's choice rather than his escape, perhaps we should make him feel comfortable about it, but help him make aloneness more self-fulfilling. And perhaps families and others should get off his back.

Umbilical cords with overprotective families must be cut. This is a problem for both parents and offspring. It may be that parents, as well as young adults, should be counseled on the ways to develop independence and self-direction, and that this should be an important ingredient in any MBD vocational project.

Is College Out?

Intellectually, many with MBD are capable of college work and at least paraprofessional employment. However, most colleges do not accept or provide for them in any special way. Exceptions can usually be traced to persistent parents finding ways to break through college barriers.

Yet community colleges, with their open enrollment and emphasis on community service, are beginning to be seen as very appropriate places for the able educationally handicapped. In California, special education funding is becoming available for eighteen-year-olds, with or without a high school diploma, who wish higher training. The need for it was shockingly apparent when an evaluation of test data indicated that approximately twenty percent of incoming freshmen were reading at fifth grade level or below.

DeAnza College in Cupertino, California, has been pioneering a program for entering students with MBD. It involves initial assessment at the Educational Diagnostic Clinic and then appropriate prescriptive teaching with the help of master tutors from the special education department of a nearby university. According to its descriptive literature, the following procedures are involved:

1. The tutors utilize media (auditory, visual, tactile or kinesthetic, or a combination of these) especially suited to the student's learning strengths to teach the subject matter.

2. The instructor guides the student to available materials on campus or elsewhere which are appropriate for his particular needs.

3. The instructor or tutor provides training experiences to build the areas of weakness determined most necessary to minimal success in his academic or vocational program.

As stated in summary, "The goals of the program in general are to help the student survive in whatever area of study he has chosen and to guide the student to a more realistic area of study if his chosen area is incompatible with his skills."

Community colleges with specific terminal vocational training are also beginning to become aware of the learning-disabled student. To assure success in such a program, special counselors with a knowledge of MBD should be assigned, with involvement far beyond that ordinarily supplied the college student. These young people are emotionally immature, still high-risk, and precariously close to despair or total apathy if not given encouragement, supervision, and specific help at any point of need. This contact should carry from the training to the job, with monthly contact after employment, if possible. Without such special help, in the face of normal competition for jobs, he still may not make it.

Barriers to Employment

Once out of school, even the job-qualified adolescent may have trouble landing a job as a result of rigid, inappropriate requirements. We know that a wheel-chair employee needs ramps and wide doors; and that a blind applicant must have someone else fill out the application form, or do it orally. But no allowances are made for a skilled job seeker who is dyslexic, dysgraphic, hyperactive, or lacking a conventional diploma—even if he has the necessary skills. Here are a few of such barriers:

1. Rigid academic requirements. An MBD eighteen-year-old with no diploma could pass the General Equivalency Diploma test, if it were given orally if he had a reading problem; or if he could read it but answer orally if he had a writing problem. But no such provision exists.

2. Inflexible apprenticeship requirements often exceed the job competency requirements. Why must plumbers have high proficiency in English? What does square root have to do with auto mechanics? Let us adapt the tests to the job; let us test for relevant knowledge.

3. Inappropriate application procedures lose many workers—both in the way they must be followed and the information required. Why throw up barriers such as "What magazines do you read?" which throws panic into the nonreader. Why require written recommendations from three friends who have known you for five years? That is devastating to a loner.

4. Inflexible working conditions often prove a barrier: hours of work, arrangement of hours, tension-producing working conditions often can be modified but are not.

These are only a few of the barriers that cut off the neurologically handicapped from a fair chance. Employment practices have been modified to permit the employment of women, third-world workers, and the physically handicapped. Let us further modify them to permit equal opportunity for the intelligent adult with skills but, incidentally, minimal brain dysfunction.

The Role of Rehabilitation Agencies

It is becoming increasingly apparent that most MBD young adults are going to need considerable help in breaking through the barriers to their employment. In fact, H. M. Sterling, MD, of the department of Physical Medicine, University of California at Davis, with years of rehabilitation experience, considers MBD a *severe* vocational disability. He is currently working with the twenty young adults involved in the CANHC pilot project and writes that there is no question that most of the young adults studied in the pilot vocational rehabilitation project for neurologically handicapped should qualify for such consideration. True, the handicapping conditions are not so grossly visible as some, but the scope and degree of handicaps is nonetheless extensive. Because of the multiple modes of impairment and the interference caused by one impairment in the remediation of the other disorders, these people require prolonged services of several professional therapists working in concert.

Just what the nature of that interdisciplinary therapy will be is still to be devised. It may be a combination of extensive counseling, sensory-motor therapy, socialization training, and vocational skills. This to be followed by job evaluation, finding of appropriate jobs, training, and finally close supervision to assure success. It is hoped that the CANHC project will result in suggested procedures to guide counselors in ways to coordinate appropriate services. The recommended designation of the term "neurological handicap" or "minimal brain dysfunction" as physical entity for easier referral by rehabilitation counselors is an important beginning.

Some Promising Social Changes

Despite a generally discouraging outlook for the MBD adolescent in today's world, there are some positive social changes occuring in which may be of benefit to him. These are apparent in society generally, and in business and education. In today's diversified culture, there is more toleration for divergent personalities and life styles than it seems there has ever been. It is no longer considered disgraceful to drive a cab or work with one's hands. Art and music are acceptable vocations. Role changes benefit the person who is untraditional. The simpler life is increasingly revered, and the material and status goals of the past are being discarded by many thoughtful and intellectually capable adults. Parents are less up-tight if their children choose ways of work and life different from theirs.

Businesses are developing more flexibility and social conscience. A few employers are disenchanted with degrees and diplomas and are taking a harder look at the job applicant himself. Part-time jobs, contracted services, shorter weeks, modified hours—all help the worker with different tolerances. Some firms are already hiring "jig and fixture men" to design work stations for paraplegics; why not adapt jobs to fit the uneven capabilities of the neurologically handicapped? It would not be hard to imagine employers putting instructions or even manuals on tape; computers could compensate for missing math skills. What else?

Schools, in a wave of reform, are deemphasizing grades and rigid class levels; they are emphasizing more individualized instruction, recognizing the existence of divergent learning styles and the need for special education. The multi-media approach is a great improvement over the visually-emphasized learning of the past. And early intervention and prevention are stated goals.

Career education, also, is a national concept that will benefit all children, as well as the learning-disabled, as it sweeps through all grades from kindergarten through adult school. In addition, the gap is closing between academic and vocational education, between special and regular education. Integrated education hopefully means that children with problems will be the responsibility of all teachers in the school.

Finally, society is looking more at the causes of crime and social failure, and by so doing is beginning to find the very people we are most concerned about. Let us hope that more money and leadership will go into useful research, successful prevention, and effective programing so as to benefit all persons whose handicap of childhood, initially minor, becomes major when ignored.

Hurrah for Families

Most families, distressed by the presence of a maverick learner in the family, feel incapable of providing direction. In fact, their disappointment over his inability to follow conventional steps to success compounds the non-learner's feelings of failure; and, by the time he is old enough to secure a job, he is not only ill-prepared, but has stopped trying.

Two alternatives are likely to follow: The unhappy, hostile teenager leaves home, defiantly declaring he will "make it on his own." Rather than success, however, he may end up on welfare or in jail. Or, by contrast, some teenagers accept their dependency with its comfortable free room and board and its avoidance of painful decision making. They develop a marginal existence devoid of satisfaction, pride, or joy. In both cases, the waste of human potential is tragic.

A few families have found a middle way, impressive as a result of the imagination and commitment involved. They have persisted in finding success experiences for their MBD child, and have found or created appropriate ways to assure financial and psychological independence. Here are a few examples.

In Orinda, California, a Spoke and Pedal Shop begun in 1970 had as its chief mechanic and cycle-assembler a young adult with no math or reading skills, but enormous efficiency in mechanics. The father, an insurance executive,bought the shop with an $800 investment for his son's skills, and three and a half years later was offered $40,000 for this same shop which had gained an enviable reputation for excellent inventory, dependable service, superior repair work. The son gained a fine reputation and a salary of $600 a month. He was able to buy himself a $3500 car and acquired enough self-assurance to leave the parent-supported shop and strike out on his own several hundred miles from home. His father considers this a supreme success, for the boy is truly independent and self-supporting, with a surprising number of friends in the small town of his choice.

Gary was a sports nut who could qualify in no way for team playing in his high school. But he was allowed to care for equipment, which he did superbly, winning the job of team manager and achieving special recognition at the time of his graduation. What then? A neighboring community college with a sympathetic administrator with a learning-disabled child of his own introduced Gary to the college coach, who promptly made him a team manager. The athletic office became his security hangout for twelve hours a day for two years, with only token courses being taken at the college. About that time an uncle in the construction business had completed a large, beautiful apartment complex that offered elaborate health and exercise facilities to the residents. A competent health manager was hired, with Gary named "assistant health manager" in charge of all game and exercise equipment. It is a full-time job, essential to the operation of the complex.

In the Sierra foothills a house is being built by a father and son on weekends. The father is an oil executive, but his fifth son had serious learning disabilities and seemed doomed to failure. Working on a one-to-one basis on weekends, father and son have been learning together the skills of the building trade; and after two years, the son has announced confidently that he wants to become a contractor. He will probably make it. In fact, he already has demonstrated success; the new family home is undeniable proof of that.

A manufacturing foreman in San Jose, California, permitted his son to leave school at age eighteen after completing only the tenth grade, because he could not hack its academic emphasis. He enrolled him in a welding course, and then personally signed welding contracts with his company for small jobs. He subcontracted the work to his son at two dollars an hour, giving him experience and supervision. The contracting was so successful that the demand increased, and now the son directly contracts his own welding jobs with that company two and a half days a week. He will be well ahead of his peers in welding experience when he graduates from the trade school into the job world.

A school principal, accepting the fact that his son could never succeed in school, turned his son's love of the country into a job-developing training ground. Back-packing was first done with the family; then with the Sierra

Club; then on individual hire. And now that the son is twenty-five, he has a firm reputation as a dependable back-packer in the non-threatening wilderness area. Pollution-free, exhilarating, paying. Who could want more?

Yes, MBD adolescents can become self-supporting; but not as a matter of course. Success seems likely only with extensive, realistic, caring help. The young adult with MBD needs marketable skills, whether they be blue or white collar; he needs good working habits; his work must be cost-productive in and of itself with no sloppy compromises. He will have to get along with his boss and coworkers.

But skills alone cannot assure success. Internal barriers characteristically interfere with his performance; and external barriers deny him opportunities. Far better to spend time and money finding ways to help him succeed than time and money on welfare checks and prison food. The barriers to success must be recognized and removed. Only then will the rich vocational potential of the bright but invisibly limited adolescent be realized.

Chapter 3:

The Specific LD Adolescent— Who is Responsible for Him?

Mary Jane O'Gara

NOT TOO MANY MONTHS AGO at a meeting of professionals concerned with the problems of the juvenile, a doctor deplored the increasing numbers of disturbed young people he was seeing. Speaking as a specialist in this field, he categorized the greater percent of these patients as specifically learning disabled. He was not objecting to these teenagers turning to him for help; rather he sees the physician as a natural counselor—someone to whom a young person can talk without the onus he might attach to a psychiatrist. What disturbed the doctor is this unmistakable indication that society is failing handicapped youth: that education, rather than being an answer to their problems, has become itself a problem.

At a time in their lives when they need to succeed in school because they look upon graduation as a necessary goal, the specifically learning-disabled adolescents too often fail. They are convinced they cannot succeed in a system in which their individual differences isolate them as surely as the wall which separates them from their peers. When their fears prove correct, their academic failure destroys egos which are already beset by frustration, tension, and self-doubt.

These young people have few options when the struggle with the system becomes too much. They look for the solution to their troubles in alcohol, drugs, anarchy, hate, even suicide. They become the school drop-outs, juvenile delinquents, or revolutionaries in a world in which they have already paid the price. They misinterpret the reasons for their failure, and they foresee no success in the future.

The price they have paid might have been extracted over the years by teachers who never learned to identify their specific areas of disability ... teachers who did not perceive the reasons these young people were different.

The price might have been the cost of an environment which was inflexible: an environment which demanded perfection of them in appearance, performance, and social skills. Or the price might have been charged of them over the years by parents who resented the demands these children unwittingly placed upon them by their "differentness."

From the standpoint of the doctor of medicine these troubled young people represent a heart-breaking loss of human resources. From the parents' viewpoint, the adolescent with a specific learning disability is a tragedy. His potential for accomplishment and his individual talents have somehow become lost between the time he entered school and now. The specific learning-disabled juvenile represents failure on the part of all those associated with him to build his ego to the point where he can accept his liabilities in some areas because he knows he has assets in others.

This young person is living proof that society must begin to emphasize the positive, or waste valuable manpower, and that educators must make their first goal the development of independent, productive human beings— young men and women who have learned how to cope with life, not just academics—and that parents must serve as active, knowledgable advocates of their children.

What they ask of society is not too different than that asked by any non-handicapped person: the right to be first-class citizens. They seek to gain from their education the kinds of skills which will prepare them to be independent, self-supporting individuals. Academics are almost secondary in their priorities.

They will learn to read and write, to compute basic problems, and to compensate or remediate spelling and writing handicaps, if they are strongly motivated. Becoming motivated to learn is more valuable to them than subject matter. They will gain the self-confidence, the security they need, if they have been trained to make judgments in an objective way. They will succeed if they have developed initiative and self-reliance.

If they have acquired expertise in conversing with adults and peers, if they have learned to listen, as well as talk, if they have overcome a basic egocentricity to form real and lasting friendships, they will have gained from their education the skills they need to be productive human beings.

They must learn to communicate with others, verbally and nonverbally, so they understand what is being said, and so others will understand them. This is the kind of learning which will enable them to be successful whether their futures lie in the vocational, business, or academic worlds. An additional benefit to be gained from this educational emphasis will be in the development of independent, self-supporting manpower for our country. Realistically we can't afford to waste any of it.

We, as parents, educators, physicians, and citizens, will profit from their achievements. Just as we are part of their failure, we will take pride in tapping a human resource which until now has lain fallow.

They are as Real as their Problems

The specific learning-disabled adolescent is more than an interesting statistic. After a decade of research into the problems of children suffering from the minimal cerebral dysfunction syndrome, he is living proof that the problem is far from solved. While he might be in better control of himself and his world at this age, he has added an entire new repertoire of deficits which support his belief that he is worthless.

These are the characteristics which parents and teachers must recognize if they are ever to help these young people. They must know the learning-disabled adolescent has a poor self-concept, that he is anxious and lacks motivation, and that he is socially immature; most important, they must be aware of those personality deficiencies which differentiate between what he can do and what is expected of him.

Because these young people are as real as their problems, I am chronicling four case histories in the hope these individuals will live for you as they do with us, their parents.

A Struggle against the System

I am thinking of bright and golden Terry who at age fourteen can ride her horse with the ease and assurance of a seasoned jockey. Her athletic ability and the companionship she gains from her association with the animal have been the only plus factors in Terry's life these past few years. Although she was diagnosed as specifically learning disabled over four years ago, parents have been unable to get any kind of educational help for their daughter. Terry has a high IQ, so she manages to achieve in the low average range. But she knows she could do better. And this knowledge, plus a growing rebellion towards teachers who she believes don't care, is pushing Terry into a corner from which she sees no escape.

Now, in the summertime, Terry is spending 18 out of 24 hours a day in bed. She eats only after arguments, which make mealtimes unappetizing for the whole family. Her parents realize she is seeking to escape from a situation which is as oppressive and confining as a prison wall. They have sought help from her doctor. He can counsel this troubled girl, but he can't change her educational environment.

Terry's case is fairly typical. Although boys with specific learning disabilities outnumber girls ten to one, Terry is proof that the problem exists. She was the fourth child in a well-to-do family—a lithe, effervescent child who manifested no exceptionalities in her preschool years. When Terry entered kindergarten, her happy attitude disappeared; and the life of her family changed. Her mother was informed by her teacher, "Terry has to live in this world; she might as well learn now."

e prediction has grown to haunt Terry's parents. Although they
that their daughter's teacher was suffering from an emotional
her own, they find it difficult to reconcile her attitude with the
h she caused their daughter.

Through the primary years, Terry apparently achieved at the same rate
as her classmates. Her teachers, for the most part, were understanding; and,
after the initial problems, she seemed to enjoy school. Not until third
grade did the first signs of any learning problem become apparent. She was
never able to complete her work, a situation which caused her constant
discouragement. By the time she entered fourth grade, Terry had become a
loner. She walked along the school walls as if she wanted to vanish into the
woodwork. Her eyes were downcast. She didn't want to see or be seen.

Her mother became Terry's strongest advocate. An intelligent,
compassionate woman, she was willing to cooperate with her daughter's
teachers in any way they advised her Terry would be helped. She insisted
Terry complete the work they sent home from school—work the girl
couldn't finish in school. Her role became that of a villian, and she soon
recognized the fallacy of the arguments, "Terry could do the work if she
tried," or "She is a daydreamer." Nights of hearing her daughter sob, "I wish
I didn't have to go to school," convinced this woman the child had a real
problem.

Terry underwent a complete battery of physical and neurological tests
in a local hospital. Her doctor diagnosed her as specifically learning disabled.
Armed with the pediatrician's report and advice, the mother sought cooperation of Terry's teachers. She knew their understanding of the girl's behavior
was primary if Terry was ever to overcome her self-hate. She sorrowed at the
change which had occurred in the first four years of school. Gone was the
happy, open child who had marched into kindergarten with an assurance
which proclaimed, "I'm here; we can begin!" In her place was a disturbed
eight-year-old who was contemptuous of herself, a girl who tried to keep
everyone at a distance to prevent further hurt.

A sympathetic teacher proved Terry's ally during the next two years.
His individual attention and his belief in her ability to succeed brought about
a better attitude and a good learning experience. Then, in seventh grade,
Terry participated in a pilot study undertaken by the school system to buoy
the confidence of youngsters who needed this type of support. All the
prerequisites for a successful program were included: interested, understanding teachers, smaller classes of students who were competing on an equal
basis, and stimulating material.

Terry's mother approved of the program, though she was aware of her
daughter's unhappiness in not being able to work above the low track. As is
usually the case, the more intelligent the child, the more difficult it is for her
to accept this type of handicap. Frustrated at not being able to achieve at a

higher level, Terry exploded, "I'm smarter than Jan" (fellow student), "but I can't make good grades." She would interact with classmates, but she fostered no friendships outside of school.

Because she found it impossible to finish a timed test, Terry was exempted from taking the *Iowa Test of Basic Skills* (ITBS) from fifth to eighth grade. This excuse was given at her mother's request. Neither her mother or her doctor believed this type of experience could be anything but debilitating to the girl. When school officials asked that Terry be required to test in eighth grade, her mother agreed but with stipulations. She wanted a record of the total number of questions in each test, the total number which Terry completed, and out of these the total number which she completed correctly. As an example, this procedure revealed the girl correctly answered 35 out of 37 questions she completed in one subject area. Although the test contained 54 questions, school personnel were pleased at her performance, and agreed with her mother that Terry only needed more time to achieve a higher score. The test was not a true indicator of her ability.

The problem of not having enough time affected many areas of Terry's life. Although she was unable to keep pace with her classmates at the junior high level, the desperately driven girl was told it would be unfair to others to lighten her load. Working through the school counselor, her mother attempted to spell out the need for an assessment of Terry's strengths and liabilities. She stressed the importance of teachers' working within the strong areas. At the end of the school year she was told by the school principal that most of Terry's teachers had failed to read the girl's cumulative folder. Not only had they neglected to make use of this information; they had complained that Terry's mother was overprotective and that the girl was using her disability as a crutch. Their consensus of Terry labeled her "lazy and spoiled."

One episode stands out as typical of her experiences. Her mother recalls her daughter's typing teacher assigned Terry to type, "I will not chew gum in typing class" two hundred times on three successive days. Terry chewed gum to relieve stress, and she had neglected to remove it before entering this class. She forgot the assignment twice. Her behavior was typical of the forgetfulness and disorganization in this type of youngster. She shrugged off the punishment with a cool "All right." The work took six hours. The damage can't be timed.

Terry's mother recognizes that her daughter is not likable at times like this. Her bravado—a cover-up for her failure—appears disrespectful. But she couldn't fault her reaction in this case. "I was actually proud she had the gumption to act as if she didn't care. They hadn't beaten her down. But, of course, they didn't know Terry comes home and goes to bed." How else to fight the growing frustration and belligerence over all assignments marked "messy" or "incomplete"? Says her mother, "If they would just once comment on what she had done well . . . I could understand if they had not been told she had a learning disability. But they feel she is disrespectful; she feels they don't care. I guess I can only agree with her."

Terry's mother has served in some official capacity in the Nebraska Association for Children with Learning Disabilities (ACLD) since its formation in 1970. Her efforts to help her daughter prompted her to accept a job as an aide in the school system where her daughter is enrolled. She was one of the chief proponents for state legislation which resulted in a legal definition of specific learning disability in children in Nebraska. With the association, she helped push for legislation in 1973 which calls for mandatory education for children like Terry.

But Terry's mother is enough of a realist to recognize the damage which has already been done to her daughter. Angry and intimidated by her failure to communicate with teachers on Terry's problem, she contends, "School is the worst thing that could happen to these kids." She would like to see college curricula require courses in this area for the general teacher. "They are the ones who see our children." These courses should be mandatory for certification, she believes.

Terry has exceptional talent in painting. One of her works took a top prize in a large city exhibition. Yet her rare ability has never been encouraged in her school. Her dancing, which is excellent, never earns her a part in school plays.

Terry continues to be a loner. Her sensitivity is poured out on canvasses; her love goes to an animal which she supports by cleaning stables.

Terry is a living indictment of our schools.

One Success Story

By contrast, there is Joy, so concrete and literal at age fifteen that not too long ago she mistakenly attempted to bleach her hair with Chlorox. Although her mother discovered the almost tragic error in time, she recognizes Joy misses the nuances of language, and will always have to rely upon oral communication to interpret the meaning of words. For her, "poison" was something dangerous if taken internally. Her mother reports Joy is aware she is missing the subtleties associated with words, and this knowledge is helping her to think things through.

The recognition of her problems and early intervention make Joy somewhat of a success story. Although her parents are quick to admit finding help for Joy was not always easy or pleasant, they believe their daughter is a better person for having learned to cope with her problem. Says her mother, "She will always have to live with it, but the one good thing we can see coming out of this experience is that she has such understanding for other children with learning problems. When she looks at people, she sees their good points."

This assessment of Joy is heartening in the light of her early background. A premature child, she joined her adoptive family at four months, a tiny, solemn baby who was immediately the focal point in the lives of her parents and a two-and-a-half year-old brother. While her growth and maturation seemed to be delayed from the beginning, the child exhibited remarkable articulation at age two. Her mother recalls Joy pronounced words beautifully, almost like a little parrot; but there was little sense or logic to her conversation. She even tells of her grandmother's experience in taking Joy on a bus trip, during which the child talked like an animated cartoon character over a period of four hours without making one word of sense.

Joy's problem became obvious when she was enrolled in nursery school between ages three and four. Although she was as bright as the materials which attracted her, she would focus on one task. When time came to change the routine, Joy perseverated. She screamed, clung to her chair, and refused to quit what she was doing. Her nursery school teacher bodily removed the child to another room where the sounds of her displeasure reverberated from every corner of the room with the tonal quality of a highly sophisticated stereo system.

Driven by an energy she couldn't control, Joy might have been a mechanical doll whose motor wouldn't shut off in those preschool days. Her mother discovered the quickest, most successful technique to combat this hyperkinetic behavior was to give the child a warm, relaxing bath. Joy's problems seemed to be washed away as surely as any dirt or grime on her small frame.

Her parents devised other methods to control Joy's perseveration. They used short, terse commands: "Stop." "Stand up." "Come here." The firm tone and the short commands proved an effective means of breaking the behavior pattern over which she had no control.

Such innate understanding and common sense would have continued to benefit Joy, but the real help she needed might not have been forthcoming if the family had not moved from their home in New Jersey to Massachusetts. In the new school system in which the mother took a position, there was understanding of children like their daughter.

Although she had taken her undergraduate degree in history and her master's degree in education, Joy's mother had gradually begun to study and work in the area of special education. She still blames herself for failing to relate Joy's language trouble to the work she was doing with aphasics in the public school setting. "Her articulation was so perfect," she recalls, "This is unusual in aphasia. It's one of the reasons I suppose I didn't realize I had a problem in my own home."

Joy's perseveration continued to be a problem in kindergarten, but fortunately her teacher was a wise and sympathetic woman who asked Joy's parents how they dealt with the situation. Utilizing the same techniques, she was able to work with the child. The school psychologist advised the family to enroll their daughter in first grade because he could find no indications from her tests that she would have trouble.

His predictions proved false. The once ebullient little girl became quiet and withdrawn, taking comfort from rocking for long hours in her mother's lap. Because her mother was employed part-time with another school system, she occasionally was not able to be home when Joy returned from school. The child's grandmother would meet her on these occasions.

Joy's mother remembers the episode which precipitated the changes in Joy's life, the changes which now prompt her parents to say their daughter lives up to her name. Her mother came home one day to find both Joy and her grandmother in tears. Joy had been assigned to write the numbers one to ten. Any child like Joy lacking fine-motor control would have failed. But the teacher insisted Joy continue over and over and over. Her teacher was an intractable individual who insisted each of her students perform identically.

Joy's parents met with the school principal to request their daughter be placed in a slower classroom. While this administrator categorized Joy as "extremely disturbed," he disagreed in her need to transfer. He suggested her habit of acting out in class stemmed from an emotional problem.

The principal told Joy's parents he had observed the girl in gym class, cavorting like a clown. This observation was true, but he failed to understand the reason for her performance. Alghough Joy could tie her shoes at three, she was unable to tell the difference between her left and right shoe. Changing clothes was a real problem. To distract attention from her inability to do what the other children did, Joy tried to divert their interest.

Although her parents spoke to the principal about Joy's auditory-perceptual and perceptual-motor problems, he could not relate these handicaps to her classroom behavior.

In the hope of securing professional support for their assessment of Joy's problems, her parents took her to a hospital clinic where she underwent a psychological and educational evaluation. The consensus was that Joy needed clinical therapy.

Joy's parents readily agree they were luckier than most people who receive this type of diagnosis. Through her position in a school system with supportive facilities and specialists, Joy's mother was able to remove her daughter from her debilitating situation and place her in a classroom where she could receive individual attention. Joy also worked part of the day in a clinic with a speech therapist and a reading clinician.

In just two weeks after the move, her mother happily recalls the sight of her daughter waving a paper she had finished in school. "It's good. It's good," she shouted. The paper. The change. The child.

Joy repeated second grade. The combination of an understanding teacher and a knowledgeable mother resulted in the child's steady advancement. Her mother recognized the necessity of working with the girl from the point at which she was assessed. Knowing the needs were individual, she was instrumental in nurturing Joy's educational growth.

Joy's mother will agree that the parent must be the chief advocate of the specifically learning-disabled child. She has her own particular war wounds—like the one she suffered when the psychologist in the school Joy formerly attended called her to ask why she (the mother) was *persecuting* Joy's teacher.

While her daughter has not needed special help since fourth grade, her mother has worked closely with all Joy's teachers. She has done patch-work repair in subject matter along a road which might have become rocky without this special follow-up.

An expert now in the area of the specifically learning-disabled child with language problems, Joy's mother voices the need for some type of continuity in the schools on the progress of children like her daughter. She bases her concern on personal experiences. Joy carried her reputation for bad behavior with her from grade to grade like most children carry the family name. But this denoted a negative connotation. Any record of her progress or weakness educationally was as nonexistent as comments or recommendations which would have helped teachers from grade to grade. If a teacher entertained negative feelings about a handicapped child, Joy sensed she was being discriminated against. And, like most persons placed in a defensive position, she lived up to her expected reputation.

Joy will always have difficulty in communicating verbally. She and her parents are realistic enough about her ability to live with the problem. She did see a solution to improving her lot, however, when her parents moved to the mid-West, when Joy was to enter junior high school. She wanted to shed her previous reputation like a butterfly does its cocoon. And, to carry the comparison further, she wanted to fly alone.

At their daughter's insistence, Joy's parents did not visit the school until the first scheduled teacher conferences. At that time they were given a similar assessment by each teacher: Joy was doing well, but she often contributed irrelevant remarks in class discussions, and her writing was poor. Their description of Joy's background and her strength in overcoming her handicap elicited many cooperative suggestions for help from the teachers. They now work closely with the school to give Joy any extra support she might need.

For the most part though, Joy goes it alone. She told her speech teacher if she could improve herself, she would like to "think quicker." When she has something very important to tell a boy friend, she rehearses what she will say so she won't make a mistake. When she is tired, she is more prone to make mistakes. And she still misses many a point. When her mother suggested she think of something nice to tell a teacher with whom she couldn't work well, she complimented the woman, "That's a nice wig you're wearing."

Highly motivated to succeed, Joy bemoaned the fact she had never received an "A" in all her years at school. When she finally succeeded, she told her parents, "You don't feel any different. You're still you." Being still "you" will always be part of Joy's life.

In the Wrong Place at the Wrong Time

If Sean had his way, I suspect he might order, "Stop the world, I want to get off." He knows as well as we do that he would have succeeded in an agricultural economy where he could have quit school in eighth grade and taken over management of the family farm.

His interest in agriculture (an interest which has already earned him twenty hours credit in animal husbandry) would have grown as naturally and fruitfully as his crops. An innate mechanical talent would have enabled him to maintain his equipment in operational order. His strong urge to succeed and the quiet, pressure-free life style would have combined to give Sean pride in himself and his work.

As it is, our son at seventeen threatens to quit school so he can accept a job delivering packages for two dollars an hour in a shopping center. If he would be happy in this job, or if he believed this choice would provide meaning to a stressful existence, we would give our permission. But Sean is well aware that type of employment would not give him the satisfaction a person receives from work which challenges his capabilities. He knows deep down inside he would be as unhappy in this job as he has been in school.

Even though Sean wants to believe our arguments that he can succeed, given proper help and encouragement, at his age he needs concrete evidence of the fact to be convinced. His threats to quit school are a way of striking back at us, at the school system, and at society in general. A way of saying: "Put up or shut up."

Sean was not always so negative. He is the victim of his times. Highly intelligent with a natural mechanical aptitude, he has never been able to achieve in school at the level at which he knows he should. As an adolescent, Sean now faces his most difficult battle: he knows he is specifically learning disabled. He has come to recognize his particular areas of strength and disabilities. To date he has been appreciative of the efforts made by his father and me to find help for him; but in this particular developmental phase, he alternates between his need for independence one day, and our support the next. Like his non-handicapped peers, he needs to be himself.

Sean can choose to take the easy way out: to quit school. Many young people like him have taken this route. It's one of the reasons teachers see less of this particular type of student on the secondary level. Another reason, of course, is because the student has been integrated into the system if he has any potential at all. In most areas special education is concentrated at the elementary level. Depending on his motivation and the encouragement he receives, Sean might be able to limp through high school to graduation.

However, a student like Sean with a history of failure belongs among the walking wounded. He might enter tenth grade with high hopes, as our son did, and with a determination that "I think I can do it," only to be shot down by his own deficits: his lack of organization, his inability to take notes quickly, his failure to understand what is being said in a lecture, his bad coordination, and his poor self-concept. His negative feelings about himself work like a fuse to blow up the whole dream of success.

Throughout his life Sean has been like a person born out of place, born out of time. From his birth as the third son in a voluable, well-adjusted family, Sean has been the child who was "different." But the differences were such that they were not liabilities—more like individual characteristics which made him interesting and lovable. He was a solemn baby (an adjective I notice often use to describe these children). He thrived on a soybean formula which was prescribed as a result of his allergy to milk. We called him "Fat Sean" when he was one year old.

When his sister was born, Sean was only eighteen months old. Like any normal baby, he resented this interloper in his kingdom; and he proclaimed his displeasure by refusing to sleep when she was awake. He rocked his crib so vehemently that it scooted across the room like some kind of motorized vehicle. Even though his father and I spent long calming hours soothing our son's distress, relief was not in sight for many months.

His pediatrician prescribed Benedryl to reestablish Sean's sleep habit, but our son was unable to relax until we discovered a way to stop the jumping. We tied two sheets together, wrapped them around his waist, and tied the ends under the bed. Sean could sit up and lie down comfortably, but he couldn't jump. This stratagem ended the jumping which we later understood was a form of perseveration.

Sean received a rocking horse that Christmas, and he rode with the intensity of a bronco buster. He seemed to need a very strict schedule with few deviations: community potluck parties, large family gatherings, and an unregulated bedtime were not for him.

When Sean could play outside in our fenced yard the following spring, I would watch him flying his glider with the same determination you might have seen Wilbur Wright's flight at Kitty Hawk. He dug in his sand box until the hole was so deep I couldn't spot his curly head from the kitchen window.

As the years passed, our son gathered beside him a merry band of friends who built disastrous clubhouses and healthy egos. He seemed to be able to analyze mechanical problems, and he shocked me by fixing our door bell when he was four. I say "shocked" because I would have expected him to be jolted! He was talkative, relishing adult conversation; and his interest range was as broad as his vocabulary.

Not until he entered school did Sean's boundless energy and endless curiosity come into any conflict. Although he enjoyed the companionship of kindergarten, his skill ran to putting goldfish in the chocolate milk. He couldn't cut, paste, draw, or print letters and numbers. His teacher gently suggested he might be an "exceptional child," something I had known all along. I thought he was a genuis!

My understanding of educational terms and learning has grown as much as our son over the past twelve years. My husband and I regret that Sean lost five years of critical instructional growth while we searched for the answer to why this bright child could not learn.

In first grade Sean was one of forty students in an overcrowded parochial school. He and his teacher worked out a kind of detente: he slept all afternoon and she maintained her sanity. The fact that he didn't learn the entire year was incidental, because he also suffered no mental anguish at that time.

At the advice of the school, we took Sean to a prominent university hospital where his educational psychological evaluations revealed a high-average IQ and a "mental block." The psychologist advised us to give him a lot of love and understanding to compensate for his failure in school. The problem would be outgrown in time, we were told. This fallacy has since been disproven, but its damaging effect lingers. Many parents and teachers still believe the inappropriate traits of these children (hyperactivity, distractability, perseveration, implusivity) will disappear with physical maturation. They believe they have only to wait for the problem to go away.

Later evaluations at mental health clinics and from other psychologists produced detailed assessments of my behavior, which was usually considered the focal point of Sean's problems. We were told to place him in a public school where the pressure was considered to be less than that in the school he attended. He repeated first grade in this new setting.

This unhappy state of affairs might have continued if Sean's father had not accepted a position in the mid-West when our son was to enter third grade. Sean was enrolled in a private school where he was placed in the low track, allowing him to compete with children of the same ability level.

Moving was a mildly upsetting experience to the whole family, but to Sean it was traumatic. A boy whose order in life came from routine would naturally shatter when the routine was changed. He vented his frustration on us and on the school. He was a rebel who had lost his war, but he wasn't going to lose the peace.

Again we took up our search for our Holy Grail, and we had an educational evaluation of Sean at a local university. His IQ still proved to be in the high-average range, though his achievement was far below. The psychologist counseled me to discontinue my support, "You're nothing but a slave. Let the boy work alone." His father and I at that time were helping Sean with his homework every night. We attempted to follow the specialist's advice, believing it to be in the best interest of our son; but hearing him sob, "I'm dumb. I'm dumb," night after night convinced us there had to be another reason for Sean's problems.

We located a reading tutor who worked with Sean for two years. He reversed letters, words, numbers. His writing was illegible. His comprehension was spotty. He was restless and inattentive one day, alert and quick the next. Sean was falling behind slowly, intrenchably; and with each reversal his self-esteem plummeted.

Sean was in fifth grade before we were referred to a pediatrician who specialized in this area of disability. He hospitalized our son for a complete battery of physical, neurological, and psychological tests. Sean's father and I wrote a detailed description of his past history to aid in his diagnosis.

Sean's designation as specifically learning disabled came almost as a relief to us as parents. We had a concrete definition at last, a point from which we could advance. Through the doctor's help we were able to work out a broad program of support between him, the school, and our home.

Sean was given medication to counteract his hyperkinetic behavior, and his improvement was dramatic. I remember a letter he wrote to us several weeks after he had begun taking Ritalin: "Thank you, Mom and Dad," he said, "Those pills really help. Thank you for not letting it go too far."

This might have been the end of the story; but, unfortunately for children like Sean, the problem is always there, much like an atrophied limb. A person learns to work around it. He needed opportunities to succeed; he needed to work in the areas in which his assets lie; and his positive efforts had to be rewarded. Because these are such broad statements, I believe it might be of help to other parents to elaborate on some of the things which worked with us and some which did not.

The farm experience was Sean's own idea. Of his own initiative he walked one day to a farm some three miles from our home where he introduced himself to the family of our eldest son's girl friend. The hard-working, perceptive gentleman to whom Sean addressed himself turned out to be one of our greatest allies.

From him Sean learned everything, from artificial insemination of livestock to pride in self. The association reaped a harvest of values because Sean learned quickly and well. Perseverence, responsibility, patience, and humor were only a few of the products which ended up at the marketplace of home. Sean became one of the few knowledgeable people in the area on the subject of "eyeball insemination." I still don't understand the process, but Sean asked me one day when he was describing a birthing problem, "You understand what I'm talking about don't you, Mom?" I understood enough to know he was learning a lot. The farmer's oral testing and assessment of Sean's performance were accepted by the school as a valid work-training program. For this he earned the twenty hours credit.

Sean's primary problems were perceptual-motor. He exhibited difficulty in differentiation, perceptual-motor match, ocular control and relaxation. He had some trouble in auditory decoding and auditory sequential memory. To improve these areas, we worked with an educational specialist who prescribed activities with emphasis on fine-motor control.

As Sean was already thirteen, a tall and muscular young man, we solicited the assistance of his sixteen-year-old brother in this exercise program. There was a dramatic improvement in Sean's coordination within a two-week period. His writing became readable, almost as if he had learned a new language. A secondary benefit was the relationship which resulted between the two boys who worked together an hour a day over a two-year period. They literally walked in each other's mocassins.

When Sean tried out for the wrestling team in the tenth grade, his encouragement was a direct result of his work with his brother. This was Sean's first voluntary participation in group activity. His coach was a gruff disciplinarian who gave each boy an opportunity if he tried—and try was the thing Sean had always done best.

It would be a happy conclusion to say Sean turned into a state champion, but in dealing with these young people a parent is elated if they succeed without too many bruises. Sean never really perfected the holds, but no one does in a year. He never won a match, but he didn't quit. He went the whole bit, being duped by his older team mates into chewing tobacco and sitting in the steam box to lose weight. It will be the kind of story he can tell his own sons. A pox on locker-room humor!

Selection of a school is most important for young people like Sean. Where the parents of a non-handicapped young person can automatically enroll their son or daughter in the public institution nearest their home, we knew the school we selected would have to be tailored to his needs. We chose a small private high school where the administrative and teaching staff was willing to individualize the curriculum in such a way that our son might succeed.

This flexibility on the part of school officials, plus their recognition of the problem in general, resulted in good communication. This might well be the key to success for all young people like Sean—young people who do not need sympathy, but who do need understanding.

The structure of the elementary classroom is gone in high school. There are different teachers every class, changeable schedules, study periods. A student presumably is prepared to adjust to this confusing scene. For Sean it would have been impossible without the support of a counselor system. One individual was assigned to work with a small number of students who he saw on a regular basis. The situation was far from ideal, and I frequently alerted the counselor to a problem situation. But it is the type of system which will work with modifications.

Sean's counselor was a former Marine sergeant who had grown up on a small farm. Their association gave Sean an opportunity to talk on a man-to-man basis. This astute gentleman followed up situations which he thought were disturbing Sean. He alerted Sean's teachers to the boy's need for recognition. In some cases, success in a class depended upon the teacher taking the time to test orally. If the test score indicated Sean had not written what he knew, the teacher would talk to him privately on the subject. This single factor has been a most important element of Sean's success to date. This, and the continuity of communication provided by the counselor.

Two experiences stand out in Sean's sophomore year which are revealing about Sean and young people like him.

Shortly after he had completed his first six-week block of courses, our son came home one night sickeningly drunk. His father and I were rocked by the experience; we had never even known him to take a drink. The reasons for his action were even more frightening. He was deliberately seeking an escape from a world he couldn't face—a world we had felt was improving for him. He wanted to die.

At the counsel of his doctor who talked at great length with him, we returned to the school and helped Sean revise his schedule. "These kids aren't seeking an easy out," the doctor warned, "but they need to be involved in subjects which give them some pleasure." He encouraged Sean's wrestling and his weight-lifting program. Sean joined an auto mechanics class which stimulated his interest and skill. I believe this need to make education relevant to life is essential if the specifically learning disabled adolescent is to remain in school.

The whole episode stands out as a nightmarish reminder that we must always be listening for what the child is not saying—as much as to what he is.

The second situation is the type of experience which can be devastating to young people like Sean. He had been employed part-time over the winter months in a shopping center doing odd jobs. In the spring he was given the opportunity to work full-time on the outdoor maintenance crew. His job took in anything which needed doing, from painting to cutting grass. When he came home after eight hours on the job, we weren't simply complimenting him when we said he was doing a "man's job." We knew this to be true.

Like all new employees, Sean was nervous but eager to please, and was conscientious about his work and hours. One day about a month after he began, he called home just before we were to leave for work. He needed a ride, and he was crying. He had been fired. Upon picking him up his father learned Sean had been given summary instructions on how to drive the large tractor and sent to cut grass. He misjudged his distance at one point and hit a road divider, breaking an axel on the machine. It was the kind of accident which could have happened to anyone.

Talking to Sean, his father emphasized the firing wasn't as important as the way he accepted it. We told him the employer had overreacted, and he had. He also wisely related a similar incident in his own life. Sean had the same choice he had: pick up the pieces or use the incident as an excuse to give up. We respect our son for accepting a baling job on a farm the next week. He told us later how much he liked working on the farm. "They tell you how to do a job," he said, "and help you if you have problems." Shouldn't everybody!

We believe that, in order to understand Sean, those working with him must recognize his inadequacy in being able to communicate his feelings to others and in understanding their feelings towards him. I asked him once why he always threatened to quit his job to go to work for a farmer who had a poor operation. He confessed, "Then if I get fired, I won't be hurt." Understanding this need of a defense mechanism is vital to teachers.

When Sean says, "I break everything I touch," he means, "I am a failure." When he says, "I'm always interfering," he means, "I need help in understanding what I am studying." When he says, "We make a good combination. I help you, and you help me," he means, "We're on the right track." Let's stay there.

A Life That Was Saved

A friend of mine relates an incident about her nineteen-year-old son which gives one a unique insight into the whole scope of the problem faced by the adolescent with minimal brain dysfunction. She and the boy were teeing off on the first hole at a nine-hole golf course when a single woman player asked if she could join them. During the ensuing round they exchanged the usual pleasantries, and Mark even suggested a change in form which helped the woman in her putting. When they finished, the stranger suggested they play again at an early date.

My friend remarked, "Isn't it ironic, life is so normal for Mark everywhere except school. That lady wouldn't have believed if anyone had said he had a handicap." Her point, of course, is that young people like Mark react to the situation. He is a good golfer. He was relaxed. And his reputation doesn't follow him on the course as it does in school. What a tragedy it is that only outside of school are adolescents like Mark accepted as equals.

Mark's story is particlarly unfortunate because it need never have happened. The adopted son of well-to-do parents, he was diagnosed as specifically learning disabled at age five by the late Dr. Newell Kephart, then of Purdue University. He was given special help in the academic areas and in motor activities from the time he was in first grade. That he graduated from high school this spring completely untouched by learning after three years in a special education class in a private school district is a crime against humanity. He was robbed in a very real sense.

As Mark's mother recounts their experiences one point is clear. Their son was the victim of lack of understanding of the problem of minimal brain dysfunction. Mark was adopted at ten days of age, legally and lovingly part of a family unit made up of his parents and a natural-born sister. According to his mother, this child with the angel face was propelled by a motor as powerful as any in the Indianapolis 500. She figured he never ran out of gas; he only took time out for repairs. By age three these repairs included: stitches on his forehead, acquired when he ran to greet his sister and fell; having his stomach pumped when he consumed a bottle of baby aspirin; x-rays when he ran into a door and knocked himself out; fifteen stitches to close the wound he received when he ran his arm through the storm door; a check-up on the goose egg and black eye earned when he fell out of the wading pool; and more stitches when he wacked his head with a golf club. She is still able to laugh, "I had my own route from our house to the emergency entrance of the hospital."

Mark's mother traces the first hint of things to come, to a characteristic she noted in her son at eighteen months. He was unable to release his grasp when he grabbed her wrist. His fingers had to be pried open. Sleep came to this busy boy with great difficulty. He banged his head constantly, and he managed to kick the slats out of his crib by eighteen months. Daily his mother patiently soothed her angry son until he could relax and recover to resume the battle he waged with the world.

Not knowing whether it was a blessing or added trial, his mother recalls Mark walked early—or, more accurately, he ran early—but always on his toes. Extremely hyperactive, he was poorly coordinated, a fact which might have contributed to his low frustration point. Though he talked at a young age, his words made no sense.

Life became a series of patchwork episodes which never fit in a pattern for this boy. His mother remembers Mark as a kind of whirling dervish who was as welcome among their friends and relatives as a tornado in a wheat field. He never walked, he ran. He couldn't concentrate on anything for more than a few seconds at a time. He heard the beginnings of records, never the end. He didn't play with his trucks, he lined them up. He enjoyed having a story read, but he latched on to an insignificant detail. As he grew older, and tried to dress himself, everything went on backwards. Like Dorothy in the *Wizard of Oz*, Mark seemed to be shipped into a vortex which was carrying him to nowhere.

The effect, of course, was as unreal as the fairytale world. His frustration rose with each failure. He would throw his clothes from his dresser drawers to register his disapproval at a world whose pressure smothered him; and after the drawers were empty, he might fling them down the stairs as an exclamation point to his unspoken statement. He couldn't walk into a room without misjudging his distance and hitting the wall.

His parents still remember with horror the Colorado vacation they took when he was three. Even though their son was bedded down in a room with his sister and an attendant, he managed to unlock the door and go into the courtyard during the night to find the pool. The desk clerk found him before he was successful in his quest, and the family returned home needing a good night's rest.

Her good humor, common sense, and downright strength sustained Mark's mother in those early years. She tells about the women in the neighborhood gathering for coffee to converse while the children played. She was the only one in the crowd wearing track shoes. She envisioned a place on the Olympic track team based on her competition with Mark.

By the time he was four, Mark was gaining strength and she was losing ground. At the suggestion of a psychologist friend, Mark's mother entered her son in nursery school. Her mother urged her to have the boy evaluated at a clinic where she did volunteer work with exceptional children. But, like mothers the world over, this determined woman preferred to believe her friends, who insisted "All boys are wild!" and the pediatrician who characterized Mark "immature." "In the back of my mind," she says, "I knew something was wrong with Mark. He wasn't retarded, but something was wrong. I just couldn't put my finger on it."

Nursery school was more beneficial to Mark's mother than to him. Each time she picked him up at the school he would react like a caged animal which had been released. His teacher assured her, however, his behavior in school was appropriate. His attempts to cut, paste, and draw were as wild as his temperament. His teacher did request Mark be excused from graduation exercises because she felt the experience might be too confusing. She also suggested his parents have the boy tested before he entered kindergarten.

Mark's tests revealed areas of adequacy and inadequacy. His parents were advised to enter him in kindergarten. They were also counseled to see a psychiatrist. This experience gave them a small view of the frsutration their son must have endured on a daily basis. After seven months of visits to this professional on a weekly basis with her son, the mother knew no more about him or his problems than when she made their first appointment. Mark was diagnosed as "emotionally disturbed." "Moderately severe," she was told, a term she could not reconcile. Mark worked with a therapist. His mother visited the doctor. She never received any advice on how to help her son at home, and could only assume her consultations were somehow a part of a grand plan to help her son—help which never materialized. The entire experience was as costly as it was unproductive.

By threading together the many small worries kindergarten brought to him, Mark enveloped himself in a cocoon of self-doubt. He could not find his materials or rug because all the cupboards looked alike. He was afraid to cross the playground because, if he saw any children rough-housing, he was sure they were waiting to attack him. He became lost on several occasions when he made a wrong turn in going to or from school. His teacher contacted Mark's parents before the first quarter ended because, like his mother, she too knew something was wrong.

The episode which changed Mark's life was as simple in origin as it was dramatic in effect. His mother read an article in a 1961 issue of *The Saturday Evening Post*. Authored by Roz Oppenheim, the story told of the family's attempt to find help for an autistic son. Mark's mother still wonders why she related this child's experiences to her son's, because Mark never quit talking; but she contacted Dr. Newell Kephart for an evaluation of the boy.

She quotes from Dr. Kephart's first examination of Mark: "Mark is an attractive, physically well-developed six-year-old boy. His response to requests to attempt tasks is normally one of resistance and noncooperation. This boy appears to have a rather severe perceptual-motor problem. Laterality does not seem to be well established. Mark shows the characteristic waddling gait of children with problems of laterality. Mark also appears to be having difficulty in directionality."

In a two-page report, Mark's mother noted references to behavior she had noticed in her son without realizing the reason for it. She knew now why he ate with his left hand when she put the silver on the left of his plate and with his right hand when it was placed on the right. She understood why he switched chalk from right hand to left when drawing a triangle. And at last she heard what she had sensed to be true: Mark was rigid, rather than hostile. He was looking for an "escape from the very real problems of perceptual-motor performance which he experiences."

Of even more import to the family than the diagnosis of Mark's problems were recommendations to correct them. An advocate for her son before the term ever became popular, this inspired mother undertook the task of stabilizing her son's disorganized world. She bought green chalkboard paint and covered one wall of a room in the basement of their home. Keeping the decor simple and undistracting, she filled it with a card table, two chairs, and a book case containing equipment, chalk, blocks, puzzles, and games. A walking board constructed from a 2 x 4 made up the only other piece of equipment.

Starting with a five-minute work period twice a day, she and Mark followed the doctor's recommended motor activities. If they suffered setbacks, they simply returned to simpler tasks and tried again. If the procedure seems time-consuming, Mark's mother speaks with singular perception, "No one can realize how good it felt to know there was something I could do to help my child. After all, I spend more time with him than anyone. Why not use that time to good advantage?

With this preparation for first grade, the boy's parents recognized the selection of a school for their son would be critical. They had already been informed by the principal of his former school that of the two first-grade teachers, one did not want him, and the other "would be willing to take him." This half-hearted welcome led them to investigate private schools.

They chose to enroll him in a new school where classes were small and both the administrative and teaching staff registered interest and a willingness to cooperate. Knowing Mark would need extra support, his parents also hired a tutor, whose compassionate assistance and genuine concern added two positive factors to Mark's elementary school success.

An episode which points up Mark's gross-motor problems is this description of his drive to and from school. The boy would sit in the front seat of the car to look out the windshield, asking on what street they were driving. He would then turn in his seat, glance out the rear window, and ask the same question. Turning around bodily turned his world.

School was a new and tiring experience for the small, confused child. He usually fell asleep on his return, but his parents were elated. He was learning, as were his principal, tutor, teachers, and family. At the suggestion of his principal, Mark was invited to be part of a pilot program for elementary children who needed special education. The child would spend part day in one school, then he would be taxied back to his home school for integration in the regular classroom.

The experiment was disastrous for a boy who needed structure to his life. He was grouped with one child who could not speak, another who was afflicted with cerebral palsy, and a third who was older and retarded. The learning for Mark became mimicry: he copied the mannerisms of the friend who was autistic; he walked like the child who was handicapped physically; and his eyes took on a dazed, glassy appearance. His teacher and his mother agreed he was deteriorating rapidly. Their recommendations returned him to the regular classroom on a full-time basis.

For Mark, the most productive learning experiences were at Glen Haven Achievement Center in Loveland, Colorado, where Dr. Kephart held summer sessions. Acceptance in the camp was based on the doctor's assessment of the parents' willingness to work with the child. Mark's parents believe the two years his mother and Mark attended camp changed their lives.

Mark's mother describes the experience as "family oriented." With only thirteen families and thirteen staff members, the emphasis was on a one-to-one ratio. The doctor was available for consultation at all times. And he was a familiar, friendly figure who observed the progress of everyone. The schedule combined a program of motor activities, readiness comprehension, sequence, swimming, lectures, games, and rest. All parents were assigned to work with a child other than their own the first week so they could be objective. The second week the parent followed her own child from session to session to observe and learn. The third week the parent and child worked together. The fourth week included consultations between the parent and staff.

Not only did Mark's mother gain an understanding of her child, but she began to see the problem in a more objective light. The experience of discovering there were many children with problems as severe as Mark's—some better, some worse—confirmed the belief she had always had in her son's ability to learn. A support to this fact was the evaluation of Mark's performance over the four-week period: "Mark learns, and learns very rapidly when taught in the proper manner."

Utilizing the suggestions made at camp, Mark's parents were able to work out a supportive program for their son in elementary school. They recognized his progress would be in direct relationship to the kind of teaching he was given. He repeated first grade because the doctor felt it better he "keep up" than "catch up." Mark's mother got all his assignments for the coming week so he would not fall behind the class—a practice she continued through elementary school.

As Mark grew older and more physically adept, his mother hired university students to work out with him. They were permitted to use the gym where they worked out on the parallel bars, balance beam, trampoline, walking board, climbing rope, rings, ladders, mats, even a bowling alley.

All this physical activity was an absolute necessity for the growing boy as a result of his problems with balance, coordination, and laterality. He was reluctant to exert pressure on his hands, and needed visual-motor exercises. Acting as a continual reminder of the need to persevere was Dr. Kephart's report, "While there is evidence of good potential, and Mark has demonstrated the ability to learn, it seems quite probable that he would have considerable difficulty getting along in a regular classroom."

The decision to move their son into a special education situation came on his entry into junior high school. His parents believed he would receive special help in the areas in which he needed individualization, and that he would participate with his class in all other areas. They now feel they were mistaken in their decision.

Mark's mother says, "Special education is definitely an ego-shattering experience. Few special education teachers understand students with specific learning disabilities, and the regular classroom teachers just assume a learning disability is another name for retarded."

Such teachers might be amazed to know Mark attended Hebrew class in preparation for his Bar Mizvah. As the entire process of reading Hebrew is the opposite of reading English, the magnitude of his accomplishment is indicative of his ability to learn, given the proper motivation and instruction.

Although Mark's mother attempted to maintain a good communication with the school through Mark's junior and senior high school days, she has come to the conclusion she was considered to be a mother who would not accept the fact her son was retarded. While she passed on the information she received about her son from Dr. Kephart, as she and Mark visited him annually, she was never successful in having his recommendations incorporated into Mark's curriculum. When he suggested Mark's mathematic requirement be filled by a course dealing with the kinds of money problems people have in daily experiences, the suggestion was refused. Mark was required to take algebra. His mother protested this was evidence of the subject being considered more important than the student. She was told, "You are the only mother who is verbal. We don't hear from anyone else. We must assume everyone else is satisfied."

Work experience for Mark was confined to the school cafeteria where all the students who participated are labeled as low-men-on-the-totem-pole. When Mark's mother suggested the program might be expanded to include experience in the office, the library, the book store, she felt as if she had opened Pandora's box.

Mark's work did prepare him for a part-time job he now holds in a delicatessen not far from his home. This opportunity came as part of the work-training program which had to be in food. Recognizing the young man's sense of responsibility, his eagerness to please, and his need to succeed, the manager of this establishment has helped Mark develop the self-confidence he had lost in school. His reaction to his job is revealing. "I feel dumb at school, but I don't feel dumb at work."

His parents would like to give Mark four more years to mature—in a vocational training institution or at some type of college where he would receive the added support required for him to achieve. They are not pushing their son, however. He wants to continue in the delicatessen this fall, expanding his hours and duties. While his parents believe he wants to stay because he feels "safe," they recognize this is a typical adolescent reaction. They believe he needs some time to mature and to feel good about himself. Such qualities do not automatically come with age eighteen or a diploma.

For Mark and his parents, the final indignity to his educational experience occurred at graduation. He was awarded a certificate of attendance instead of a diploma. Of 760 graduating seniors, only four students were singled out for this differentiation. His mother says, "Our son not only attended school, he participated, he studied, he worked hard, he completed assignments. We believe that he earned a diploma and that a certificate of attendance will be detrimental to his future."

Mark's mother admits she is often envious of parents who do not have a child with a specific learning disability. But then, she remembers her son did not choose to have one.

Chapter 4:

Different Points of View

Mary Jane O'Gara

IN WRITING ABOUT THE ADOLESCENT with a specific learning disability, I am acting in the role of advocate for my own seventeen-year-old son. The experiences of my husband and myself in seeking ways to help him have led to our association with knowledgable, concerned professionals in many fields. Several have assisted me in developing suggestions which would not only benefit our children . . . but all children.

A Doctor's View

A specialist in juvenile medicine, who is an authority in the area of specific learning disabilities, believes a critical goal of the dynamics of adolescence must be to make counseling a natural part of the office health setting. Here he is convinced the young person would be able to talk freely without overtly requesting help.

As he sees it, a doctor is in a position to convey ideas which will contribute to the child's success. He recognizes the very real problems of teenagers in accepting any blemishes which set them apart from their peers. He is aware the biggest area of discouragement to these young people is in their feelings of self-worth. To talk of their problems is to downgrade themselves. Thus the doctor provides an opportunity for them to discuss problems without any onus attached.

Ideally, the physician can play a very positive role in contributing information about the student to the teacher, information which will make it possible for him to succeed. He believes this kind of cooperation between the medical and educational communities is essential considering the lifelong consequences of their action.

According to this specialist, "Solving the minimal brain dysfunction problem will mean one of the greatest answers to mental hygiene and mental health phenomena which now overlap from childhood to adulthood. The more severe the disability, the more disorganized, the more chaotic are home and school, the more apt the child is to be schizoid or autistic, because he can't do anything in an organized and constructive fashion."

The doctor urges the parent to be the child's advocate because he believes only parents can give continuity to how the child learns best. He also considers it the responsibility of the parents to explain to the teacher how the child learns in areas of difficulty. This doctor attaches great value to the array of knowledge which is in the parents' hands; and he advises them to help the teacher, utilizing their experience and skill.

The doctor is concerned about the need for deep insight on the part of the teacher in her handling of these young people. He considers her understanding essential if the student is to build on the strengths which will enable him to cope.

He asks, "How much insight does the teacher have in requesting conferences? Does she call at the first sign of a problem, before it becomes unsolvable? How much insight does she have into the quality of the child's work—or is she associating it with quantity? Does she allow for individual differences?

His years of experience in working with young people as a professional, as a member of the community, and as a parent prompt this doctor to note, "The teacher who has this flexibility can work with these young people so they can achieve near potential. Without her understanding, they go the other way into defeat. The teacher must build on their strengths and lend them support in the areas of difficulty."

"These young people need so much support because they are rather worthless in their own eyes. They must learn to adjust, adapt, cope. Our whole goal must be to help make them self-productive, adapted to their own needs. This is why so many people must look at this situation from different points of view."

A School Nurse's View

Supporting the doctor in his determination to approach each young person as an individual is a registered nurse who supervises the health service program in a public school setting. She explains, "I can see the nurse in the role of a liaison between the doctor and the school, and between the home and the school. She could be an advocate of the child *and* teacher; and all of us would be working together to help the teacher realize the seriousness of this problem."

Drawing on her experience in the school system over many years, this perceptive woman points out an urgent need for a place within the school building for these young people to go to relieve tension. She recalls incidents in which the nurse's room served this need, cases of a child who would visit her when things were going badly. The teacher was understanding and tried to gear the work to the boy's speed, the nurse relates. "When he needed a change of pace, she sent him to me. I gave him small jobs to do. When he had relaxed, I asked him, 'Are you ready to go back?' He returned to the class able to cope."

She believes the nurse and the teacher must establish a close working relationship to help children and youth. The nurse must be sensitive to the child's individual needs and help the teacher to differentiate between the child with the handicap and the child who is acting out. "The teacher must recognize that some young people need a flexible schedule. When she gains insight into the signs that a student needs a change, she might send him to the nurse's room. She must be able to judge when he needs a break."

This nurse believes the ideal situation would be a room where the student could visit when the pressure became too great for him to function. In this setting he might jump rope, throw a basketball, paint—but only until he was calmed. But until this facility is a reality, the nurse's room could serve.

From her background a nurse is aware of the medical reasons a doctor might prescribe medication for a child. This nurse believes she could advise the teacher of the child's need. She recommends teachers keep anecdotal records of children's behavior, narratives of their progress which would be of aid to a doctor in diagnosing this type of problem. Her reports can be a valuable aid for both parent and physician.

There are occasions when a nurse can give the teacher the kind of professional support she needs in visiting parents to suggest their child would benefit from a complete physical examination. She believes this examination should be the first step in any effort to determine a child's problem.

A Teacher's View

Anyone seeking a cook-book-type recipe to apply to all specifically learning-disabled children and youth will fail the student and themselves, according to a master teacher in a large public school system. "The first step is to understand the student," she emphasizes. "You may not know the cause of the problem; but you assume there is a cause; and you seek a solution."

With some thirty years of teaching experience to her credit, this sensitive woman contends she acts instinctively. "There are no fundamental patterns. Helping the student find a way in which he can be successful is exploratory. You must try until you find the method that works with the individual."

Although there are no concrete rules, the teacher believes true individualization will be the answer for all students—and most especially for those with specific learning disabilities. "An individualized program will involve good work habits. There will be reachable tasks, attainable goals, and success," she explains. "Even if a student completes only a quarter of an objective, he is credited for this work. He does not fail."

The teacher emphasizes the need for persons who serve in the role of "guides." Whatever the name, "group guide" or "counselor," this individual is involved with discipline, attendance, tutoring, and scheduling tasks. He even assists the teacher in determining the student's problems. He must combine a unique understanding of human personality, a sensitive approach to which the student will respond, and a broad range in methods and materials to solve the instructional problems.

Endorsing a close working relationship with parents, this teacher fosters personal contact with the parents of her students at the beginning of each term "I like to know the parents before there is a need. I think a parent should be notified at the first signs of any problem, so we can work together to prevent its worsening."

A Psychologist's View

Although the function of the psychologist has been traditionally to assess the child for placement, one psychologist who combines an educational career and private practice believes that the role should be expanded.

"As well as child study, there should be opportunities to consult with the teacher and parent, opportunities to assess the child's strengths and weaknesses in learning, and opportunities to interpret his perception of himself in his environment."

She believes the result of this broadened study would help the parent and teacher to be more supportive of the child. Her understanding of the problem of all those involved made the psychologist the obvious person to conduct inservice classes for parents and teachers. He could focus on effective practices of child rearing for parents and on a humanistic approach to teaching for teachers.

This psychologist foresees herself in the role of the child's advocate. She could act as a liaison between the student and the teacher, between the school and home. She could help teachers to recognize these children and young people as individuals.

"Teaching is really a communication process. The knowledge the student receives relates to the effectiveness of the teacher: whether she is truly individualizing."

A Parent's View

Speaking before various university classes this summer as part of a parent panel, I have been asked what changes I would like to see made in the school system for our children. To have the opportunity to express my view to persons who can be instruments of change is an exciting experience.

Many of the changes I would ask have already been voiced by the professionals who contributed their suggestions: the doctor, the nurse, the teacher, and the psychologist. From all of them came the same basic advice: view this young person as an individual. I do not like fragmentation: treating this student for the language problem . . . the motor deficit . . . the perceptual impairment. He has been torn too many ways already. These problems are all part of him, and the solutions must reach into each area in order for them to relate to his complete entity.

With this adolescent, as with all young people at this age, there must be an understanding attitude on the part of all those associated with him. Negativism acts like charcoal fuel igniting his feelings of worthlessness. Parents and teachers need to ask themselves what they like about him. Listing these qualities might be very revealing. Too often we fail to focus on his good points, and prove to be the young person's worst critics.

Perhaps because our children are a reflection of ourselves, we expect them to react in the same way we do. We might not admit it, but we really want perfection. We must accept the fact we do our best, we try to instill values, but the adolescent must have the right to his own choices. Our acts of trust in him and our respect for his judgment can be highly important in the direction he chooses. We need to discuss our differences, but also must let him know we care for him. He needs to know we care. We must determine how much freedom to allow and how much control to keep. We need a lot of wisdom, a lot of courage, and a lot of faith.

In the school setting I believe a primary concern is vocational counseling. This young person needs to be directed into the areas in which his skills will be given full play. There are hundreds of areas in which he could be successful, given proper direction. But he can't wait until he has stumbled or been pushed through high school to begin planning. Career planning must start at the elementary level, and career education is only relevant insofar as it gives meaning to his life.

Because this student works best in a structured situation which allows him some freedom of movement, I would like to see more subjects programed. Sequential instruction is the only way for this student to go. Systematized reading and math programs help young people of all ability levels.

His records need to be passed from teacher to teacher so that he does not lose precious time each year while the new teacher analyzes his problems. (The parent has been urged to provide this continuity by the doctor.) I see a difficulty in communication with all the students' teachers at the secondary level. My own son changes courses and instructors every six weeks. After an initial parent conference, I would like to see a person within the school system who would have the responsibility of carrying progress reports of these students to new teachers on a continuing basis through the year.

Having an advocate—whatever her or his position in the school—is critical. But I caution the individual in this role to be aggressive in pressing the student to tell his problems. Empathy is the secret to a good association. The specifically learning-disabled adolescent will not ask for help or admit to a problem, because putting words to his feeling increases his feelings of worthlessness. His needs must be voiced by an advocate who will be sensitive enough to understand him. This person must communicate with the parent regularly. And, incidentally, any good news he might report will make his bad news more palatable.

My major concern is in the recognition of this child or youth within the school. I believe the general teacher must have training at the college level in order to be able to recognize this student in her classroom. Such training should be required for certification.

Because it is the colleges and training institutions who have the responsibility to prepare teachers to meet the educational needs of children, it follows they must revise their curricula to meet this changing emphasis on the individual child's differences. Teachers must be trained to recognize the overt signs of specific learning disabilities: to differentiate at an early age between the child who isn't achieving because he isn't trying, the child who isn't achieving because of his ability range, and the child who has the ability and who is trying but who is not achieving.

There will be extra demands made on teachers. They will have to extend themselves to give such extra efforts as oral testing, checking to see if the student has been able to do his assignment, and being sensitive to the number of directions he can take at one time. If the teacher is aware of this type of student, and if she knows he is as different from others with the same types of handicaps as he is from his non-handicapped peers, then she will be looking for him when she goes into the classroom.

Perhaps we as parents could offer our assistance to the colleges. We could tell them to use our homes for training sites. Student teachers could serve internships with our families. In this close situation they will feel the full impact of the specifically learning-disabled adolescent. No one truly appreciates his total effect without living with him. Those teachers who are subject-oriented would soon become child-oriented in this type of situation.

There are other methods which could help our children within the school system. These are methods which would have far reaching effects even though implementation would be fairly simple. These young people need Big Brothers on entering school: peers who can steer them to the right class, provide a friendly transition from the closely structured elementary setting to the chaotic junior and senior high school. They need to be invited to participate in discussions, to attend games, to join clubs, because they are not assured enough of their own worth to impose themselves on anyone. Their whole school experience could be eased by this program. Furthermore, they should be invited to be Big Brothers themselves after this experience so that they could feel the esteem which comes of being a leader. A one-to-one relationship is good for them. Large groups are too stimulating, and the handicapped teenager feels intimidated in this type of situation.

Sports are another area where these young people need to participate. But, not being natural athletes, they are neither sought after, nor will they volunteer to take part and admit to their clumsiness. The types of activities which should be encouraged are those which are individual or small group: golf, bowling, tennis, wrestling, weight lifting, swimming, and gymnastics.

These young people who need the coordination, discipline, self-control, and success from such endeavors seldom are enrolled. Coaches should be made aware these young people need their help desperately. And chances are when they finish school their ability to golf will be a social asset. Football is seldom a plus after graduation.

One word of caution though: the locker-room ridicule is OUT with these kids. A coach has the same characteristics as any teacher, so he must be aware these kids don't need being put down. Dragging them up by their bootstraps and building their egos through physical education is as important to the parents of these children as any team standing!

A Word for the Parent

Any parent of an adolescent has acquired his own particular battle scars based on the assessment made of him by his own child. He recognizes his opinions carry little weight with his own teenaged judge. He either is trying too hard or too little. He acts too old or too young. He is too strict or too lenient. His measure is determined on a rigid scale which classifies him either "all right" or "all wrong." He is wrong more often than right. He exists in a world adjudged to be all black or all white with no greys for soft contrast. He survives despite the indictment because he remembers his own inflexible attitudes at the same age.

The lot of the parent of the non-handicapped adolescent is easy, however, compared to that of parents of the learning-disabled teenager. For them life is a series of ups and downs, a kind of roller-coaster existence whose crests represent their child's successful forays into the real, unprotected world, and whose valleys signify their failures. They are still the major support of their child; and he, like the non-handicapped teenager, might resent his need. The parent continues to be a necessary model, even when his child wants to establish his own individuality.

When the learning-disabled adolescent successfully maintains a job, or when he volunteers his service or advice without prompting from the sidelines, his parents share in his achievement. Their world is up. When he takes it on the chin, in job, friendship, scholastically, their world is down. Not just a bit up or down; like all teenaged measurements, the registration is on the far side of either scale.

The parent might have survived the years with the non-handicapped youngster, but he begins to question his stamina with this one. He wonders if his child will ever be moderate in his judgment, and if there will ever be an end to his role. He wants to break away, to grow old with the dignity of the village sage. But he feels honor-bound to fill his dubious place as an intecessor for an adolescent he worries might never grow up.

He is criticized for holding too tight, for being too demanding, for not permitting his child to be independent. On the other hand, if he takes a chance and allows the learning-disabled adolescent more independence, he might suffer self-recrimination when the young person fails again. His only solace is in his recognition that he has no guidelines to follow. Others might have trod the same path, but no one has pointed the way. He knows the youngster needs to be given opportunities, and he prays he will have the courage to stand back and let him try.

He should take heart in the fact that he is one of a large population. Joining the local Association for Children with Learning Disabilities (ACLD) will provide two major functions: allow him the opportunity to meet others whose problems are similar or worse, and give him the opportunity to learn more about his own child. He will find solace in talking out his problems. He will find hope in working to change them.

A Community Approach

Looking back on five years of active work in this field—work which has been directed primarily towards informing those who do not understand the problem—I am convinced the only real help for our children will have to come from a completely dedicated community. This kind of dedication can only be inspired by better communication and understanding of the problems involved.

I recall a meeting not too long ago at which I suggested one of the major difficulties confronting our young people was the absence of a person in the school system who could act as an advocate for them with their teachers. One of the committee members took issue with my statement, arguing that, if a child had the proper diagnosis and help at the elementary level, he would require no help at the junior high and secondary levels. She charged parents with the blame if the young people found themselves in this untenable position at adolescence.

My retort is that we are not looking to place blame, we are not even seeking the cause of the problem at this point, but we *are* trying to find ways to help these young people. I would say to anyone in the school system who doubted their existence, "These young people are a reality. They are alive and well and going to our schools."

Fortunately, the negative attitude such as was expressed by the committee member is rare. In my job as a public information specialist with a large public school system, I have the opportunity to work with people whose responsibility is to provide equal educational opportunity for all children and youth. I see dedicated efforts being made to meet the changing needs of our times. I am convinced that the future of our children will be better served if more parents act in the role of advocates. Their voices are heeded by educators, particularly those in administrative positions who feel a heavy burden of accountability for the types of programs which are ongoing in schools. These people recognize the need for more expertise in the area of specific learning disabilities. Their foresight can be discerned in the increasing trend to individualization in reading, math, and some vocational areas.

School people and members of the medical community deplore with parents the waste of talent when our children go unaided. In Omaha a community approach to the problem came about through the formation, in December, 1968, of the STAAR Central Planning Committee (Skills, Techniques, Academic Abilities, and Remediation) to seek an answer to the problem of children with the minimal brain dysfunction syndrome. Educators, doctors, psychologists, and some parents from four counties representing approximately 600,000 people meet periodically to exchange ideas and formulate long-range plans. Their goal is the diagnosis, identification, remediation, and eradication of specific learning disabilities. While a better spirit of cooperation has developed between the various participants, I would say the major thrust of this group has been in the area of dissemination of information.

From this nucleus, a parent association was organized locally in 1970. With the strong support of the Central Planning Committee, parents inaugurated a communication program to reach all segments of the community. While the STAAR name identifies the Omaha Council, the association has become affiliated nationally as the Nebraska Association for Children with Learning Disabilities (NACLD). There are five councils in the state. Their organized efforts have brought recognition to the plight of these children. Speakers with expertise in this field from both local and national levels have been commissioned by the parent groups to address local and state workshops directed mainly at educators.

With the financial help of several community organizations, the parent organization sponsored its first state conference in the spring of 1974. Featuring a multidisciplinary approach to attract members of the medical, educational, and parent communities, the meeting registered a capacity audience of 585 persons. Another 600 hopeful registrants had to be turned away for lack of space. This venture has resulted in an overwhelming number of requests by parent groups and school districts for more speakers who are knowledgeable on the subject.

The NACLD has formed a parent panel of speakers to take their story to the community. Available to speak before university and college classes, civic groups, inservice classes for teachers, and Parent-Teacher Association meetings, these individuals do not tell anyone how to solve the problem. They say, "This is how it is with us. This has worked. This hasn't."

A Physicians' Panel which addressed the state conference has been invited "to take its act on the road." These experts direct their remarks to members of the medical profession, and they have found there is a thirst for knowledge in the small towns of this state from general practicioners to school nurses. The suggestions of all these people (pediatrician, neurologist, psychologist, opthomologist, and a moderator who is a specialist in juvenile medicine) is positive in nature, highlighting the importance of good mental health in dealing with the social, emotional, academic and vocational factors affecting these children and youth.

As a point of interest, it might be well to note this emphasis stems directly from the personal experiences of many of the panel participants. The doctor who is seeing more of our children is not the only person who is witnessing the evidence of their increasing numbers. Parents too are discovering at this age the tragic consequences the years of failure have wrought on their children. When they ask for changes in the educational system, they base their request on agonizing personal experiences. Young people who have low self-esteem are temperamentally unsuited to meet the demands of adolescence. And so we see them encountering real problems.

Life has been tough on these kids. They need, as I said of my own son, a slower time, a slower world. But since this isn't possible, they need us. All of us. To show them they are important to us and with our help they can succeed. In today's world.

Chapter 5:

A Preface to Recognition, Remediation, and Restoration

Sylvia Bleiweiss

THE DESIGNATION "learning-disabled adolescent" encompasses a section of the population that has not only a wide range of ages, but a broad spectrum of psyches, personalities, histories, and levels of achievement and non-achievement. Chronologically, the age levels are considered to be from twelve to about twenty; within this group are variables of size, sex, maturation, interests, outlook, goals, responsibilities, attitudes, peer relationships, home life, academic background, previous remedial efforts, and present standing.

It should be apparent that planning for such a diverse population requires a great variety of programs and approaches. Programing could embrace the education and retraining of a fifteen-year-old reading at a first-grade level, a twelve-year-old performing at a fourth-grade level, or a nineteen-year-old in community college who is unable to cope with that level—each with his own set of variables. While there are no blueprints of specifics for each person, there are common underpinnings essential for success. There must be awareness of individual differences, requirements, and the special needs of this age group; programs must be very flexible, carefully thought out and structured, be multidimensional, and be skillfully administered.

Some parts of this presentation apply to the broad range or common aspects of the problem; others are directed to specific segments. The opinions and advocacies represent mainly insights gained from my own participation in education as a teacher, specialist, administrator, and consultant, as well as from personal research and study. Throughout this discussion, the learning-disabled adolescent will be indicated as "he," and the teacher and other personnel involved as "she," no sexist discrimination intended. These terms are being utilized as handles, rather than labels.

Overview

Traditionally, the term "3R's" described *what* was to be taught and often was the essence of a teacher's training and preparation. A psychoeducational approach to cope with learning disabilities, however, considers the *what* sometimes less important than the *how, why, where, when, who*, and *for whom*. Focusing on these as guideposts gives us an outlook and philosophy which can be distilled into a more pertinent "3R's": *recognition, remediation, restoration*. While it is true that these categories house the basic considerations for the education of the learning disabled of all ages, they will be examined here in reference to the particular needs and behaviors of the adolescent.

Obviously, the first step in recognition is knowledge of the existence of the problem: the fact that there is a significant group of students with various degrees of learning handicaps, caused by conditions other then mental defectiveness, primary emotional disturbance, or physical deficiency of hearing or sight. They are found in almost every classroom in almost every school. They are educable, but they need an appropriate academic environment for maximum development.

The umbrella term recognition also includes awareness of the following: the syndrome of symptoms which includes perceptual, behavioral, physical, emotional, and organizational characteristics and patterns, which may appear in various combinations. These students have accumulated long years of frustrating non-accomplishment, to which now is added the overlay of adolescent emotional "yo-yoism" and agitation. The fact is that they have reached crucial decision-making stage in which they must decide whether to keep on struggling or drop out.

Remediation is the effort to enhance existing abilities, overcome, alleviate or compensate for deficiencies, and create new skills. It is scarcely enough to know pedagogic techniques, systems, or programs; the approach must have a philosophy, a psychology, as well as a pedagogic orientation. Involved in remediation are testing, diagnosis, and evaluation, and an eclectic working knowledge of methods, materials, systems, supplementary activities, and alternative programs. Of equal importance are the relationships to be established, which necessitates a positive learning *climate* as well as the physical accoutrements conducive to development. To work with the teenager in a meaningful sense, it is essential to cope with moods, to overcome resistance, to motivate, to prove relevance, to communicate, to develop a sense of trust and hope, to develop two-way communication, to create areas of success, to encourage, assure, and reassure. The program must be individualized; it must start with where he's "at," and then build up the skills he needs, while at the same time keeping him honestly informed of his strengths and weaknesses. Part of the remediation is the reshaping of attitudes, which leads us to the third pillar of the triumvirate.

Restoration is an integral but special part of remediation. What is meant by the use of the word in this context? It means a conscious effort to help the student become a "whole," social person, not only by leading him into appropriate channels, but *out* of established inappropriate ones. Changing his basic attitudes in regard to himself, his peers, the learning situation, the school, the future, is essential. It involves the attempts to create a realistic outlook, a better self-image, and appropriate activities and goals. This is not only the province of the guidance personnel, but should be inextricably contained in the daily regimen of learning. Again, this has to be a concerted effort on the part of all school personnel with communication between all areas, as well as with the parents and outside therapists or other interested parties.

In sum, we must help the student become a social human being in the true sense of the word; with self-esteem; confidence; ability to interact; ability to plan ahead; awareness of his shortcomings, but also willingness to persevere; and with optimism about his future. Ideally, he should have realistic goals and the inclination to try to attain them. We must foster this with great doses of encouragement and the opportunity for many successes. The keywords are *change* and *hope*. We'll now examine all three foundational constructs in greater detail, hoping by this delineation to help create a fuller understanding of a workable psychoeducational approach and outlook.

Chapter 6:
Recognition

Sylvia Bleiweiss

A CHILD WHO CANNOT SEE or hear well, or one who needs a crutch or brace, is always given special consideration in the classroom. Why then should the dyslexic child, whose handicap is just as great and whose problem is just as severe to him, not warrant and get special help also?" I second this question posed by George M. Bright in his work on the adolescent.[1] Stanley Sherman, who works with teenage dropouts in Boston, puts it bluntly when he maintains that schools which do not meet the needs of all students are perpetuating a criminal act, since students are required by law to attend school.[2] It is obvious that the learning-disabled adolescent as a member of the educational system, equal but with special problems and needs, deserves and is legally entitled to receive the most productive educational experience consistent with the limits of his inherent intelligence. What may not be so obvious is the cost and repercussions to the individual *and* society when these needs are not met. The neglect of this portion of our population results in school drop-outs, whose emotional upheavals often lead to commitment in institutions, disruption of families, and—in many cases—juvenile delinquency, drug-taking, and more serious criminal activities.[3]

What percentage of our school population falls in this special category? The recent literature gives varying estimation of from five to twenty-five percent—a sizeable amount![4] Do we claim that all of these students will become a statistic in the list of young offenders or drug takers? Of course not. But let's be aware of the possiblities in a situation which affects a fairly large portion of our vulnerable adolescents. The problem is not peculiar to any one school, any one academic level, geographic locale, or any one economic class. It is global.

The intense emotions and the new needs of the pubescent student are the latest incidents in a long history of having his condition unrecognized or poorly handled. Recently, at a symposium in Toronto on the subject of adolescents, one of the speakers emphasized the alarm that teenagers feel at the "differences" they notice: pubic developments, sexual urges, physical growth, new attitudes, feelings, awarenesses, etc.[5] Often a gulf is created between them and their parents and authority. Their refuge generally is with their peers; being and doing with people with the same happenings alleviates some of the anxiety—hence the urge for conformity. The parents, as indicated by some of the ensuing discussion and questions, often do not understand either the need for peer conformity or the basic turmoil of their children.

Imagine the plight of the learning-disabled adolescent who has to cope with all this newness, with parental alienation, and with an added "difference." He needs accomplishment, to feel necessary and to be part of his peer world. Yet, in an area where he spends a good part of his day, he can't perform on par with the others. There now is an academic gulf between him and them. He is worried about appearing a fool, being considered and even called a "dummy," and being rejected by peers, teachers, and parents. By now, he is becoming increasingly aware that he cannot coast along, getting by on verbosity, cuteness, or other compensatory devices. He cannot cope with the voluminous reading required in the content areas, with problem solving, or with the necessary conceptualization. He is faced dramatically with difficulties and inadequacies. His poor school performance, of considerable duration, convinces him that he will never amount to anything, that he can't make it, either in school or out in the world. Feelings of vulnerability and defeat, accompanied by frustration, worry, and anger, often lead to both inner- and outer-directed hate. These inner tensions in turn exacerbate the the learning deficiencies; and, pronto, we have a vicious cycle.

Now, in the midst of this turmoil, he finds himself confronted with weighty question: Should he continue to face this daily grind, making little or no progress and seeing no doors opening of any consequence to his future? Should he drop out of school and find any kind of a job just to pass the time? (Remember, we speak of students with average or above-average intelligence.) Should he seek other avenues of escape from this gnawing dilemma? Very often there is a fruitless search for a job, which compounds the depression he already feels. He will fight with his teachers, his parents, the authorities; and perhaps not the least of his reasons for doing so is a feeling of having been betrayed by them.

In making an analogy between psychological and physical energy functioning, a bulletin of the Robert Louis Stevenson school states, "Frustrated emotional energy, denied its natural outlet, is not eliminated but only dammed up, and often sets the individual at war with society or with himself. The cost to him, to his family, and to the community, is enormous."[6]

Educators must be aware of the extent, the severity, and the possible consequences of disregarding this problem. In truth, we are faced with a choice between dynamic guiding of the education of the individual toward a gestalt of productivity, accomplishment, and positive outlook and aspirations, or allowing the impoverishment of the potential to continue, the individual thereby losing the opportunity to actualize inherent abilities to the point of possible destruction of chances for any sort of fulfilling life. We can really choose only one direction, can't we?

How Do We Identify?

If the learning-disabled adolescent has not been correctly diagnosed or specified, it will take an extremely capable teacher to make the identification. Not only will the student have accumulated many adaptive and compensatory mechanisms, but his previous records usually will have ascribed other labels to the condition. He may have been described as bad, unruly, mentally deficient, low IQ, a behavior problem, an underachiever, minimal potential, minimally brain damaged, neurotic, chronic absentee, incorrigible, resistant, a ring leader, and possibly even autistic. How, then, does the teacher (or others working with the student) tune in? She must listen, observe, record, think, and integrate; but she also must know for what she is listening and observing, and how to integrate the information she gathers.

Listen to oral reading—what types of errors are being made, how fluent is the reading, is there comprehension? Listen to explanation, expositions, views, definitions—are they logical, organized, coherent? Listen to answers—are they to the point; is the language valid? Listen to the speech—are the patterns acceptable; is there a speech impediment? Listen to excuses, fears, refusals, and defiances, and think about what prompts them. Look at written work—what is the nature and frequency of the errors, particularly in spelling? Observe the angle of writing, the way the pen and paper are being held, and the handwriting itself. Is there evidence of poor organization, poor work habits, poor use of time, space, and materials? Is there evidence of perceptual difficulties? Does he exhibit behavioral and emotional problems? Does he appear unmotivated, uncomfortable, unhappy? Is he absent or late excessively? Observe his communication with his peers. Look at the way he moves—is he awkward, unsure of spatial relationships?

These are just some of the areas which can give clues to an alert teacher, who, if she begins to analyze them, will see a pattern emerging. For easier identification, we will now list the more common symptoms specifically and divide them into two major categories—the emotional/behavioral, and the perceptual/learning—recognizing that there is a great deal of overlapping of causes and resultant behaviors.

Emotional and Behavioral Performance

Angry, defiant, and tense: makes derogatory remarks about peers and teachers; is sullen or explosive; overreacts; unable to enter debate or discussion, loses temper, calls names; uses strong language; refuses to work, refuses to cooperate; refuses to take tests; refuses to read aloud or write compositions; is easily provoked—may fight or throw things; provokes, taunts, and dares; resistant to suggestions; makes unnecessary errors during oral reading resulting from tension.

Embarrassed: refuses to read aloud, or to have anything he's written read aloud; refuses to bring books home; refuses to enter discussions; doesn't want anyone to see his work; complains of the level of the materials and the work.

Frustrated: tears up paper or marks it up, rather than correct errors, or admit errors; hates to get low marks; cannot cope with competition; seeks attention by performing in non-academic ways—may be class clown; dislikes to repeat anything he has said or done.

Vulnerable: makes excuses for inability to perform or accomplish; tries to hide feelings and reactions; is afraid to make errors; antisocial—refuses to "buddy up"; does not like to be touched, or wants excessive body contact.

Uncertain: resists change; is afraid to try something new; will follow the lead of others; will change allegiances, to follow group.

Moody: uneven behavior, feelings and reactions—often goes from a peak to a trough; extreme enthusiasm changes to disinterest; can go through several mood changes in one day.

Easily distracted: looks at other students; is disturbed by sound, movement, interruptions; loses his place when reading; forgets what he was about to say or do.

Hyperactive: taps floor, desk; wiggles, jumps up and down; leaves his seat; perpetual motion—will write or draw on anything available, including his own body or the person nearest to him; may have a spell of incessant talking, laughing, or making sounds.

Impulsive: speaks out when others are speaking; may walk out of the classroom, either saying nothing or mumbling; will suddenly stop working, or do work other than what class is doing; disrupts class with witticisms or behavior; starts and stops activities on the spur of the moment.

Poor self-image and feelings of defeat: may call himself a "dummy"— often accepts the role; considers himself "bad" or different; associates with younger children or those in a lower grade; won't plan ahead—feels there's no place for him to go; refuses to believe he can succeed at anything—may feel he can succeed only verbally.

Disorganized: frequently late or absent—doesn't wake up on time; forgets homework, books, equipment; neglects homework, or does it incompletely; undisciplined; forgets special activites such as trips, even though planned; leaves money at home; forgets to bring lunch.

Immature: uses inappropriate responses; has unrealistic goals; interrupts others; enjoys getting others into trouble—will "tattle"; wants all the attention; wants the teacher to himself; whines and complains about minor things; does not know how to handle money; sulks; allows others to use him; cannot function socially with his peers.

Poor spatial orientation and coordination: is clumsy and awkward; bumps into people, furniture; can't find things; turns in messy work—ink blots, etc.; makes a mess wherever he sits—drops and spills things.

Perceptual-Learning and Academic Performance

Poor auditory and/or visual discrimination: does not hear differences in sound, particularly vowel sounds; cannot reproduce sound; confuses letters and words.

Poor auditory and/or visual memory: faulty output of material seen or heard.

Sequencing: deficient in reproducing things.

Deficient visual-motor abilities: cannot copy or draw what he sees; has difficulty in tracing, completing, or reproducing forms.

Cannot blend sounds: hears them as individual sounds, but has difficulty putting them together in word form.

Poor eye-hand-foot coordination: shows up often in athletic activities.

Fine- and gross-motor deficiencies: has trouble with writing, prefers to print; cannot assemble parts of mechanisms; has problems with activities like hopping and skipping; holds paper at unusual angles, grips pencil too hard, holds head too close to paper, tilts head; falls; bruises himself; misjudges.

Mixed dominance: does some tasks with right parts of body, and others with left (hands, feet, eyes).

Confused laterality: cannot always distinguish right from left in own body, or in space; often organizes and performs work in right-left progression; has tendency to write letters such as "o" from right to left.

Space, time, directional disorientation: unable to tell time and has poor sense of timing; has poor judgement of spatial relationships; confused about concepts of up, down, back, front, over, under, etc.

Poor conceptual and integrative skills: cannot form abstractions.

Perseveration: does not stop reading or writing at indicated point, as directed, but continues as though unaware of limits.

Eye movements: sometimes too many fixations.

Poor retention of learned material and practices.

The operational concommitants of these deficiencies may show up as follows:

Sequencing: may change the order, omit items, or backtrack; an uneven level of work from day to day, and between subject and subject; verbal responses and intelligence far superior to written work and reading.

Reading and writing: makes reversals, omissions, inversions, deletions, insertions, and substitutions; skips words or whole lines of print, and loses his place frequently; lip-reads, and points his finger; in eagerness to decode harder words, often omits or miscalls small words, especially prepositions, leaves off word endings; fluency in reading is poor: flat tone, hesitation, disregard for punctuation, slow and labored pronunciation; sometimes charges ahead at break-neck speed, disregarding meaning.

Reading—Word Recognition and Comprehension: does not syllabicate, and can't apply phonics or use context clues for meaning; comprehension is poor—struggles even with literal meanings; has great difficulty with inferences and critical analysis. (If the student is below the third-grade reading level, emphasis is largely on literal meaning with some lesser work on inferences. At higher levels, a more sophisticated understanding is called for.) For most, comprehension is usually superior to word recognition; some have better word recognition; and some can word-call with virtually no attention to meaning. Poor recognition and use of explanatory clues and connectives.

Writing and problems in punctuation, usage, syntax: finds it difficult to organize ideas and express them in sentences; sentences are usually short and choppy; uses limited vocabulary, and words out of context. Writing is limited to the shortest possible amount—even then, there is poor letter formation; cannot make capitals; and struggles with cursive writing; sometimes will switch from upper- to lower-case letters; often, writing is illegible: sometimes too big, other times too small.

Spelling: omits letters; does not retain sight words; can't apply phonetic analysis; reverses, inverts, and does not recognize patterns or families of letters as related to sound.

Problems in following directions: oral and written instructions are difficult to follow; also, cannot take dictation.

Organization: does not put ideas into logical order; has no system for use of time, space, or resources; likewise, does very little preplanning of his work.

Integrative deficiencies: ability to conceptualize is deficient; often cannot easily follow math, social studies, or science concepts unless they are presented in very concrete terms. Also, has trouble with complex sentences, so that he cannot extract central ideas plus supportive details—ability in doing book reports, summaries, taking notes, and making outlines is hampered. These, and other related study skills, usually begin to be presented at about the fourth-grade reading level, but the learning-disabled adolescent often is deficient in this area, not only at this reading level, but above as well.

At the lowest levels, some do not know the letters of the alphabet, cannot give the days of the week or the months in sequence, or even name all of them, cannot give their address or telephone number, and in some cases cannot even print their own name correctly.

The most handicapping symptoms can be grouped in four categories:

- Poor sequential memory
- Difficulty with sound-symbol relationships
- Deficiency of organizational skills
- Integrational deficits

Some of these symptoms are primary deficiencies; others, particularly the behaviors, have been acquired consequentially over the years. The learning-disabled adolescent will exhibit some combination of these difficulties, of varying nature and severities, but will not just have one or two in isolation, any more than he will have them all.

Now that the plot's been presented, it's time to put on the play! How do we go about working with and for these students?

Chapter 7:

Remediation

Sylvia Bleiweiss

THIS SECTION ON REMEDIATION is not meant to be a syllabus or a teachers' guide in terms of specific lesson plans, delineation of skills, or techniques for skill-mastery, but rather to attempt to convey an understanding of an outlook and orientation necessary for a psychoeducational approach to the education of a particular group of adolescents. In truth, this might prove effective for the larger group as well; but, for the learning-disabled adolescent, it is imperative.

Once a group of the symptoms is recognized, the exploration begins. By this time, the teacher should be conferring with resource services and the administration to apprise them of her observations, and to start the necessary diagnostic work-ups. To her subjective findings, there must now be added a study of the student's history and records. It is necessary to become acquainted with the academic, medical, psychological, and familial history through reading the files, and speaking with previous teachers, the parents, resource people who may have known the student, and therapists. Sometimes, this will be done by the teacher, sometimes by the guidance counselor or school psychologist, and sometimes by a resource person. Some of the pertinent background information to be obtained is: the length of time the problem has been known; how much and what kind of remediation has been tried; how he responded to previous procedures; what special "problems" or weaknesses have been identified; whether he has shown special interests or strengths at school; what sort of peer relationships have been noticed; what his general level of achievement and intelligence has been as indicated by previous testing. The teacher should ask whether there are any special situations in the home which could be influencing his performance; what the relationship is with siblings; are the parents derogatory, disheartening, resentful; is he being compared to others? In addition, family records or conference should disclose whether there is a history of learning disabilities in the family; if his behavior was unusual during infancy and childhood; illnesses; and the parents' understanding, feelings about him and their ambitions. The parents could possibly shed light on his nutritional habits as well.[1] A medical history should discuss not only illnesses and accidents, but also the type of drugs he may be taking, and possible allergies.

One should be able to obtain behavioral insights from all people previously involved with the student. In discussing her son (who, incidentally, displayed the classic symptoms of dyslexia in the classroom), a parent told me that, of her eleven children, this son was the only atypical one in behavior, being overactive to the degree that she found it almost impossible to keep him on her lap during infancy. Once, during some particularly vigorous bouncing, he broke several of her teeth! Of course, there were many other evidences of this overactivity, and they were apparent in class in many ways. Also, she reported, he had always been uncoordinated, impatient, and disorganized, but loveable and bright. Parents can clue us in. Physicians, therapists, resource people, previous teachers, and sometimes the administrators, can provide us with a description, as well as a running history of the behavioral-emotional life, which will give us indications of the severity, and acceleration or deceleration of these concomitants to the learning difficulties over the years. To summarize the nature of the data sought, it should include:

Academic record: grades, test scores, weaknesses and strengths, schools attended, behavioral aspects, interests shown, and activities; all reports and comments.

Family record: siblings; unusual behavior or traits displayed; home milieu—attitudes, goals, interests of family; exposure to learning materials or stimuli; birth data, health and accident information; eating habits, amount of sleep, anxieties, frictions; others with similar problem; developmental history.

Medical report: a medical history; unusual findings, any signs of neurological impairment, allergies, drugs previously taken or presently prescribed.

School resources: behavioral and/or emotional history, all tests, reports on conferences and meetings regarding the student; records of previous remedial work and achievements; psychological evaluations.

Additional: findings of any agency, therapist, summer camp, clinic, or center the student may have been attending.

At the same time that this information is being assembled, the student should be tested and evaluated for as much specific data as can be made readily available. Time is of the essence, and the remediation must begin, and should begin, without much delay. If the records show recent testing (within two years), it is usually not necessary to retest extensively. In any event, it is a good idea not to subject him to extensive psychological testing, meetings, and nit-picking. If not done recently, it also is advisable to test hearing and sight acuity and perception, professionally. When it is established that the student is not mentally retarded, not severely disturbed, has adequate sight and hearing, is not physically disabled, and has a history of learning handicaps, we are quite safe in assuming he is learning disabled, by whatever label we may designate it. The evaluation at this point can be conducted by a knowledgeable reading or learning disabilities person, a supervisor, a psychologist who is familiar with these informal procedures, or a combination of school personnel who have been trained in the procedures and approach.

If a student is just entering a program or facility, or is being evaluated as a result of his lack of progress, in order to prescribe a program, he can be tested and interviewed according to the following procedure, which will be offered as a sample, not necessarily a model. This should be done under optimum conditions regarding time, place, and comfort.

Reading—word recognition, fluency, and comprehension: Have the student read aloud, using either the *Gray* or *Gilmore Oral Reading Test.* These are informal reading inventories which supply graded passages with comprehension questions to follow. An alternative is an informal reading inventory which the examiner can construct quite easily with the same format. While conducting this reading test, make notes of errors in word recognition, comprehension, fluency, and evidences of speech defects, for later referral. This will establish a reading level and will provide insight into repeated errors and into the nature of comprehension. If the student is reading at third-grade level or above, it is wise to have him read silently as well, to test comprehension more accurately. These passages can be used for vocabulary skills as well. Another quick diagnostic measure is the *Cloze* procedure, which will give insights into comprehension, word knowledge and application, and which can also be used as a teaching device at a later time.

Sequential memory and ability: Ask the student to repeat groups of letters, numbers, or words as dictated. See if he can give the letters of the alphabet, days of the week, and months of the year. (Here is an interesting sidelight: many students omit the month of October, even if they know all the others. They have offered a number of reasons whenever it was called to their attention. One young man said it was because there are no holidays in that month. Another said the reason might be that it begins with a vowel. When I pointed out that April also begins with a vowel, he adroitly answered, "But that's a long vowel.") At the same time you ask for the alphabet or months, you might suggest that he stop at a particular letter or month, so that you may get a clue to his ability to stay within limits, possible perseveration, and ability to follow directions. After this, see if he can repeat, in writing, sequences that you present orally, and then written ones. Show groups of numbers, letters, or other symbols. Increase the number of items to the limit of the student's ability to reproduce them.

Auditory discrimination: Ask him to identify the only first sound of the words you give him; then, try him on final sounds in the same manner. Make sure that he understands that you wish him to say only the sound and not the name of the letter. Present him with two vowel sounds, and ask if they sound the same or different. Change the vowel sound in a medial position within the same word and ask him if the word is the same or different, like *get* and *got*. Also, supply a word and see if he can rhyme.

Visual discrimination: Present a horizontal column of words or groups of letters; ask him to circle every one that is the same as the first one in each line; this can serve to illuminate some of the common reversals, inversions, and sequential errors. There are many variations to this procedure, such as asking him to find words which begin or end with the same letters as the sample word, or to find the combination of letters which is different from the sample in a group.

Vocabulary: Have the student define some of the words in a passage he reads, or use words from the glossary of a reading book. If at higher reading levels, see if he can handle vocabulary related to content areas such as science and social studies.

Blending: See, if upon hearing separate parts of a word, he can integrate and make a whole word. Start with a three-letter word; say each letter separately, with a hesitation between each; and ask the student to tell the word. This can be escalated by saying syllables separately and having the student repeat them together as a word. Nonsense words can be used as well.

Writing and spelling: If he is unable to write much, have the student write letters of the alphabet or his name, if possible, or copy. At lower levels, dictate a short, easy sentence or phrase. At higher levels, the student should write a short composition. For multiple purposes, he might be asked to write on themes such as "If I Had Three Wishes," or "What I Hope to Achieve by Coming Here." This exercise will help provide clues to his thinking and planning. Examine the output for spelling errors, punctuation, syntax, usage, and organization. View his handwriting: is he able only to print; does he intermingle upper- and lower-case letters; is he unable to make capital letters; are the spelling errors consistent? At all levels, one can look for the student's ability to spell sight words, as well as his vowel confusions, letter reversals, and inversions. While the student is writing, the examiner should be observing the performance itself. Look for unusual positions of the paper, the writing hand, the grip on the pen, a labored effort. Also, notice how he forms his letters: does he write in the usual flow or does he reverse the motion in many letters; does he have trouble joining them?

Laterality, directionality, orientation: Put a row of pennies on the desk; ask him to pick them up one at a time; and see if he goes from left to right; observe which hand he uses. See which foot he hops on, which hand he extends to receive something, and through which eye he sights. (To do this last item simply, roll a piece of paper into a cone shape. Ask him to look at something across the room, and notice which eye he uses.) Throw a pencil across to him and note the hand used for catching. This could give you some idea of whether there is mixed laterality. Test him with simple activities to observe his facility with concepts of up and down, left and right, over and under. Can he tell time, estimate space?

Auditory-visual-motor coordination: The student can be asked to copy geometric forms, complete unfinished forms, trace, or connect lines or areas. He can be given oral directions for motor activity. At higher levels, dictation can be utilized, but in small segments, possibly one, two, or three words at a time, to eliminate element of sequential memory.

Study Skills: If student can work above third-grade levels, an assessment can be made of ability in use of skills related to book usage, note-taking, and various other skills, dependent on particular level of the students. When he is asked to read a passage in a book, let him find the title in the table of contents; observe when he looks for the page—whether he knows how to find it efficiently. One can quickly determine whether he knows the parts of a book. He should be able to state the main idea of the covered material and a summary in his own words. He should know how to use the dictionary. These are basic skills, and it would be helpful in giving a total picture of his attainments or deficiencies.

Psychological Information

Some important clues to the youngster's mental state can be obtained by having the student draw a person after receiving the simple, unannotated instruction, "Draw a person." Give as few instructions as possible which might be hints. When he finishes, ask him to draw someone of the opposite sex. If you wish, the Goodenough *Draw-A-Man* or the Machover *Draw-A-Person* tests may be used with their interpretations. The purpose of these tasks is to provide insight regarding self-concept, and to show ability in handling an unstructured task. Students at higher levels can use a check list or work up an attitude sheet which will give information regarding feelings about reading; feelings about school; which subjects are their best or to their liking; what they consider their biggest problem in school, at home, socially; objectives; aims; and similar pertinent issues. At lower levels, this can be done verbally in conference. Delineating three wishes, as suggested previously, can be a clue for anxieties, fears, or very unusual thinking. One teenager wrote three wishes which asked for good health for him, good health for his family, and a long life with good health. When pressed, he said he just hasn't any other wishes, which led me to the pseudological conclusion that I finally had met the man who has everything. Seriously, though, such answers as these might be a clue that there possibly is a hypochondriacal home milieu, or that he may have been a very sickly child. It is worth exploring!

Very often the behavior during testing or interviewing will give hints of disturbances: a child may refuse to take the written tests; may blow up during testing and refuse to continue; may tear up his work; write or mark up his work, rather than correct it; or complain unrealistically of others near him or of physical conditions. During conference, some will refuse to answer, some may whisper, some may let the parents do all the talking, and will not answer questions put to them. Others may become extremely verbose, trying to steer the meeting into directions to suit their purpose, or hoping to avoid being tested in areas of low or non-accomplishment, while still others may pretend to have more difficulty than they really have, hoping for rejection. All of this has to be observed, noted, and integrated when evaluating and planning.

To this informal testing, there could be added an achievement test such as the *Stanford Achievement Test* or *California Achievement Test*, and there should be given a *Wechsler Intelligence Scale for Children* (WISC) or *Wechsler Adult Intelligence Scale* (WAIS).

Comments, Suggestions, Advice, Helpful Hints

Reading: When testing, it is better to start at a level fairly easy for reader, to avoid failure and anxiety. Scanning his records should give you a fairly good idea of present reading level. Allow for nervousness; if he's off to a shaky start, allow him to read a bit longer than planned, or drop it and come back when he's more relaxed.

Parents: Try to direct only the necessary questions to parents, and to have the student answer as much as possible. If a parent is present at interview, ask the parent to leave before testing.

Atmosphere: Try to have testee at ease. Make him comfortable; engage him in conversation; inform him of purposes for testing; and assure him that testing is for diagnostic purposes, not for marks or comparisons. Give him some orientation regarding the testing situation and programs offered. Allow him to discuss or ask about anything of interest to him, but put limits to discussion if he seems to prolong it to avoid other activities.

Mechanics: Have the necessary books, materials, tests, and pencils with erasers available. Be certain that any directions given are clearly understood before proceeding. If the student makes errors, either observe or record them; do not attempt to teach during testing period.

Observations: As previously stated, there may be behavioral manifestations during the testing or interviewing that may be illustrative of difficulties, anxieties, fears, and other reactions. Listen to answers, listen to the tone of voice, watch facial expressions, notice reactions, and observe writing. A note of caution: in addition to allowing for the tension of testing, it's well to remember that most tests are culture- and language-bound.[2] Consider this in your evaluation as well as accents and dialects.

This method of testing, with virtually no reliance on formal structures, is efficient, fast (should take no more than about three hours, including the achievement test), and quite accurate for assessment. By combining the results of the testing and interviewing of the student with the information gleaned from careful reading of previous records, and from the consultations with parents, previous teachers or therapists, where possible, the program for remediation and upgrading can begin and should begin. There are many formal tests which can be given for accurate pinpointing of strengths, weaknesses, levels (see Appendix B); and of course there should be psychological data supplied by a trained person, to help not only to understand the functioning, but also to evaluate the degree of disturbance. The course of action to be embarked upon must include measures for coping with the psychological factors simultaneously with the academic, and eventually with career guidance. At this point, start to "accentuate the positive"!

Chapter 8:

Remediation II

Sylvia Bleiweiss

ONE OF THE FIRST TASKS to be done, after testing and assessment, is to communicate with the parents or guardians. Their understanding and help are an important part of any program, as adolescents, by and large, still are living at home, or in a home. There should be an avoidance of discussing test scores, but rather the focus should center on particular skills, weaknesses and strengths, and the proposed placement or program. It is better to give the parents the awareness that scores may in themselves be influenced by low reading ability; that it is more important to use the test diagnostically than as a "be-all." The program should be thoroughly explained, including proposed or necessary therapy, counseling, and guidance.

Parents

Parents usually are emotionally involved, even when supportive; and there are familial pressures in all strata. In the disadvantaged homes, there are often tensions of poverty, unstable relationships, bewilderment, and lack of language; in the more affluent homes, one often finds frustration, parents with great drive and ambition, comparisons with more accomplished siblings, and resentment. It is necessary, therefore, to give as positive a picture as possible, without being unrealistic. In spite of the reaction to labeling by many professionals, I found parents much relieved when I explained the symptoms and called them "dyslexia," if I felt the term was warranted. They were so relieved to learn that the child was not retarded, "stupid," "crazy," and that he could be helped, albeit it would take time and patience.

Many of the adolescents who still are functioning at lower levels, will go on to vocational schools, rather than colleges; and parents should begin to think positively along these lines. For those able to go on to higher education, supply the parents with names of and information regarding colleges, universities and community colleges.[1]

It is urgent that parents learn to remove pressures; and one of the devices to accomplish this is to try to remove their own anxieties in respect to academic attainment. There has been much emphasis recently, on courses, seminars, and study programs for parents to increase their knowledge and cooperation. Many working-class parents, however, do not have the time; and some parents do not have the inclination. Many a time, have I suggested subtly to a parent that he not help with homework, giving as the reason the fact that it was important to see what the student retained, and also to evaluate his shortcomings, as evidenced in the homework. While this in itself was not untrue, my main thrust was to break the pattern of parents screaming or feeling despair at mistakes or poor performance. By all means, let's educate and involve the parents; but let's not expect miracles; and let their participation be enlisted with discretion.

The Group and the Individual

Learning in a class or group is the most desirable pattern for the adolescent. In a group he will continue to have social and academic interaction with peers; there will be more stimulation; it will more closely approximate a school or job relationship; and it always is of solace to find others with the same problem. There are certain conditions, however, which would justify individual instruction; but, even then, this should be terminated as soon as feasible, by transfer to a group. If the student has dropped out, if he needs his confidence restored before joining a group, if he is badly deficient in one area, if he is unable to cope with group dynamics, or if there is no group structure available, then instruction could start on a one-to-one basis.

In addition to the personal advantages of the group, there are budgetary considerations. School systems would hardly have either the personnel or the money to provide the services required on an individual basis. They would only be able to cope with part of the problem or just some of the students.

Classes should be small; if students are reading at very low levels, they should be in a group of six to eight. If above third-grade level, classes could have 12 or 14, if necessary. At community college level, where often the drawbacks of the student are lack of study skills, and poor organization, rather than word recognition, the students could work in labs, with looser arrangements, and with more programed instruction.

Homogeneity of both age and reading level is most desirable. This will be of help both academically and psychologically in that those of similar age will share many interests and experiences; younger children will not fear the older ones; and the older ones will not have to be ashamed at being with those much younger. Also, while the program should be prescriptive and individualized, many students, working at the same levels, will have common deficits which can be worked on in group learning sessions, which will lessen the need for one-to-one instruction. If a student is far superior or inferior in any one specific area, however, he could receive individual help, or perhaps join another unit for that subject or skill.

The Learning Climate: Personnel and Personality

Those who work most effectively with learning-disabled adolescents have a special type of artistry. To create an optimal milieu, a teacher (ideally), would have the following qualities:

"Unflappableness": She would not be thrown by strong language, unusual happenings or behavior, emergency situations, or ups and downs.

Sense of humor: It's important to be able to laugh, to enjoy, and to give and take ribbing or share in a joke.

Voice control: Pleasant voice quality is a decided asset. Students react negatively and with irritation either to screaming or whispering. Some teachers through nervousness or fright get a shaky quality in their voices, which the students quickly detect. Some, when they feel they are losing control of the class, escalate their volume; and bedlam often ensues.

Flexibility: Accept unexpected changes in routine, unusual demands; be able to deal with many types of people and situations, able to change style and plans.

Fairness, impartiality, and honesty: Students will usually accept censure, help, criticism, decisions, if the teacher acts in good faith and if they have learned to trust her. Do not show favoritism; be open and honest; and try not to make empty promises.

Empathy, simpathy, strength: Even though she has understanding and insight into the students' plight, the teacher must not become an instrument for them to manipulate. Kindness and sympathy must be coupled with strength and determination to accomplish the job at hand.

Resourcefulness: There will be unexpected questions, unexpected answers, boredom, and challenges concerning methods, materials, and plans. The instructor should not only have answers, but should vary materials, create interest, and vary style of presentation.

Interest and curiosity: There must be geniune concern about what the student is thinking, how he is reacting, his feelings, his needs, particular stresses, and even his out-of-school activities. In a special program, with a group of older students, I encouraged a discussion of their particular work plans in relation to the course of study we were following. They not only discussed their individual goals, but we looked at the program in view of future needs of the jobs. This resulted in a two way-way benefit: I geared my program to fill their specific needs; they in turn became much more motivated and interested in the studies; and the level and output improved dramatically, to the point of even reversing their former reluctance to write more than three sentences!

Radar: A built-in sensitivity—the ability to get "messages"—is absolutely essential, and is one of the most important assets: when to start, when to stop, when to continue beyond planned work because the group is going full-steam and enjoying it; when to work, when to play; when to insist, when to retreat. How to break tension, when necessary, to remove someone from the class; whom to group together, whom to make sure to separate; when to push, when to pull; who needs and appreciates physical contact, a pat on the head or shoulder, and who resents the slightest touch. Teachers must sense the fitness of things. Two illustrative examples: a teacher, whom I was to observe one afternoon, had designated a student to take over the class for part of the day. That particular morning the student and another were feuding. Not recognizing the possible danger of following the planned course of action, she allowed the student to lead the class. When I entered the room, the teacher was shaking and helpless, and the two battling students were on the floor, with no holds barred, while some of the class were trying to separate them, and others were cheering them on! The age range of this group was 15 to 18 years; they were reading at about a second-grade level; and there were tremendous frustrations, antagonisms, and anxieties in all of them. The signals were there, but the teacher was not receiving.

The second example is that of a young man of 15 in one of my classes (a full-day class). He was disruptive and abusive, and created a great deal of turmoil in the classroom. In trying to grapple with the problem, I noticed that his behavior and attention usually improved when he returned from the scheduled break at 11:30. After working with him and commending him for his efforts in the afternoon, I scheduled a meeting with him—after 11:30! Putting someone in charge of the class, we went to an unoccupied room to talk. I found out that home conditions were intolerable for him, and that almost every morning he had a fight with his mother's "friend" before leaving home. Realizing that it took him the better part of the morning to simmer down, we arranged to have quiet work for him without participation in group work until after the break time. It worked beautifully; not only was he successful academically, but his social behavior began to change, and furthermore he became quite devoted to me, and championed my cause in the classroom. It takes time, determination, hard work, soul-searching, a great deal of personal fortitude, a desire for professionalism, and a basically empathetic person to approach this "ideal," this paragon. We have delineated a set of goals, towards which a truly interested, dedicated teacher might strive. We have been fortunate enough to have met and worked with a few who have, over the years, grown and developed along these lines, and endowed their work with accomplishment and inspiration.

These are but two of many examples that I and others could give of the necessity of being tuned in to "vibrations" from your students.

Action and Interaction

Above all, it is the *people* who work with the student who will make the difference. The materials, the housing, the programs (pedagogy) all help;

but it is the stimulation, motivation, and understanding that make a student desirous of, excited about, and involved with his academic growth. Many a fine teacher acts and reacts instinctively, but it is well to examine the constructs of working relationships.

Communication: There are several layers of communication; the give-and-take of the classroom, the unspoken messages, the conferences. When issues arise in the class, stop the work and thrash them out. The students should be allowed to discuss their feelings and opinions. It is well to encourage the quiet ones, sometimes by a direct question, or even by a vote to express their convictions. Time spent in discussion is time well spent, as many of the students have never felt free or competent enough to make their voices heard. Discuss your feelings, needs, what you as the teacher expect, and what you can offer. Allow the class to express displeasure, dissatisfaction, but encourage them to be aware of positive aspects as well. For some, this will be quite a change. Operate on the premise of the self-fulfilling prophesy, "The Pygmalion Effect": expect positive results.[2] Be aware of your speech; make an effort to articulate clearly, to speak at a rate that is not too fast or slow, and be audible. Make it clear that the student can let you know if he doesn't understand or cannot hear you.

The unspoken communication is now commonly known as body language. There can be two-way communication, by facial expression and body gestures; be alert to these. There may be a subtle form of message-giving by the student if, for instance, he does not do homework or comes late. Receive the clues.

In addition to conferences that you may schedule, inform your students that you are available for private discussions whenever needed. I encouraged my students to get to me even by letter, and promised to answer all letters by personal or written reply.

Certainly, when classes begin, meetings should be held individually. Explain the level at which the student is operating, the deficiencies, the program, and of equal importance listen to what he thinks is wrong, his goals, ambitions, hobbies, past experiences. Draw him out regarding family and peer relationships, special problems. Encourage and reassure him, but level with him. Explain that it will take hard work and patience, that the work may sometimes be repetitious, that the materials may not always be fascinating, and that realistic aims are important. Reassure him that he will and can learn. It also is important to make him aware of the nature of his problem, that it is not a disease, or mental retardation.

If yours is a special school or program, discuss what it has to offer, how it can relate to his needs, what the mechanics are, the nature of the student body, the physical set-up. At New York University, the remedial facility is called the "Reading Institute" (although actually the full-day program is for the remediation of learning disabilities). We discovered that many adolescents were confusing the word "institute" with "institution," and that it was a matter of concern to them. In the orientation sessions for new students, therefore, we took pains to differentiate between the two words, which helped overcome the anxiety about the nature of the place.

Often, one will find a complete blackout between the student and parents. Adolescents will often complain that they cannot talk to their parents, or that the parents won't listen or understand. The school can try to open up channels between child and parent by suggesting ways to approach the parent, or by concretely discussing subjects or issues that the young person has been afraid or reluctant to tackle with his parents, and by stressing that there can be much better relationships if these are brought out in the open. Time and again, I have seen this work.

Motivation: Although the word is sometimes bandied about, let's be fully aware of the role it plays. There have been many studies made and a great deal of literature written on the subject. What do we mean by motivation and what are the instruments for furthering it? To motivate is to make a student willing to attempt, to want to do, to be interested in, to continue once started, to be enthusiastic about his work, and to understand and apply himself when working, even when it's not particularly pleasureable. The tools are materials and methods.

Materials of all sorts can be used, and often those which are most relevant to daily living are the most effective. Newspapers, menus, bank forms, applications, advertisements, labels, directions, recipes, ad infinitum. For the higher-level student, correlating the remedial program with other academic pursuits, with hobbies or interests, and with occupational reading or activities, can prove of great interest. At lowest levels, handling money, learning to write one's name and address, even the use of pictures and cartoons can be stimulating.

Games, puzzles, riddles, songs, recordings, all sorts of audio-visual equipment, symbols such as traffic or hazard warnings are all possibilities.[3] Consider also the use of humorous material and imaginative devices such as story boards, which show abstract forms and from which a story can be devised. Poetry, drama, song lyrics—all can be utilized.

Every teacher can devise methods for stimulation with a little thought and research. Varying routines; explaining the impact or reasons for the assignments; basing the program on the expressed needs or interests of the individual; allowing students to take over as teacher; creating "buddy" systems where students work together, or teach each other; planning interesting trips; or having the group create a newspaper or a magazine, are some of the devices. Occasional competitive activities, with clear understanding of the procedures and with groups involved rather than individuals, can be productive. Create a United Nations in your class, and have the students research their country, always a group representing a country. Let them be public relations people, and see who does the best selling job. These activities can be oral, or written, or both; and there are unlimited possiblities for variations. At times, have the students select their own activity or suggest topics or areas they would like to explore. Another motivating measure is to allow students to score their own tests, to keep charts and records of their progress. In addition, there are the practices of behavior modification: rewards, incentives, promises. The procedures would differ for different age levels; one would hardly offer candy to students in their upper teens! At lower levels, sometimes charts, letters of commendation, or prizes can be very effective. Judy Kupersmith relates a pilot attempt to effect behavior modification in college, where the reward was free time, a very meaningful prize.[4]

Jerome Bruner tells of a junior high school course in which relevance and motivation were combined to create great interest.[5] In studying the times of Julius Caesar, the class was divided into two camps: those who thought he should cross the Rubicon, and those who were opposed to this. They had to reason like politicians; they compared the heroes of that time to people they knew of; they found they could analyze corruption in the Roman system; and they were caught up in the excitement to the point of doing research into the era. Incidentally, the article states that the leather-jacket motorcycle kids related completely to Caesar, and thought "Pompey was a fink without guts."

Creating interest is one of the prime keys to reaching the learning-disabled adolescent. There can be no program unless it is a basic ingredient; the methods and materials may very to suit the age and developmental level; but motivation must be considered essential. This will result not only in a willingness to work; they will also produce more, pay more attention, be less disruptive, be more involved, attend more regularly, and arrive on time. They will finally have the courage to try new frontiers.

Attitudes, Agonies: Alleviation

These troubled learning-disabled adolescents are happy to see others fail, are ashamed of the level of their work, hate to make mistakes, are wary and afraid of books, are easily embarrassed, resistant to change, do not trust teachers and other adults in their contacts, may lie, cheat or taunt, are overly sensitive, and are failure-oriented. Not each one will have all of these hangups; but, if they have not been helped, and are not accomplishing, they will have many negative feelings about themselves and the world. The educator must reverse these tendencies; this must be a conscious part of the planning.

The past: Inform the student that you and he are going to forget the past completely (not easily done). Whatever is said and done *now* is important. The teacher will find herself countering remarks such as, "My other teacher showed us another way," "In my other school we were told never to do that," "Oh, I had that before," or "I read that book before." (Try to avoid using previous materials, as one way of coping with this problem.) After a few dozen times of explaining why it is being done the way it is, the best thing to do is make an arrangement for a clue signal that in essence will mean, "Forget it." Treat it lightly, but firmly. Of course if the student says, "I already learned all that, and I know it," make him prove it. He will realize that there's more to do. Impress him, however, with the fact that he has turned a corner and is now on a brand new road.

Resistance: This will take many forms; sometimes expressed, sometimes through action, sometimes through nonparticipation. Students will say that they don't want to do something, that they don't know how, that they are too stupid, or that they've never been able to learn that particular thing and never will. They must be coaxed, encouraged, and led into trying it. Start with a very simple act which they can master, and then build on that. Try to have another student work with the student and suggest ways of learning which have helped him. Another means of starting is to work individually with that student, do part of the work for him, and gradually give him more and more of it to do. He may need additional explanation, or another method he has never used before to give him the spurt to try. If students resist covertly, it's best to have personal talks, making them aware of the self-defeating elements. Sometimes, if this technique is not successful, it works to change the tactics and raise the issue in the classroom. One term, I inherited two "sleepers." Their previous teachers informed me that they had been sleeping through half the day, and sitting with heavy-lidded eyes the other half. After a few days of this in my class, I shook them awake one morning, walked to the front of the group, and in an "Ethel-Mermanish" voice, making the walls tremble, declared, "No one sleeps in my class! I've got too much to give, and you've got too much to learn. If you don't want to make it—out!" They immediately sat upright, eyes wide open; and I shook with internal laughter watching their efforts to stay awake. It worked, however; and within a relatively short time they stayed alert, with a few exceptions, the entire day. They told me later that they themselves were surprised to find that they could stay awake, which made me conclude that conking out had become a habit, induced by non-accomplishment and non-participation in classes where they could not function, or where nobody cared.

Flaring up and cooling off: Anxiety, anger, frustration, sensitivity, are often manifested in fights, blowing-up, taunting, withdrawal, or exaggerated reactions. If the incidents do not happen too often and can be controlled within the classroom, then it can be handled by group discussion of the roots of the disturbance, suggestions for alternative reactions, or even group censure. In addition, it often is important to discuss such matters calmly in private meeting, when one might learn more of the causes. If the situation is out of hand, however, efforts should be made to remove the involved persons from the room. No attempts should be made for rational discussion if the moment is heated. Only when people are calm and fairly rational are they able to listen and absorb. The supportive personnel should be involved as well; they can defuse potentially troublesome activities by coming into the class for an "encounter" session, or working with individuals apart from the class. A supervisor can perform this function too, and should work with the teacher in prevention and cure.

Sensitivity—pressures, practices: If we can create a milieu in the classroom of sustained endeavor, free of anxiety to the greatest possible extent, we can hope for improved social and academic attainment. There should be an awareness of pressure spots and sensitivities. If a student is ashamed of his reading level, wean him into oral reading, where desired, by allowing him to read silently first, reading to the teacher alone, or finding answers to questions and reading them when he is confident. Allow time for the students to become accustomed to work, to share, to cooperate.

Marks, tests, homework, all can be focal points of tension. It is often better to give marks of "excellent," "good," and so forth, than to give number marks. There should be a directed discussion on testing. This should include the reasons for testing: to see how much was learned this week, and what still remains to be taught, learned, and reviewed. A scheme that worked very well for me over the years was to test once a week, covering mainly that week's work, with a small amount of review, and with the assurance to my pupils that there was no intensive study required if they had been conscientious all week. A special day and time was decided in advance, and the tests were scored immediately following the exam period, so that there was optimum reinforcement. All directions and instructions were perfectly clear and completely understood before the writing began. There were always some questions built into the test specifically designed for maximum success.

Homework should be given in small amounts; and here, too, it is well to explain the need for homework as a reinforcer and practice. Analogies can be made with learning to play the guitar, or participating in a sport; all require more than just instruction to be good.

Students should be prepared in advance for any changes, since they become concerned about a shift in schedule, change of room or teacher, new materials or methods, trips—in short, departures from routine may be upsetting. It is wise to give not only explicit information and directions about proposed changes, but to give reasons as well.

Students will resent anything that appears to be a discriminatory practice. Give equal time to all for work, answers to questions, and your personal time and attention. Call all students by name: avoid just nodding in their direction, or saying "you." Don't call on just a favored few students becuase they are volunteering, or always seem to have the answer. I have observed students become upset and discouraged when a teacher did not listen fully to an answer, or did not accept an answer. The teacher must not make the mistake of expecting or awaiting set replies. Very often, the student will interpret the question or the material in a novel way, and can become agitated over the instructor's failure to recognize his point.

The use of group dynamics can help relieve intense concerns. Talk sessions should be encouraged, with interchange of opinions between students, and between student and teacher. Open discussions of tattling (a common practice), of angers, of ethnic or racial slurs, of "hang-ups," of dissatisfactions, can often serve to alleviate emotional reactions. It is better not to have these talks as openers for the day, since many adolescents come to school in the morning bringing the tensions of the home or outside world with them, and are therefore not ready at that time for objective rap sessions.

Withdrawal is another sign of inner turmoil. This problem is as acute as acting out, and is a signal for the school to become concerned. Treat such a student with kindness, with understanding, with attempts to involve him slowly with the group and with the work at hand. Sometimes, it works to seat him close to the teacher, or to find another pupil with whom he can relate. Allow him successes, commend him, pat him on the back (literally), bring a book or a game especially for him, and certainly have him in touch with the school psychologist. The others must understand and sympathize. Some final words: most learning-disabled adolescents have feelings of horror at the thought of a report card. Therefore, it is wise to eliminate standard report cards with emphasis on marks and group standing, and instead create a sort of progress report, which should show the progress made in specific skills, and which might act as a guide for the future program.

Create a milieu of security and assurance, with honest and open interaction, and caring.

Order out of Chaos

"Every authority says in speeches or in writings that children with severe learning difficulty [sic] need to live in a structured environment, that they need structured tasks, that their lives should be structured." So writes Angie Nall, in an article titled "What is 'Structured'?"[6] She goes on to say, ". . . not knowing their limits frustrates them." I agree with the latter premise, but must take issue with the fact that all authorities accept the need for structure; in fact, the literature is replete with opinions for and against, although often the controversy is largely based on semantic rather than pedagogic or philosophic precepts. Let's discuss what we mean by the term and how we can employ it as an effective tool. My experience has been that adolescents with learning difficulties not only accept the guidelines which we'll be discussing, but they respect the concept, and benefit from its implementation. In a fairly recent issue of one of Toronto's major newspapers a counselor in a school system was quoted as saying, "Lately there's a shift in the thinking of many people back to developing more structure. . . . For the young adolescent, it's vitally needed. They're so involved in their social maturation that they really need more structure at that age."[7] His concern is basically with truants; some learning-disabled adolescents do become truant when school becomes too rough for them; but this thinking applies to all, truant or not.

An efficient teacher can organize structure which will not exclude freedom; she will set limits, inform the students of the demands that will be made upon them, what will be accepted and what will not, create a plan of operations, a routine for work, a basic set of rules (not too overwhelming), and know what she, herself, is about. She will make known her position on matters of deportment, tardiness, bringing necessary materials such as paper and pens, eating in class, etc. Once the teacher has discussed her intentions and feelings, she and the class together can work out a further set of rules, including privileges and responsibilities. The students must understand that they have certain obligations to fill in order to receive certain freedoms. For instance, they might work out mutually the question of how much free time they are to have, what they can do, and where they can go during this time, and how not to abuse it. It's also a good idea to ban food and drink from the class, since sometimes volatile children may resort to spilling drinks, snatching food, and other annoying practices. A compromise might be arrived at, however, which would allow a pupil to have food in the room under certain circumstances, or to allow gum chewing, at appropriate times. For some, gum chewing is almost a necessity, particularly needed in times of stress. If food or drink is in the class, then the students have the responsibility for cleaning up and seeing that refuse is placed into the waste basket.

Another maxim to discuss is the question of respect for others. For instance, when one person talks, the others must listen and allow him or her to finish. The teacher should make it clear that here, too, there is mutuality of interest. "If you want me to listen when you talk, then you must listen when I talk." This applies between the students as well. The responsibility for their own behavior includes an obligation to the others.

Students should feel free to challenge any part of the regulations or suggestions; but they must realize that they are to do this rationally, and at the proper time. If the instructor has well-thought-out and prepared plans for homework, testing, the day's activities, the calendar for the day, ways of involving the students, and is able to cope with the unexpected, she will earn the respect of the students, which in turn enhances their self-image. The very fact that there is a plan, that there are limits, that there are expectations, that there is a person in front of the group who knows what she's doing, and who is going to see to it that they do, too, serves to provide students with encouragement, courage, assurance, a sense of self-worth, a renewed confidence in the possibility, and even belief in the probability of accomplishment.

There is another kind of structure to consider: physical aspects of the rooms and facilities. Seats and desks should be comfortable, with adequate leg room; rooms should be in as quiet a spot as possible, with good air, light, and ventilation. Don't overdecorate the room; distractions and visual stimuli should be kept to a minimum. It is important to have adequate storage space with easy access. Space should be provided for individual work, or where small groups may carry on activities, apart from the mainstream. There should also be a place for students to be alone when they are cooling off; this should be outside the classroom.

Additionally, library space is necessary in the classroom, and there should be special library rooms. (It is a good idea to have many soft-covered books available; most students look upon a hard-covered book as a burden in more than one way.) It's helpful to have space and a program for physical education, music, art, audio-visual materials, and a common meeting room. Make these readily available to your students. The place does not have to be new, or elegant—just pupil-centered.

Expand the Horizons

There is a world outside the classroom which should be explored. Visit museums, government bodies such as city councils and the courts, local industrial and commercial enterprises, vocational high schools, and colleges, if possible. This will give the learning-disabled adolescent not only an idea of the world in which he lives, but a glimpse for the future. He may realize that there is more opportunity than he thought possible, and these trips may show him paths of which he wasn't aware. Extracurricular activities can add interest and develop skills in a way variant from the classroom. Music, art, dancing, dramatics, gym work, producing a newspaper, all can serve to enhance the student socially, physically, perceptually, intellectually, emotionally. These improvements, in turn, will have a salutory effect on the learning process.

Encourage the students to become involved with the school: they should have governing bodies which truly govern. This can start with the classroom, with perhaps a class president who will take the suggestions and criticisms of his group to a student council which can act upon them. They should feel free not only to bring their recommendations, gripes, and plans to the teacher and the administration, but to an advocate as well. Many a school has benefitted in valuable ways from the deliberations and actions of student government, and for some students it has been a remarkable experience. They are being listened to, consulted, working out problems within the context of the group and the overall considerations of the school, and feeling worthy. The school should give this opportunity to as many as possible, guarding against the job becoming a sinecure by establishing some sort of rotational basis.

Remediation, should contain as an integral concept, the aim of improved functioning of the individual, not only academically, but as a total person—in other words, "another beginning." One cannot divorce the academic from the social and emotional life of the student.

Chapter 9: Restoration

Sylvia Bleiweiss

IT IS NOT ONLY THE TEACHER and learning disabilities specialist who is involved with the student with a learning dysfunction, but the administrator, the supervisor, the psychologist, the counselor. They may not always be aware of the roles they should play. There should be interaction, sharing of knowledge and insights, and mutual planning, to create an integrated atmosphere, program and aims. In many cases, a good in-service program is a necessity for both new and old personnel. W. Cruichshank and G. Johnson, in agreement, state, "It is vital that all secondary school personnel obtain knowledge and understanding regarding exceptional children."[1] For instance, it is only when content area teachers understand the needs, the shortcomings, the anxieties of the student, and his strengths and weaknesses, and in addition, have been taught how to prepare the type of lessons needed, how to create materials, or how to employ audio-visual materials, that they can meaningfully implement the prescribed program. In their booklet on inservice education in relation to reading, W. Otto and L. Erikson give pointers which can be valuable for our concerns, regarding training objectives to reach the maximum number of involved people.[2] Because the learning-disabled adolescent needs special materials, special methods, and a very special milieu, it is incumbent upon all the people working with him to be knowledgeable, cooperative, and open-minded to each other's suggestions and advice.

The teachers should exchange information, the psychologists and counselors should know of changes and accomplishments in the class; in turn, they should feed back to the teacher any relevant facts or feelings; and the administrator should be informed of developments, of thinking, of insights, of plans, and of needs—after all, he or she is handling the budget! It is because restoration is inextricably bound to the remedial process and is an integral part of it, that we are considering here the education and participation of the entire staff at all levels of operation.

It is the teacher, first and foremost, who is the crux of the "rehabilitation." She is the one who will create challenges, inspire interest, soothe ruffled feelings, stimulate, assure, calm, have patience, hold conferences, create opportunities for success, group and separate people, and listen, day in, day out. Many issues will lend themselves to discussion in class, such as why a student is being scapegoated (and every class seems to have one); the destructive effects of racial or ethnic slurs that students may be making; the real motives for informing on a fellow classmate; why some students will do better than others in different skills; the fruits of hard labor; the fact that making mistakes is part of learning (the wise teacher will be sure to make some mistakes herself, hoping that someone will point them out, giving her a chance to explain that no one is right all the time); the mutuality of problems and needs of the members of the class. Subjects for discussion will be plentiful, and must be dealt with. On the other hand, there will be the need for conferences on a very personal, private basis. Following is a suggested basis for differentiation between private and group discussions, whether led by teacher or counselor.

Private Meetings

1. The problem is an exclusive one for the individual, which might not be important for the others.

2. Certain things can only be told in the strictest of confidence, and must remain secret.

3. The student wants or requires the undivided attention of the listener.

4. The subject would prove to be embarrassing if discussed publicly.

5. The request is for *specific* vocational or career guidance.

6. Something is to be revealed, and the student is afraid of retaliation by another.

7. The teacher might want to give some personal advice, or send a message home.

Group Discussions

1. Common problems can be thrashed out as they arise.

2. Discussion in order to stimulate interaction and interrelationships, which may not always happen during instruction.

3. Group censure can be more effective than that of the teacher.

4. When there is need for peer acceptance or sympathy.

5. There are certain irritations to be eliminated.

6. To discuss suggestions for improvement by teacher, by students.

7. To have a general discussion of plans for the future.

8. To plan a specific event or project.

9. To discuss dissatisfaction with the work or deportment of the group, and why; to not only inform them of the facts, but to have them *examine* them as well.

Some of the devices to use in the class, other than discussion, are role-playing; psychodrama; debates; showing of films; writing a story or play; putting on a TV or radio show; a suggestion box; a regularly scheduled gripe session; having former students come in to talk and tell of their experiences and present status; having student government; allowing students to take over the class at designated times, and with well-understood conditions; and grouping students in effective working relationships.

Barry Metcalf, in discussing role-playing, suggests topics such as "Who am I?" "What am I Doing?" "Trouble," "The Mistake," "Saturday Night."[3] Results may be increased language skills and writing. He also says that role-playing frees the constricted personality, and we can add that it often leads to a new way of seeing an old problem, and an awareness of shared dilemmas.

A "buddy" system where two or more can teach each other, work together on a project, correct errors, and read to each other can obviously be a wonderful instrument for creating a socializing experience. William R. Page notes two important values when he writes, "The responsibility of playing the teacher role plus the self-concept involved in being 'teacher' is an especially worthwhile activity."[4] A "buddy" system should be instituted slowly, with care in the selection of people who work well together, and have skills which can be of help. This can be the weaning away from the isolation of a "loner."

Psychodrama is another effective vehicle for thrashing out problems or illuminating them. Rather than holding a discussion, a topic is selected; parts are assigned; and there is an acting out, which is then followed by discussion. In an article which describes eight interesting and unusual dramatics activities, Jane Schisgall relates that they have been used with adolescents to loosen up their inhibitions and to increase their self-awareness.[5]

Let us not forget that, in addition to all the conditioning we may devise to ameliorate the student's emotional and behavioral negatives, there must be academic growth. In finding himself able to read, write, or perform any of the things he couldn't do before, the student will find satisfaction and solace. Patrick Lane tells of a project in which 11 junior high school boys, mostly nonreaders, were taught in a special class, largely on a one-to-one basis. After four months of instruction there was significant improvement for most. "Behavioral improvements were marked. Truancy was cut in half. . . . The boys emerged from the project with a healthier self-image."[6]

Supporters

The Supervisor: I believe in a participating role for all administrators. The supervisor would be expected to conduct in-service training, be responsible for selection of materials, advise on methods, create innovations, expand the program, keep abreast of the literature, and pass new information on to the faculty. In a special school or facility, however, her role would be larger. She would be involved in meetings and conferences with parents; teachers should feel free to seek advice from her regarding a difficult situation or student; she might, on occasion, teach a demonstration lesson in the classroom, particularly if requested by the teacher; she can create an exchange of information between teachers; she could suggest intervisitation by teachers and wisely arrange teachers to visit the classes which will be of the most help to them; and she might help a teacher who may not be adept at handling audio-visual equipment. In observing a class, it is important for the supervisor to notice the rapport of teacher and students; the teacher's ability to motivate, creating involvement for all, making eye-to-eye contact, fostering a positive atmosphere, and if some of these things are lacking, suggestions might be forthcoming from the supervisor in a most constructive spirit, for improvement.

Direct contact with and knowledge of the students is one of the major aspects of supervision. How can she get to know them all? In a small facility, she will probably teach some, and the proximity itself will make for contact. In a larger place, she can be in the halls during break or lunch time, and attend student council meetings and special activities; and of course there will be a never-ending parade of those seeking special permission, forms for signature, planning groups for special events, and inevitably, those who cannot be contained within the classroom, at a particular time.

In sending a student out of the classroom, it is important for the teacher to designate whether he just needs a breather, needs help, or is creating an intolerable situation. There should be a place to settle students into, if they just have to be alone to let off some steam. If they need to be "dealt with," it should be done right then and there. It is a good idea, in order to give the necessary undivided attention to not answer the phone, and to meet in an office with closed doors, minimizing interruptions. An adolescent needs this privacy and will be more prone to talk and to listen under these circumstances. If he comes in raging, furious, or even incoherent, he should be allowed to calm down before discussion begins. Often, I would say to such a student, "Would you please excuse me for a minute, I must put these important papers away," or invent another such activity, to avoid the necessity for either one of us to speak at this time. It has worked every time. When the student has had a few minutes to calm down, the talking can begin. The phrasing of the questions put to him is most important. "Do you want to tell me what happened?" or "What is the problem?" are much better openers than "Oh, it's you again," "What's wrong with you?" or "Why are you giving us trouble?" After discussing the issue, sometimes it may be important to get other students in to settle the matter, particularly if accusations are being made or they are being implicated. Students, as a group in the office, can often not only get to the bottom of things, but can work out ways of meting out justice, or taking disciplinary measures; and what is better than self-imposed discipline?

The supervisor really needs many of the important attributes of the teacher in order to "reach" the youngster. She has the advantage of being able to cope individually with the students at time of difficulty, but must be adroit in the handling of each situation as it arises, has to be calm, empathetic, strong, a good listener, and be genuinely concerned.

Upon learning of my resignation from my last position in New York, one of the young men (who had been sent out to see me many times during that year, allowing us to know each other quite well) went to the psychologist to discuss my leaving. She suggested that he tell me of his feelings; and, after lamenting my planned departure, he commented on what he considered my prime value, saying, "When we talk you listen, and when you talk, we listen. How can you leave?"

The supervisor must understand her role in terms of the students, to be a mediator, a conciliator, an advisor, at times a teacher, sometimes a psychiatrist, her aim being to help develop functioning students who can participate in class and school activities for their best possible growth.

Counseling, guidance, direction: These functions may be assigned to one or more people as a specialty, although it is not uncommon that they be part of the duties of the administrator. The psychologist will often participate in, perform, or expand the previously described functions of the supervisor. In addition, implementing the goal of considering the "total" person, she should interpret reports; evaluate actions; act as liaison with other therapists; suggest and encourage therapy when indicated; supply lists of therapists or agencies; provide advice on after-school pursuits which might complement or supplement the shcool programs; hold rap sessions or lead encounter groups; conduct defusing sessions in or out of the classroom; and be available for consultation with teacher, parent, student. If there are enough psychologists on the staff, individual therapy might be undertaken; if not, perhaps group work might be done.

One of the ways to open a door to the future for the learning-disabled adolescent is to offer vocational, career, and academic counseling. He must clearly understand the time involved in preparation for a career or continuing to a school of higher education, the skills he'll need, and a course delineated which will be planned realistically on the basis of his age, deficiencies, strengths, interests, and potential. The potential should not be underrated, nor should the desire to go to college be dampened if there might be a chance. The counselor must know which schools to recommend, entrance requirements, whom to see, and what to do in preparation; and she should help him fill out forms and applications. If the student is best suited for a vocational school, he should be impressed with this fact and informed of the choices of occupations and their requirements, with an attempt made to match his choice with his proficiencies and leanings. I once had the arduous task of trying to dissuade a seventeen-year-old from planning to attend law school. He was struggling with third-grade level exercises, trying to take high school subjects at night in a local high school, and failing miserably in spite of our help. His reason for wanting to go to law school was that the "big money" was there, and that it was prestigious. Obviously, knowing his potential, which was realistically evaluated by some of us who were normally optimistic and hopeful, we had to try to lead him into obtainable objectives. Very often a balance must be struck between those with unrealistic values and aspirations who feel that vocational school is demeaning and therefore set their sights too high, and, on the other hand, those who fail to see or work with the true potential of a student who may, with sweat and determination, make it to college, and therefore guide him into lower levels of attainment.

Harry Kreel, writing in *Special Education in Canada*, describes the school of which he is principal. It is a vocational school which provides for personal, academic, social, and career growth, and which offers a tremendous variety of vocational programs and athletic activities. "Although the school teaches saleable skills, it is more concerned with making it possible for students to be trained and retrained in any area of employment."[7] He further writes that the school functions in the same way as other high schools do in that community. A school of this kind might be a fine goal for some learning-disabled adolescents, and counselors would do well to seek out schools of this caliber.

If the school does not offer sufficient remedial help, any special service person should be able to recommend other facilities: hospital clinics, university clinics or schools, remedial help offered by private organizations, the "Y"s, private practitioners, neighborhood centers, and—in some cities—store-front centers or other funded clinics. Don't let the condition of the student deteriorate.

Direction comes from the top. The administrator, be he or she principal or director, must be thoroughly familiar with the aims, needs, and workings of his project. As responsive individuals, they will make budgetary provisions for special materials; provide for needed space; understand the necessity for small classes and for special groupings; make available therapeutic and counseling services. Knowing the proper criteria for evaluating staff and program, they will hire the right kinds of personnel, which might include tutors, aides, and consultants. They'll be sympathetic and helpful, be realistic about hoped for gains, and understand and implement the aims and values of faculty and staff. They must make sure that all lines of communication are always open: between teachers, between teachers and administration, between students and administration and resource people. They will inspire a concerted team effort on the part of all, for the interest of the student.

Some Words on the Community College Student

Older students, particularly in high school and community colleges, may find their problem is less one of word recognition, but more lack of study skills and organization, and psychological factors. Often, on retesting, we will find evidences that the gap between the verbal and performance sections of a test like WISC, for instance, has narrowed; and perceptual difficulties may have been somewhat attenuated. The need for guidance and counseling, however, is often greater than at some of the lower levels. To my knowledge, there has been no successful program that has not included significant amounts of both. To accommodate the large numbers of students who need help, the community college makes use of programed instruction, labs, and audio-visual aids—all of which are good components of a program. This must be coupled, however, with personal counseling and career guidance, with sympathetic teachers and personal relationships. Advice and counseling should not be given only at entrance time, but should continue on an on-going basis.

The Tally

When we test and diagnose, we are trying to assess the needs of the total person; when we remediate, we try to fill those needs; and, if we have restored, we have been successful. Let's examine what we might have accomplished. In addition to, or as the result of, creating and enhancing skills and abilities, we might have achieved any of the following:

Group participation: He will listen, talk, debate, play, work in cooperation with others, and be aware of the rights and need of others.

New self-assurance: He will voice opinions, attempt new levels, repeat work he had abandoned, make new friends, improve his appearance, laugh more, be able to take criticism, be able to acknowledge mistakes.

Peer relationships: He may seek out new friends and they may seek him out; he may get friends closer in age and interests; he may plan to enter into sport and social activities with his peers; and there may be a mutual cessation of mockery and scapegoating.

Emotional life: There will be diminished guilt, self-doubt, self-hate, frustration, anger, feelings of vulnerability, resentments; he will be less inhibited, less fearful, and will have increased confidence, assurance, and a happier frame of mind. He will be more apt to like or love.

Behavior: He will be less explosive, less taunting, less threatening, less sulking, and instead, he will be more calm, patient and reasonable. The withdrawn may become more outgoing, the passive more aggressive, and the aggressive less so.

Physical appearance: He will look less grim, smile more, walk "taller," and pay more attention to his clothing and his general appearance.

Attitudes: He will have more dignity; he will accept necessary rules or decisions of teachers and peers more readily; he will resist less; there will be more acceptance of his family; he will be willing to correct work rather than destroy it, and willing to try something hard, something new.

Maturity: He will think about and try to resolve personal problems; he will be more apt to accept advice; he will be more willing to have realistic goals and embark on the necessary path of action to obtain them; he may accept the necessity for therapy, cope with the unexpected, be willing to try for working papers, drivers license, job; and accept advice on how to go about it.

Academics: He will be more willing to read, write, and try new skills. If not overjoyed at having to read or write, he at least knows he has the ability, and accepts the "chore." He will be more organized in thinking about and planning more activities; more aware of bringing necessary equipment; more willing to answer questions, to take tests, and do homework; and greater ability to study.

A "People" Point of View

Unfortunately, the learning-disabled adolescent may be educationally disabled; not just in terms of poor physical plant or materials—but by educators who didn't care, didn't try, had no expectations, set no boundaries, set no goals. I cannot stress enough that it is the *people* who work with the student who are going to make the most difference. We have to be aware that we are teaching people, not subjects. We are *teaching Edward to read*, we are not *teaching reading*. People teach; people learn; people work together; people create; people understand; people talk to each other; people make it work. We learn in the doing; we learn from each other. People are the helpers, teachers, classmates, friends, therapists, guidance counselors, administrators, siblings, parents. Let's enlist them all.

Part Two / Notes

Chapter 2:

1. Camilla Anderson, *Society Pays: The High Cost of Minimal Brain Dysfunction in America* (New York: Walker & Co., 1972).

Chapter 6:

1. George M. Bright, "The Adolescent with Scholastic Failure," Reprint 33 (Pomfret, Connecticut: The Orton Society, Inc., n.d.): 65.

2. Stanley Sherman, "Caterpillars Cannot Fly Yet" (position paper; Boston: Center for Alternative Education, n.d.): 8.

3. Specifically, "More than one third of all children in America drop out of school before high school graduation. One of the basic failures is the failure to learn to read and write," from *Secondary School Guidelines* (Framingham, Massachusetts: Massachusetts Association for Children with Learning Disabilities, 1971-72). Further, "Children with learning problems constitute a large proportion of those who seek mental health services," is stated by Lillie Pope and Abraham Harkavy, in "A Followup Study of Psychoeducational Evaluations Sent to Schools," *Journal of Learning Disabilities* 7:4 (April 1974): 56. *CANHC-Gram* 8:3:1, published by the California Association for Neurologically Handicapped Children, states that 77 percent of 155 tested inmates in Rhode Island training schools showed evidence of neurological impairment. In Colorado, 90.5 percent of the delinquents were learning disabled, as compared with 18 percent in the state's public schools.

4. William R. Page, "Junior High Programs—Instructional Systems for Students with Learning Disabilities (a reprint of the Canadian Association for Children with Learning Disabilities) (St. Ann, Missouri: U.S. Department of Health, Education, and Welfare, Office of Education, Central Midwestern Regional Education Laboratory, Inc., 1968): 1, claims that 20 percent of the school population is learning disabled. *Raspberry Report Card* (January 25, 1974) of Nashville, Tennessee, states that 7.5 percent of the typical school population is learning disabled. Doreen Kronick, in *A Word or Two about Learning Disabilities* (San Rafael, California: Academic Therapy Publications, 1973), claims that between 8 and 20 percent of children in the classroom have specific problems in learning. *Back To School*, an Associated Press newsfeature, states that it is generally accepted that, among children with average or above-average intelligence, 10 percent suffer from learning disabilities. Harry S. Valentine, director of the Churchill School in New York, feels that the figure is closer to 20 percent. The Bureau of Education for the Handicapped, U.S. Office of Education, claimed that 20 percent of the students had learning disabilities, and an additional 5 percent had minimal brain damage. H. Silverman and K. G. O'Bryan, *Perspectives on Learning Disability* (Toronto: The Ontario Institute for Studies in Education, 1973): 1, say that estimates of the number of children suffering from learning disabilities range from 1 percent to 40 percent of the total school population.

5. M. Wolfish, MD, and others at a seminar sponsored by The Hospital for Sick Children Foundation (Toronto: May 21, 1974).

6. "A New Frontier of Education," (New York: Robert Louis Stevenson School, n.d.).

Chapter 7:

1. There has been an upsurge of interest in the effect of nutrition on behavior and learning which has been reflected in the current literature. A publication of the Ontario Association for Children with Learning Disabilities, *Communique* (March 1974): 5, and (June 1974): 3, reports on the work and findings of Benjamin Feingold, MD, director emeritus of the department of allergy at Kaiser-Permanente Medical Center in San Francisco. Dr. Feingold has been trying out restricted diets with children who have behavior problems. While his studies are not conclusive, in one group he found that, by removing artificial additives, 15 of 25 children returned to normal behavior. He advocates the elimination of all artificial dies and flavors from the food supply of children. *CANHC-Gram* 8:5:6, reports on an article in *Psychology Today* 7:11 (April 1974): 83-88, which says that children with learning disabilities who are hyperactive have been helped by the use of megavitamins. Dr. E. Rees of Castro Valley, California, reports great improvement in his patients by using a diet of natural foods and vitamins. Helen and Martin Weiss, in *A Survival Manual* (Yorktown Heights, New York: Board of Cooperative Educational Services, 1974): 51, mention the fact that research is delving into the connection of nutritional factors and learning disabilities, and assert that "all experts seem to agree that diet plays an enormous role in the chemistry of behavior and brain functioning." *The Wall Street Journal* of June 28, 1974, reports that the National Institute of Nutrition wants to finance research on the role of additives to food in causing hyperactive behavior.

   My own experience with teenagers has been that they favor very inadequate and lopsided diets, with great amounts of sugar, carbohydrates, and manufactured foods, rather than fruits and vegetables. The Churchill School in New York City has been active in providing parents and children with information on nutrition and recommending reduced intake of sugar and carbohydrates. There is still much research to be done.

2. Many educators have become increasingly concerned about the linguistic and cultural aspects of traditional IQ tests, which are inherently Anglocentric, and which do not always give a true picture of students from minority cultures. Gustavo Gonzalez, in "Language, Culture, and Exceptional Children," *Exceptional Children* 40:8 (May 1974): 565-570, suggests that both standard and minority culture tests should be used for more accurate assessments, and mentions two tests based on minority culture values: one, constructed by Antonio Gomez, relates to Chicano beliefs; and the other, by Robert L. William of the Washington University (St. Louis, Missouri) Black Studies Program, is based on the urban Black cultural experience.

Chapter 8:

1. Martin and Helen Weiss, in *A Survival Manual* (Yorktown Heights, New York: Board of Cooperative Educational Services, 1974): 150, list the College of the Ozarks, Clarksville, Arkansas, and Curry College, Milton, Massachusetts, as offering college programs for dyslexic and learning-disabled young adults. The Association for Children with Learning Disabilities, also, can often supply information concerning higher-education facilities. Especially, the Massachusetts ACLD, 1296 Worchester Road, Box 908, Framingham, Massachusetts, has published a list of colleges which do not have foreign language requirements for admission.

2. Robert Rosenthal, "The Pygmalion Effect Lives," *Psychology Today* 7:4 (September 1973): 56-63, as cited in *Communique* 2:4 (March 4, 1974): 4.

3. Eric Haughton, "Curriculum Options: International Symbols," *Special Education in Canada* 48:2 (February 1974): 12.

4. Judy Kupersmith, "Gold Stars, M&M's, and the Junior College Student," *Forum for Reading* [a publication of the International Reading Association Special Interest Group for Two-Year Colleges] 3:1 (December 1974): 19-29.

5. Jerome Bruner, *The Relevance of Education* (New York: W. W. Norton, 1971): 75.

6. Angie Nall, "What is 'Structured'?" (reprint; Toronto: Canadian Association for Children with Learning Disabilities, n.d.).

7. Wally Freel (as cited by Harvey Schacter), "Truancy Can Be Cry For Help," *The Toronto Star* (March 13, 1974): C-3.

Chapter 9:

1. W. M. Cruickshank and G. Orville Johnson, *Education of Exceptional Children and Youth* (2nd ed.) (Englewood Cliffs, New Jersey: Prentice Hall, 1967): 101.

2. Wayne Otto and Lawrence Erickson, *Inservice Education to Improve Reading Instruction* [Reading Aids Series] (Newark, Delaware: International Reading Association, 1973).

3. Barry Metcalf, "Language and Reality in High School," *Orbit* [a publication of the Ontario Institute of Special Education, Toronto] 3:5 (December 1972): 24-25.

4. William R. Page, *Junior High Programs—Instructional Systems for Students with Learning Disabilities* (St. Ann, Missouri: U.S. Department of Health, Education, and Welfare, Office of Education, Central Midwestern Regional Education Laboratory, Inc., 1968): 8-9.

5. Jane Schisgall, "The Creative Use of Multimedia," *Teaching Exceptional Children* 5:4 (Summer 1973): 162-169.

6. Patrick R. Lane, "Educational Therapy for Adolescent Non-Readers," *Educational Therapy* 6:2 (Winter 1970-71): 155-159.

7. Harry Kreel, "School Offers Varied Program," *Special Education in Canada* 48:3 (April 1974): 25.

Appendices

Appendix A

(Exclusive of sources in chapter notes.)

Brogden, J. D. *Developing Communication Skills in Non-Committed Learners.* West Nyack, New York: Parker Publishing Co., 1970.

Clarke, Louis. *Can't Read, Can't Write, Can't Takl Too Good Either.* New York: Walker & Co., 1973.

Cowin, Pauline and Virginia Graff. *Comprehensive Treatment of the Older Disabled Reader.* Reprint 128. The Orton Society, Towson, Maryland.

Deno, Evelyn N. (ed.). *Instructional Alternatives for Exceptional Children. Reston,* Virginia: Council for Exceptional Children, 1973.

Doohan, Joseph, E. "Some Practical Guidelines for Effectively Teaching Low Achieving Students at Secondary Level." *Journal of Special Education* (November 1970): 335-336.

Hartman, Nancy C. and Robert K. "Perceptual Handicap or Learning Disability?" *The Reading Teacher* (April 1973): 684-693.

Jackson, M. S. *Reading Disability: Experiment, Innovation and Individual Therapy.* Sydney, Australia: Angus & Robertson, 1972.

Jones and Pikulski. "Cloze for the Classroom." *Journal of Reading* (March 1974): 432-438.

Meredith, Patrick. *Dyslexia and the Individual.* London: Elm Tree Books, 1972.

Money, John (ed.). *The Disabled Reader: Education of the Dyslexic Child.* Baltimore: John Hopkins Press, 1966.

Pope, Lillie. *Program Profile.* Reprint from *Urban Review* (November 1971).

Rawson, Margaret, B. "Teaching Children with Language Disabilities in Small Groups." *Journal of Learning Disabilities* (January 1971): 22-30.

Smith, R. K.; Drummond, R. J.; and Pinette, C. A. "Assessing Community College Reading, Students' Reading Attitudes, Interests and Techniques." *Forum for Reading:* Special Interest Group for Two Year Colleges. International Reading Association, December 1973: 6-14.

The report of the Ontario Committee of the Commission on Emotional and Learning Disorders in Children. (Toronto: September 1970).

Appendix B

Reading Tests

Gates-MacGinitie Reading Tests
 Teachers College Press, Columbia University
 1234 Amsterdam Avenue, New York, New York 10027.
  Speed, vocabulary, comprehension. Grades one through twelve.

Gilmore Oral Reading Tests
 Harcourt, Brace, Jovanovich, Inc.
 757 Third Avenue, New York, New York 10017.
  Oral reading for evaluation of fluency and accuracy, to assess general level of reading for group placement at instructional reading level. Grades one through ten.

Gray Oral Reading Tests
 The Bobbs-Merrill Co., Inc.
 c/o Howard W. Sams & Co., Inc.
 4300 West 62nd Street, Indianapolis, Indiana 46268.
  Similar to *Gilmore*. Grade one to adult.

Science Research Associates Diagnostic Reading Tests
 SRA
 259 East Erie Street, Chicago, Illinois 60611.
  Grades four through thirteen.

Triggs, Frances O. Diagnostic Reading Tests
 Mountain Home, North Carolina 28758.
  Tests various reading skills. Elementary grades through college freshman. Also, survey test, silent reading. Grade seven to college freshman.

Davis Reading Tests
 The Psychological Corporation
 c/o Harcourt, Brace, Jovanovich, Inc.
 304 East 45th Street, New York, New York 10017
  Tests comprehension in relation to content subjects (Word knowledge, comprehension, and appreciation, literature, social studies, real life, and others).

Achievement Tests

Jastak & Jastak Wide Range Achievement (WRAT)
> Guidance Associates
> 1526 Gilpin Avenue, Wilmington, Delaware
>> Reading, spelling, and arithmetic computation. Reading ability is less of a determining factor in the overall score. Takes less time and is easier to score than some of the others, such as *Stanford*. Pre-first-grade to post-college.

Adult Basic Learning Examination (ABLE)
> Harcourt, Brace, Jovanovich, Inc.
> 757 Third Avenue, New York, New York 10017.
>> Vocabulary, reading comprehension, spelling. Battery includes arithmetic computation and problem solving. Geared for *adults* at educational levels one through twelve. Might be of interest to Canadians as well as Americans.

Intelligence Tests

Wechsler Intelligence Scale for Children (WISC)
Wechsler Adult Intelligence Scale (WAIS)
> The Psychological Corporation
> c/o Harcourt, Brace, Jovanovich, Inc.
> 304 East 45th Street, New York, New York 10017.
>> Two major areas; one, performance; one, verbal. Manipulation of symbols. Good objective measure.

Language Aptitude

Illinois Index of Scholastic Aptitude
> Western Psychological Service
> 12031 Wilshire Boulevard, Los Angeles, California 90025.
>> Measures language ability at secondary levels.

Verbal Power Test of Concept Equivalents
> Western Psychological Service
> 12031 Wilshire Boulevard, Los Angeles, California 90025.
>> Gives insights into language usage and college readiness of students performing at grades ten through twelve.

Learning Disabilities, Phonics

Slingerland Screening Tests for Specific Language Disability
> Educators Publishing Service, Inc.
> 75 Moulton Street, Cambridge, Massachusetts 02138.
>> Identifies potential dyslexics through screening of auditory and visual modalities. Grades one through six.

The Neva Malcomesius Specific Language Disability Test

Educators Publishing Service, Inc.

75 Moulton Street, Cambridge, Massachusetts 02138.

Useful in identifying specific defects which interfere with learning. Many similar aspects to the *Slingerland*, but more suited to adolescents. Grade six and above.

Bender Visual-Motor Gestalt Test

Follett Publishing Co.

1010 West Washington Boulevard, Chicago, Illinois 60607.

Measures integration of perceptual functions.

Roswell-Chall Phonics and Word Analysis Skills

Essay Press

Box 5, Planetarium Station, New York, New York 10024.

Assesses phonics skills. Discrimination of sounds, ability in blending, and syllabication.

Gillingham-Childs Phonics Scales

Educators Publishing Service, Inc.

75 Moulton Street, Cambridge, Massachusetts 02138.

Measures phonics skills, shows deficiencies. Can be used for teaching, too.

This list of tests, while far from being an exhaustive list, offers an example of the type of evaluation tools which can further amplify or inquire into the the findings of the informal testing. Personnel not conversant with informal procedures, or who are not experienced enough to evaluate on this basis, may find the formal tests a necessity, since they offer manuals, or explicit procedures for administering, scoring, and interpretation or rating scales, as well. Tests of the nature of the *Wechsler* and an overall achievement test should always accompany any diagnostic evaluation. Testing should be kept to the essential minimum; further testing can be undertaken where indicated by preliminary results. Further information which may be of help in testing: The International Reading Association publication: *Tests of Reading Readiness and Achievement*, by R. Farr and N. Anastasiow. This provides a critical evaluation of tests such as the *California Reading Tests, Stanford Achievement*, etc. SRA Testing and Measurement, Extension Service, 259 East Erie Street, Chicago, Illinois 60611, provides a free series of booklets available which discuss many aspects of standardized testing. *The Mental Measurements Yearbooks* by Oscar K. Buros (Highland Park, New Jersey: Gryphon Press) contains a comprehensive list of published tests accompanied by reviews. Also by the same author, *Reading Tests and Reviews*, is available, but is limited to reading and reading-related tests.

Appendix C

The Association for Children with Learning Disabilities (ACLD) has branches throughout the United States and Canada; sometimes the branches, while affiliated, call themselves by variant names.

CANHC-Gram is the newsletter of the California Association for Neurologically Handicapped Children, P.O. Box 604, Los Angeles, California 90053. Very informative on current issues, views and research; as overview, rather than in depth.

Communique is a publication of the Toronto ACLD, 2323 Yonge Street, Toronto, Canada. Similar to *CANHC-Gram* in content.

Massachusetts ACLD published a well-thought-out, professional booklet, "Secondary School Guidelines, 1971-2," which offers a guide for community and school to meet the needs of secondary students with learning disability. 1296 Worcester Road, Framingham, Massachusetts.

Many ACLD branches publish lists of books which can be ordered, plus filmstrips, lists of schools, camps, and other similarly helpful material.

The Council for Exceptional Children (CEC)
1920 Association Drive, Reston, Virginia 22091

The CEC Information Center, a major program of the Council offers many services. It is the Clearinghouse on Exceptional Children in the ERIC network, and is a member of the Special Education Instructional Materials Center/Regional Media Center. It responds to requests for information from individuals. It also publishes *Exceptional Children*, eight times a year, and *Teaching Exceptional Children*, quarterly, and the *Exceptional Child Education Abstracts* and *Exceptional Child Bibliography Series*. Their information and publishing systems are very extensive and of great help for general and specific information on learning disabilities. The Canadian Committee of the Council, located at One Danforth Avenue, Toronto, Ontario, publishes *Special Education in Canada* four times a year.

The International Reading Association
800 Barksdale Road, Neward, Delaware 19711

This organization publishes:

The Reading Teacher (elementary level)

Journal of Reading (secondary level)

Forum for Reading (special interest group, two-year colleges)

Reading Research Quarterly

It also publishes many books and booklets of professional interest, as well as bibliographies. Local chapters publish bulletins and newsletters, as do regional groups.

The Orton Society
8415 Bellona Lane, Towson, Maryland 21204

This group publishes the *Bulletin of the Orton Society* annually, with a wide variety of articles regarding specific learning disabilities, and with reviews of materials, articles, and books which have appeared in the current year. It also publishes important abstracts, original writings, and reprints. A helpful publication is the revised (1974) edition of *A Bibliography on the Nature, Recognition and Treatment of Language Difficulties* by Margaret B. Rawson, published by the Orton Society. It has sections on testing, remediation, specific learning disabilities, journals, bibliographies, instructional materials, and allied disciplines. It is a fine source book. Local chapters also publish.

Journals

Academic Therapy. John I. Arena, Editor. Academic Therapy Publications, 1539 Fourth Street, San Rafael, California 94901.

Journal of Learning Disabilities. Professional Press, Inc. 5 North Wabash Avenue, Chicago, Illinois 60602.

Journal of Special Education. Buttonwood Farms, Inc., 3515 Woodhaven Road, Philadelphia, Pennsylvania 19154.

Psychological Review. American Psychological Association, Inc., 1200 17th Street, N.W. Washington, D.C. 20036.

University Press

Child Development. The University of Chicago Press, 5801 Ellis Avenue, Chicago, Illinois 60637.

Harvard Educational Review. Harvard University Press, 13 Appian Way, Cambridge, Massachusetts 02138.

McGill University Press, 1266 Pine West, Montreal, Quebec, Canada.

University of Michigan Press, Ann Arbor, Michigan 48106.

Syracuse University Press, P.O. Box 8, University Station, Syracuse, New York 13210.

Teachers College Press of Columbia University, 1234 Amsterdam Avenue, New York, New York 10027.

University of Toronto Press, St. George Campus, Toronto, Canada; publications of the Ontario Institute for Studies in Education, University of Toronto, 252 Bloor Street West, Toronto.

Yale University Press, 302 Temple Street, New Haven, Connecticut 16511.